AWESOME
ALMANAC™
ALMANAC
THE GREAT SEAL OF THE STATE OF OHIO
OHIO

Created by
Jean F. Blashfield

Compiled and Written by
Marjorie Benson

B&B Publishing, Inc.

B & B Publishing, Inc.
820 Wisconsin Street
P. O. Box 96
Walworth, Wisconsin 53184

Additional Materials – **Roxanne Walsh, Nancy Rockwell**
Copy Editor – **Irene Keller**
Photo Researcher – **Ramona Uhlenhake**
Production Manager - **Katy O'Shea**
Computer Production – **Katy O'Shea and Ramona Uhlenhake**
Original Cover Design – **Gary Hurst**

Publisher's Cataloging in Publication

Benson, Marjorie.
    Awesome almanac: Ohio / Marjorie Benson.
    p. cm.
    Includes bibliographical references and index.
    Preassigned LCCN: 92-074711.
    ISBN 1-880190-19-2

1. Ohio—History—Miscellanea. 2. Almanacs, American—Ohio.
I. Title.

F491.5.B46 1995   977.1
                                   QBI95-20088

Printed in the United States of America

95 96 97 98   5 4 3 2 1

AWESOME ALMANAC is a trademark of B&B Publishing, Inc.

TABLE OF CONTENTS

On the Ohio River near Marietta

MOTHER OF PRESIDENTS

When the Northwest Ordinance was passed in 1787, the Continental Congress had created a plan for orderly land sales and paved the way for annexing new states. All that was needed was for people to move west—and that didn't take much coaxing.

The governor—General Arthur St. Clair—arrived in the Northwest Territory in 1788, when the population included 300 white settlers. By 1803, Ohio had the required 60,000 people to become the first state carved from the huge territory. In 1850, the population was 2,000,000 and Ohio had already sent one Buckeye to the White House. In the years to follow, seven native-born sons would lead the nation, giving Ohio the nickname "Mother of Presidents."

The king was ignored

The land west and north of the Ohio River was part of the Province of Quebec before the Revolutionary War. France ceded this province to Britain in 1763, and Britain hoped to maintain it as a place for Native Americans and fur trading. The English monarchy wanted no colonization in the west. So King George III made a polite request of his American subjects in a proclamation dated October 7, 1763. "Leave the land east of the Alleghenies for the "use of the Indians," he said. Furthermore, " … on pain of our displeasure, all our loving subjects … are forbidden … from making any purchases or settlements whatever, or taking possession of any of the lands above reserved, without our especial leave and license." Few listened. Dreams of freedom, money, and self-sufficiency pulled stronger than fear of the king's "displeasure." By 1783, it didn't matter anyway. The western lands were ceded to the United States when Britain lost the Revolutionary War and the movement west continued.

THE LAND

Area – 41,328 square miles in total area (34th in the United States)
On the north – Ohio claims 2,097,000 acres of Lake Erie and 320 miles of its shoreline
On the south and southeast – 436 miles of the Ohio River
Longest distance north to south – 245 miles
Widest distance east to west – 230 miles
Northernmost town – Conneaut
Southernmost town – South Point
Geographic center – Centerburg in Knox County
Highest point – Campbell Hill, 1,550 feet
Lowest point – Near Cincinnati on the Ohio River, 433 feet

Water made it bigger

After the 1990 census, Ohio became about 8.5 percent larger in total area. That's because "territorial waters" were counted for the first time as part of the state's total area. For Ohio, that meant that the part of Lake Erie from the United States boundary south to Ohio's shores was counted as part of the state's territory. The state is now 34th in size among the states, instead of 35th.

An island border

Off Marblehead Peninsula and north of Sandusky are about 20 oddly shaped islands—and some of them are part of Ohio's northern border. Discovered by French missionary Gabriel Segard in the 1600s, Britain acquired the islands in 1765 and passed them on to the United States in 1783. Today, Canada claims Hen and Chickens, Pelee, and several others. The state of Ohio has Green Rattlesnake, Starve, Ballast, Sugar, Gibraltar, and Mouse. Most of these are mere specks of land that birds use for nesting grounds—or wealthy people use for very private summer homes. (Civil war financier Jay Cooke built his summer "cabin" on Gibraltar.)

The larger islands—Kelleys Island (7 miles across at its widest) and the three Bass Islands—weren't settled until the mid-1800s. Datus and Irad Kelley bought the island now named after them, planting grapes in 1846 and establishing the first wine cellar north of Cincinnati in 1851. The Bass Islands—North, Middle, and South—are named after the fish once plentiful in the waters of Lake Erie. Some fairly important people have vacationed here including Presidents Hayes, Cleveland, Harrison, and Taft.

THE PEOPLE

Total population – 10,847,115, ranking seventh in the nation

1990 population

Male – 5,226,340
Female – 5,620,775
White – 9,521,756 (86.5 percent)
African American – 1,154,826 (10.6 percent)
Hispanic – 139,696 (1.3 percent)
Asian or Pacific Islander – 91,179 (0.8 percent)
Other races – 58,996 (0.5 percent)
American Indian, Eskimo, or Aleut – 20,358 (0.2 percent)

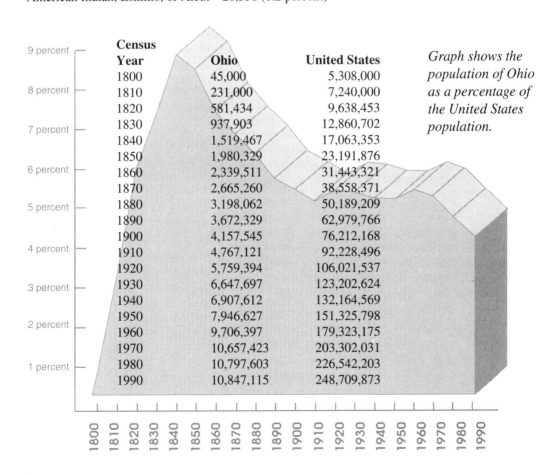

Census Year	Ohio	United States
1800	45,000	5,308,000
1810	231,000	7,240,000
1820	581,434	9,638,453
1830	937,903	12,860,702
1840	1,519,467	17,063,353
1850	1,980,329	23,191,876
1860	2,339,511	31,443,321
1870	2,665,260	38,558,371
1880	3,198,062	50,189,209
1890	3,672,329	62,979,766
1900	4,157,545	76,212,168
1910	4,767,121	92,228,496
1920	5,759,394	106,021,537
1930	6,647,697	123,202,624
1940	6,907,612	132,164,569
1950	7,946,627	151,325,798
1960	9,706,397	179,323,175
1970	10,657,423	203,302,031
1980	10,797,603	226,542,203
1990	10,847,115	248,709,873

Graph shows the population of Ohio as a percentage of the United States population.

NAMES AND NICKNAMES

It's shorter than the book title

Although it can't be proved conclusively, many believe French explorer René Robert Cavelier, sieur de La Salle, was the first white man to see the land between the Ohio River and Lake Erie in 1669. He may have named the region "Ohio" after the name Native Americans had given the river. In any event the word "Ohio" probably came from the Iroquois word, *O-he-yo*, which early settlers interpreted as "the beautiful." The Wyandots also had their version, *O-he-zu*, which translated as "great, grand, fair to look upon." The English word "Ohio" was printed in 1756 for the first time in a book authored by John Shebbeare entitled *A Fourth Letter to the People of England on the Conduct of the M–RS in Alliances, Fleets, and Armies, since the First Differences on the Ohio, to the taking of Minorca by the French.*

A touch of New England

If you travel through Ohio, especially in the northeast region once called the Western Reserve of Connecticut, you'd think you were in New England. With their oval village greens, white clapboard churches, and white shuttered houses, towns such as Canfield look like New England villages. Other towns with names such as Danbury, Streetsboro, and Greenwich, reflect that same New England heritage. Yankees "flooded" Ohio buying land as speculators or coming to live, thus giving the state the nickname—the Yankee State.

Native presidents

Seven United States presidents were born in Ohio, giving the state the proud nickname "Mother of Presidents." Perhaps that should be lengthened to Mother of Republican Presidents since all seven claimed allegiance to the GOP. Civil war hero Ulysses S. Grant led the way to the White House with his election in 1868. He was followed by Rutherford B. Hayes, James A. Garfield, Benjamin Harrison, William McKinley, William Howard Taft, and finally Warren G. Harding. If you add William Henry Harrison, grandfather of Benjamin, who moved to Ohio and was elected president in 1840, the state claims eight chief executives—as many as Virginia. You probably don't remember any of these presidents as the best we've ever had. A poll conducted in 1962 by a Harvard professor, ranked two Ohio presidents, Grant and Harding, as the "only failures in our history." Ohio Democrats have tried to win the Oval Office with no success.

Where's Metropotamia?

In 1783, Thomas Jefferson was asked to come up with a plan of government for the "Western Territory." His idea called for dividing the land into 10 states—named Sylvania, Michigania, Assenisipia, Illinoia, Polypotamia, Pelisipia, Saratoga, Chersonesus, Metropotamia, and Washington—along parallels of latitude. Present-day Ohio might have been four states under his plan—Washington, Metropotamia, Saratoga, and Pelisipia. Jefferson's territorial government ordinance was adopted as a forerunner to the Northwest Ordinance of 1787, but Congress thought each state should choose its own name. Just think, it could have been Cleveland, Metropotamia!

Everyone's heard of the Buckeye State—or at least the Ohio State Buckeyes! The moniker derives from the Ohio buckeye tree felled by pioneers to build cabins. Not commonly found east of the Allegheny Mountains, the Ohio buckeye is related to the Asiatic horse chestnut. Native Americans thought the tree's big, thick brown nuts resembled the eye of a male deer. They called the tree *hetuck*. White settlers called it "buck eye." Colonel Ebenezer Sproat was the first official Buckeye when Native Americans took a liking to Marietta's new sheriff in 1788. They named the lawman "Hetuck" as a sign of respect. It wasn't until William Henry Harrison's presidential campaign, however, that the term "Buckeye" was applied to the state and its residents. His political campaign successfully used log cabins made of buckeye wood as a symbol for their candidate ... and Ohio has been the Buckeye State ever since.

The Buckeye State

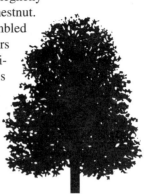

GOVERNMENT IN OHIO

On March 1, 1803, Ohio became the 17th state. Ohio was the first state admitted from the Northwest Territory and the first in which slavery was illegal from the state's inception.

Statehood granted

Admitted to the Union

Although Ohio became a state in 1803, it was "officially" admitted to the United States on August 7, 1953. The admission of a state requires, according to the Constitution, a final vote on the part of Congress. Somehow that formal resolution didn't happen in 1803. Representative George Bender introduced a resolution during the state's 150th birthday year that said Ohio had really become a state March 1, 1803, when the first elected legislature met for the first time. President Eisenhower signed the bill and Ohio was legal. But that didn't satisfy Pearce Holton, an academic from Georgia, who argued that this late attention to legal detail was not constitutional. Holton filed a lawsuit in federal court claiming that the "people of the Territory of Ohio were masquerading as a state and sending delegates to Congress to vote, unlawfully ...." The court ruled otherwise, however.

The Ohio constitution establishes an executive branch headed by a governor. The chief executive serves for four years. He cannot hold office for more than two consecutive terms. (A 1954 constitutional amendment ended the two-year, unlimited number of terms for governor.) For a salary just over $100,000, the governor administers more than 20 different agencies or departments. The original state constitution written in 1802 gave very little power to the governor. He had no veto power until 1902. Remembering Governor St. Clair's dictatorial abuses, the writers of the first state constitution gave more power to the General Assembly.

The chief executive

Constitution

Straight-talkin' Lausche Son of a Slovenian-born steelworker, Democrat Frank Lausche was the first Cleveland mayor elected as governor and the only Buckeye to serve five terms—when terms were only two years. Often called "Ohio's Lincoln," Lausche was first elected in 1944. He moved on to the U.S. Senate in 1957, serving two terms.

The Cabinet until 1999 Governor – George Voinovich (Republican)
Lt. Governor – Nancy Hollister (Republican)
Secretary of State – Robert Taft (Republican)
Auditor of State – Jim Petro (Republican)
State Treasurer – Kenneth Blackwell (Republican)
Attorney General – Betty Montgomery (Republican)

A new kind of leader

Governor George Voinovich (right) is a new kind of leader—he makes government work. Born on July 15, 1936, in Cleveland, Voinovich began his political career by winning a state representative seat in 1966—in a Democratic district. The second Cleveland mayor elected to the governor's office, Voinovich—"the guy who saved Cleveland" in the 1980s—became governor in January 1991. During the 1994 gubernatorial race, Voinovich faced a colorful opponent. Independent Billy Inmon—a former used-car salesman who was hired and fired as director of the the Ohio State Fair—staged a hunger strike on the capitol lawn when the governor wouldn't debate him. Columbus DJs broadcast live from the statehouse grounds as they ate pastries in front of Inmon's tent. The challenger gave up his fast after 27 days when he realized he could die.

The Legislature The General Assembly is the state's legislative body, consisting of a House of Representatives and a Senate. Legislative sessions begin on the first Monday in January. Representatives are elected every two years and serve two-year terms. Half the senators are elected every two years and serve four-year terms. There are 99 state representatives and 33 state senators.

The Courts The state judiciary consists of the Supreme Court, Courts of Appeals, and Courts of Common Pleas. The legislature also created one Court of Claims in 1975 (located in Franklin County), County Courts, and Municipal Courts. Judges, including Supreme Court Justices, are elected to serve six-year terms. The Supreme Court consists of a Chief Justice and six associate justices, all of whom must have practiced law for at least six years prior to their election.

Cases begin their journey through the legal system in the Municipal and County Courts, and in the Courts of Common Pleas. Every county has a Court of Common Pleas. The other constitutionally established courts—Courts of Appeals and the Supreme Court—are for appeals. There are 12 districts served by the Courts of Appeals, with a panel of three judges hearing and ruling on cases appealed to their jurisdiction. The Chief Justice of the State Supreme Court appoints judges for the Court of Claims, which hears only cases against the State of Ohio.

Elected to Congress
Ohio sends 19 representatives and 2 senators to Congress.

THE SHAPE OF THE STATE

Above the law

An Ohio squatter, John Amberson, thought he was above the law— as did many frontiersmen. Settling on the upper Ohio River in 1785 at "Amberson's Bottom," he declared that anyone has "an undoubted right to pass into every vacant country… and Congress is not empowered to forbid them …."

From territory to state

The Northwest Territory spanned 263 million acres from Pennsylvania all the way to the Mississippi River—a huge expanse for the young United States to administer. The states gave up their claims to western lands when Congress promised that revenue from the sale of these lands would be used to benefit the whole nation.

On July 13, 1787, the Continental Congress, meeting in New York, passed what is commonly called the Northwest Ordinance—before the nation's Constitution was signed. Its six articles affirmed freedoms that would later become the Bill of Rights, and prohibited slavery. "…Not less than three nor more than five states…" would eventually be established as equals to the original 13 states. The determinant for statehood was a population of at least 60,000 people. Parcels of land no smaller than 640 acres at $2 per acre were sold to individuals. Congress wanted to make the land expensive enough to discourage "antisocial squatters." Huge areas of land were sold to big companies. In order to vote or hold office, people had to own land.

The first division of the Northwest Territory was made May 7, 1800. The Indiana Territory (present-day Indiana, Illinois, Wisconsin, and part of Minnesota) was organized with its capital at Vincennes. The smaller eastern division of the Northwest Territory (present-day Ohio and south Michigan) had its capital at Chillicothe. The western boundary line to Fort Recovery was temporary and followed the boundary set up by the Treaty of Greenville in 1795 separating Native Americans from white settlers (see map p. 12).

Congress passed an "enabling act" April 30, 1802, authorizing the citizens of the "eastern division" of the Northwest Territory, now called Ohio, to write a constitution. Ohio was the only state admitted from the Northwest Territory that never existed as a territory under its own name.

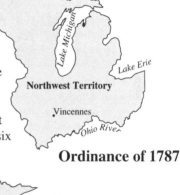

Ordinance of 1787

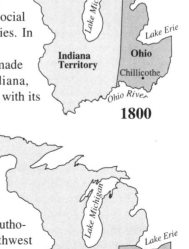

1800

1803

Land divisions in Ohio country

Like pieces of a huge cake, the Northwest Territory was divided into various sections for different reasons. The main land divisions included:

- Virginia Military Tract – Established in 1784, this 4-million-acre section was never ceded by Virginia to the federal government. Land warrants were issued to Virginia's Revolutionary War veterans in lieu of cash payments. This was the only part of the territory not surveyed in the rectangular pattern set up by the Land Ordinance of 1785.
- Western Reserve or New Connecticut – About the same size as the Virginia Military Tract, the Western Reserve was established in 1786 for war veterans and homesteaders. The Fire Lands, a section on the west, was reserved for people from Norwalk and Fairfield, Connecticut, whose homes had been burned by the British.

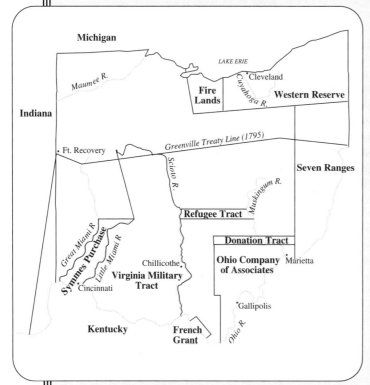

- Seven Ranges – Established in 1786, this section was triangular in shape and established the surveying guidelines (range is a surveying term for 6 miles) for the rest of the territory. Quakers, Irish, and Dutch settlers from Pennsylvania moved here.
- The Ohio Company of Associates – In 1787, this group purchased 1 million acres. The contract required that each township set aside 640 acres for "educational and religious purposes" and 46,000 acres for a university.
- Symmes Purchase – Also called Miami Purchase. A Trenton, New Jersey, judge turned real estate promoter, John Cleves Symmes obtained 312,000 acres between the Little Miami and Miami rivers in 1788. Early settlements included Columbia, established by Symmes' New Jersey neighbor Benjamin Stites, and Losantiville (Cincinnati) in 1788.
- Donation Tract – Settlers willing to use guns against Native Americans could earn their land by doing so. If they defended themselves for five years, the land was theirs.
- The French Grant – Congress allotted 12,000 acres to the original French settlers of Gallipolis who were duped into coming to Ohio. (See p. 69)
- Refugee Tract – Congress set aside 58,000 acres for Canadians who supported the American Revolution. The British had confiscated their lands.

Apparently, the tip of Lake Erie was drawn too far south and the bottom of Lake Michigan too far north on early maps of the Northwest Territory. Unaware, Congress accepted Ohio's 1803 request for statewood. But the "boundary" article of Ohio's constitution had a little addition—it stated that the northern boundary was an east-west line that "should in no event strike Lake Erie below the northern cape of the Maumee River." While working on the document in Chillicothe, the writers found out that early maps were wrong, and they quickly added the new boundary provision. Michigan rightfully claimed this narrow wedge of territory as its southern boundary—the Northwest Ordinance had set it. A dispute over the 6-mile-wide strip of land began because Toledo and its harbor were at stake.

The Toledo War

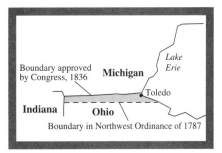

Boundary approved by Congress, 1836 **Michigan** *Lake Erie* Toledo **Indiana** **Ohio** Boundary in Northwest Ordinance of 1787

The festering dispute almost became a war in 1835 when soldiers from both states headed for Toledo. Before any fighting occurred, President Jackson's representatives arranged a truce. If Michigan wanted statehood, the disputed strip should go to Ohio, they said. Michigan didn't have much political clout then and Ohio did. In return for giving up its claim, Congress promised Michigan the present-day Upper Peninsula. At first Michigan's representatives protested—they thought the Upper Peninsula was worthless. But Congress had the upper hand and the dispute was finally settled when Michigan wanted statehood more than Toledo. In 1837, Michigan became the fifth state from the Northwest Territory and Toledo was incorporated as an Ohio city.

CAPITALS AND CAPITOLS

A humble Capitol

Chillicothe's Capitol Building wasn't anything grand in 1800. The ground floor of Bazel Abram's two-story log cabin housed the legislature and the court. On Sundays it was a church. The upper floor was described as a "place of resort for gamblers"—it housed the state's first billiard table. There's no record as to whether the legislators made frequent visits upstairs.

A radical place

Deputy-surveyor of the Virginia Military Tract Nathaniel Massie founded Chillicothe—named after the Native American village of Chalahgawtha—in August 1796. Though Governor St. Clair didn't like this "hotbed of Jeffersonian radicalism" with its "liberal Republicans," the town served as the capital of the Northwest Territory from 1800 to 1802. Chillicothe became the state's first capital in 1803. After a brief stint in Zanesville from 1809 to 1812, the capital came back to Chillicothe from 1812 until the permanent move to Columbus in 1816.

Five capital cities

Between 1788 and 1816 the capital moved four times. Marietta, Cincinnati, and Chillicothe were capitals of the Northwest Territory. Chillicothe was also the state's capital twice—Zanesville interrupted its rule for two years.

A very temporary capital

On February 19, 1809, the General Assembly designated Zanesville as the state capital. But the very next day they changed their minds by passing a resolution for a permanent capital "… not more than 40 miles from what shall be … the common center of the state." Zanesville didn't fall within those guidelines. The Capitol Building, nicknamed Old 1809, was patterned after Philadelphia's Independence Hall. After the capital moved back to Chillicothe, the structure became the Muskingum County Courthouse. It was replaced in 1874.

Clean and pretty

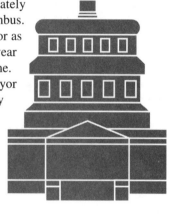 A bustling commercial center on the west bank of the Scioto River, Franklinton—established by Virginia surveyor Lucas Sullivant in 1797—could have been the new capital. But a group of Franklin County realtors—Lyne Starling, John Kerr, Alexander McLaughlin, and James Johnson—wanted the capital on the other side of the river. They surveyed a town site, set aside 10 acres for a Capitol building, 10 acres for a penitentiary, and promised to build both buildings by December 1, 1817. On February 14, 1812, the legislature couldn't resist their offer. The new town was named Columbus—Franklinton ultimately became part of the west side of Columbus. In June 1812, the first lots were sold for as high as $1,000 and by the end of the year 300 people called the new capital home. Jarvis Pike became the city's first mayor in an election at the Columbus Inn. By 1842, when Charles Dickens passed through, the capital had grown into an agricultural trading center that he described as "clean and pretty."

The original Capitol was a plain two-story brick building, with the penitentiary to the southwest.

Politics as usual

The General Assembly stipulated that the capital would remain in Columbus until May 1, 1840, and after that—if the Assembly desired. During the 1839 session a political squabble exploded that almost moved the capital again. Samuel Medary, the state printer, was accused of stealing some of the state's paper for his own use.

An investigation exonerated Medary, but his friends—incensed at the purely political flap—demanded that Whig legislator William Lloyd be thrown out of the legislature. They suspected Lloyd of tampering with the state's books to make Medary look guilty. Lloyd was guilty but he wasn't expelled—he had friends in the legislature and plenty in town who mounted a demonstration for him. Opposing legislators were mad enough at the interference of local citizens that they passed a bill to stop the erection of the new Capitol and to organize a committee to find a new capital. Lengthy discussions began as Newark worked hard to be named the capital in 1842. But the political fight ended on March 6, 1843, when the Assembly passed a resolution to stay in Columbus.

Where's the dome?

In 1838 the legislature decided a new Capitol was needed. Sixty plans were submitted and Cincinnati architect Henry Walter won the $500 first prize. When the final plan came out of the legislature, however, it wasn't Walter's, but a combination of ideas from architect Alexander Davis and painter Thomas Cole, who hadn't won the competition. Walter became the supervising architect—and he made some changes too. The Capitol cornerstone was laid on July 4, 1839. Before the building was

finished 22 years later, 12 governors and 5 architects had come and gone. When the old Statehouse was destroyed by fire in 1852, legislators decided things had to move faster so a railroad was built to haul limestone from Marble Cliff. On November 15, 1861, the Capitol was officially completed, although the legislature had been meeting in its chambers since 1857.

The Greek Revival structure with Doric columns at each of its four entrances cost $1,644,677. Foundation walls, 12 to 15 feet thick, indicated that the building wasn't going anywhere. The original plan called for a dome "surrounded by a colonnade that would match the building's style." But again legislators argued about the details and the cost. Instead, the building was crowned with a less expensive structure—some call it a cheesebox and others a hatbox. Renovations to the building are scheduled for completion in 1996.

Shafted!

When the legislature began meeting in the Capitol in 1857, they started worrying about their water supply. Rainfall was scarce, a drought was forecast, and the state was paying the outrageous sum of $30 a week for the building's water. Statehouse Architect Nathan Kelley convinced the legislators that drilling an artesian well for a mere $3,000 was the answer. Drilling started on July 23, 1857, and didn't stop until October 1, 1860, after about $14,000 had been exhausted. The third well shaft—about 90 feet northeast of the Capitol—did set a record. It plunged 2,775 feet, deeper than any shaft at the time, but there was no water. If legislators had listened to the state geologist, they could have saved a lot of money and had water too. He said that there was a large water supply in an aquifer under the Capitol and installing a pump at 150 feet would give the lawmakers all the water they needed. But the idea of a "noble fountain" of free-flowing water was just too grand a project not to fund and so the legislators wasted money and time on a project that yielded no water at all.

THE OHIO COUNTY ALMANAC

Total number – 88

Largest in size – Ashtabula, 711 square miles

Smallest in size – Lake, 232 square miles

Largest by population – Cuyahoga, 1,412,140

Smallest by population – Vinton, 11,098

Oldest county – Washington, established July 27, 1788

Youngest county – Morrow, established March 1, 1848

Strangest county seat name – Washington Court House, county seat of Fayette County. It was originally called Washington but when the first Court of Common Pleas was held there in 1810 in John Devault's cabin, Court House was added to the town's official name. By the way, the jury reached its verdict in a hazel patch outside the cabin!

County	Population	County Seat	Sq. Miles	Founded	Named after
Adams	25,371	West Union	586	7/10/1797	Pres. John Adams
Allen	109,755	Lima	405	3/1/1820	Col. John Allen
Ashland	47,507	Ashland	424	2/14/1848	Estate of Henry Clay
Ashtabula	99,821	Jefferson	703	6/7/1807	Ashtabula River
Athens	59,549	Athens	508	3/1/1805	Athens, Greece
Auglaize	44,585	Wapakoneta	398	2/14/1848	Auglaize River
Belmont	71,074	St. Clairsville	537	9/7/1801	French meaning "beautiful mountain"
Brown	34,966	Georgetown	493	3/1/1819	General Jacob Brown, War of 1812 hero
Butler	291,479	Hamilton	469	5/1/1803	Gen. Richard Butler
Carroll	26,521	Carrollton	393	1/1/1833	Charles Carroll, signer of Declaration of Independence
Champaign	36,019	Urbana	429	3/1/1805	French meaning "level land"
Clark	147,548	Springfield	398	3/1/1818	Gen. George Rogers Clark
Clermont	150,187	Batavia	456	12/6/1800	Clear Mountain, France
Clinton	35,415	Wilmington	410	3/1/1810	Vice Pres. George Clinton
Columbiana	108,276	Lisbon	534	5/1/1803	Combination of Anna and Columbus
Coshocton	35,427	Coshocton	566	1/31/1810	Delaware word for "Black Bear Town"
Crawford	47,870	Bucyrus	403	4/1/1820	Col. William Crawford, R.W.*
Cuyahoga	1,412,140	Cleveland	459	6/7/1807	Native-American word meaning "crooked"; Cuyahoga River
Darke	53,619	Greenville	600	1/3/1809	Gen. William Darke, R.W.
Defiance	39,350	Defiance	414	4/7/1845	Fort Defiance
Delaware	66,929	Delaware	443	4/1/1807	Delaware tribe
Erie	76,779	Sandusky	264	3/16/1838	Erie tribe
Fairfield	103,461	Lancaster	506	12/9/1800	beautiful "fair fields"
Fayette	27,466	Washington Court House	405	3/1/1810	Marquis de LaFayette
Franklin	961,437	Columbus	542	4/30/1803	Benjamin Franklin
Fulton	38,498	Wauseon	407	4/1/1850	Robert Fulton
Gallia	30,954	Gallipolis	471	4/30/1803	Gaul, early name of France
Geauga	81,129	Chardon	408	3/1/1806	Native-American word for "raccoon"
Greene	136,731	Xenia	415	5/1/1803	Gen. Nathaniel Greene, R.W.
Guernsey	39,024	Cambridge	522	3/1/1810	Isle of Guernsey
Hamilton	866,228	Cincinnati	412	1/2/1790	Alexander Hamilton
Hancock	65,536	Findlay	532	4/1/1820	John Hancock
Hardin	31,111	Kenton	471	4/1/1820	Gen. John Hardin, R.W.
Harrison	16,085	Cadiz	400	2/1/1813	Wm. Henry Harrison
Henry	29,108	Napoleon	415	4/1/1820	Patrick Henry
Highland	35,728	Hillsboro	553	5/1/1805	highlands between Little Miami and Scioto rivers
Hocking	25,533	Logan	423	3/1/1818	Native American word meaning "bottle"; describes shape of Hocking River
Holmes	32,849	Millersburg	424	1/20/1824	Major Holmes, War of 1812
Huron	56,240	Norwalk	495	3/7/1809	Huron tribe
Jackson	30,230	Jackson	420	3/1/1816	Andrew Jackson
Jefferson	80,298	Steubenville	410	7/29/1797	Thomas Jefferson
Knox	47,473	Mt. Vernon	529	3/1/1808	Henry Knox, Sec. of War
Lake	215,499	Painesville	231	3/6/1840	Lake Erie
Lawrence	61,834	Ironton	456	12/21/1815	Capt. James Lawrence, War of 1812
Licking	128,300	Newark	686	3/1/1808	Salt licks near Licking River
Logan	42,310	Bellefontaine	458	3/1/1818	Gen. Benjamin Logan
Lorain	271,126	Elyria	495	12/26/1822	French province of Lorraine
Lucas	462,361	Toledo	341	6/20/1835	Gov. Robert Lucas
Madison	37,068	London	467	3/1/1810	James Madison
Mahoning	264,806	Youngstown	417	3/1/1846	Native American for salt licks, salt licks near Mahoning River
Marion	64,274	Marion	403	4/1/1820	Gen. Francis Marion, R.W.
Medina	122,354	Medina	422	2/18/1812	city in Saudi Arabia
Meigs	22,987	Pomeroy	432	4/1/1819	Gov. Return Jonathan Meigs, Jr.
Mercer	39,443	Celina	457	4/1/1812	Gen. Hugh Mercer, R.W.
Miami	48,800	Troy	410	3/1/1807	Miami tribe, miami means mother
Monroe	15,497	Woodsfield	458	1/29/1813	James Monroe
Montgomery	573,809	Dayton	458	5/1/1803	Gen. Richard Montgomery, R.W.
Morgan	14,194	McConnelsville	420	12/29/1817	Gen. Daniel Morgan, R.W.
Morrow	27,749	Mt. Gilead	406	3/1/1848	Gov. Jeremiah Morrow
Muskingum	82,068	Zanesville	654	3/1/1804	Delaware word meaning "a town on the river side"
Noble	11,336	Caldwell	399	4/1/1851	Political leader Warren P. Noble
Ottawa	40,029	Port Clinton	253	3/6/1840	Native American meaning "trader"
Paulding	20,488	Paulding	419	4/1/1820	R.W. militiaman John Paulding
Perry	31,557	New Lexington	412	3/1/1818	Oliver Hazard Perry, Battle of Lake Erie hero
Pickaway	48,255	Circleville	503	3/1/1810	misspelling of Piqua
Pike	24,249	Waverly	443	2/1/1815	Zebulon Pike
Portage	142,585	Ravenna	494	6/7/1807	From Native-American for portage meaning "carrying path"
Preble	40,113	Eaton	426	3/1/1808	Capt. Edward Preble, R.W.
Putnam	33,819	Ottawa	484	4/1/1820	Rufus Putnam, R.W.
Richland	126,137	Mansfield	497	3/1/1808	richness of the soil
Ross	69,330	Chillicothe	692	8/20/1796	James Ross, Pennsylvania gubernatorial candidate
Sandusky	61,963	Fremont	409	4/1/1820	Native American "at the cold water"
Scioto	80,327	Portsmouth	614	5/1/1803	Native-American for deer
Seneca	59,733	Tiffin	553	4/1/1820	Seneca tribe
Shelby	44,915	Sidney	409	4/1/1819	Gen. Isaac Shelby, Gov. of Ky.
Stark	367,585	Canton	574	2/13/1808	Gen. John Stark, R.W.
Summit	514,990	Akron	412	3/3/1840	Portage Summit, highest point on the Ohio Canal
Trumbull	227,813	Warren	612	7/10/1800	Jonathan Trumbull, Gov. of Ct.
Tuscarawas	84,090	New Philadelphia	569	3/15/1808	Native American for "open mouth"
Union	31,969	Marysville	437	4/1/1820	parts of 4 counties joined to form this county
Van Wert	30,464	Van Wert	410	4/1/1820	Isaac Van Wert, R.W.
Vinton	11,098	McArthur	414	3/12/1850	Samuel F. Vinton, Ohio statesman
Warren	113,909	Lebanon	403	5/1/1803	Civil War Gen. Joseph Warren
Washington	62,254	Marietta	640	7/27/1788	George Washington
Wayne	101,461	Wooster	557	8/15/1796	Gen. Anthony Wayne
Williams	36,956	Bryan	422	4/1/1820	David Williams, R.W.
Wood	113,269	Bowling Green	619	4/1/1820	Col. Wood, Fort Meigs engineer
Wyandot	22,254	Upper Sandusky	406	2/3/1845	Wyandot tribe

*R.W. – Revolutionary War

STATE SYMBOLS

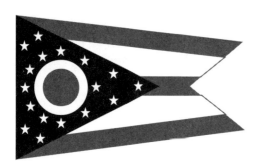

The rising sun

William Creighton, the 21-year-old secretary of state, used his own seal on official papers. While visiting Thomas Worthington's home, Governor Tiffin, Creighton, and others spent the night talking and playing cards. The following morning the men walked across the grounds as the sun rose above Mount Logan. Impressed by the scene, Creighton remarked, "The rising sun of a new state!" He incorporated the sun rising above Mount Logan on a field of wheat when the state seal was designed. A bundle of 15 arrows and a sheaf of wheat are in the foreground. One of Ohio's newest state parks, the Great Seal State Park, was established in 1980 to commemorate the events in 1803 that led to the design of the state seal.

A motto and a slogan

The state's first motto, adopted in 1865, was *Imperium in Imperio* meaning "Empire within an Empire." It didn't really fit the state and was abandoned. A new motto, suggested by 12-year-old James Mastronardo of Cincinnati, was adopted in 1959. It's taken from Matthew 19:15: "With God, All Things Are Possible." But most people are more familiar with the catchy phrase penned by a Columbus advertising agency—"Ohio, the Heart of It All."

Buckeye burgee

Every state flag is square, except Ohio's. Buckeyes have a burgee-shaped flag (pennant with two points), designed by architect John Eisemann in 1901 for the Ohio Building at Buffalo's Pan-American Exposition. The flag's sharp tips represent the state's hills and valleys. The white circle is an O for "Ohio" and also the shape of a buckeye. The 17 stars indicate Ohio's entrance to the Union as the 17th state. The red and white stripes stand for waterways and roads.

More state symbols

State Flower – scarlet carnation, adopted in 1904, in honor of President William McKinley's favorite flower

State Bird – the cardinal (*Cardinalis cardinalis*), adopted in 1933

State Tree – Ohio buckeye (*Aesculus glabra*), adopted in 1953

State Animal – white-tail deer, adopted in 1987

State Fossil - the trilobite, adopted in 1985

Sate Gem Stone – flint, used by Native Americans for arrowheads, adopted in 1965

State Herb Capital – Gahanna, designated in 1973

State Insect – ladybug, adopted in 1975

Beautiful Ohio

The music for the state song, "Beautiful Ohio" adopted in 1969, was written by Mary Earl (a pseudonym for Robert Kind) with original words by Ballard MacDonald. In 1989, several words were rewritten by Wilbert McBride. Most Buckeyes are probably more familiar with Ohio's state rock song, "Hang on Sloopy," because it's a favorite of The Ohio State University Marching Band. Written by Ohio's own Rick Derringer, the popular 1960s song was adopted as a state song in 1985.

Beautiful Ohio

I sailed away;
Wandered afar;
Crossed the mighty restless sea;
Looked for where I ought to be.
Cities so grand, mountains above,
Led to this land I love.

Beautiful Ohio, where the golden grain
Dwarfs the lovely flowers in the summer rain.
Cities rising high, silhouette the sky.
Freedom is supreme in this majestic land;
Mighty factories seem to hum a tune, so grand.
Beautiful Ohio, thy wonders are in view,
Land where my dreams all come true.

Drink up

Ohio had a huge tomato harvest in 1965 and honored the red fruit by adopting tomato juice as the state beverage that year. When Governor James Rhodes was in office, he encouraged his fellow citizens to drink up. "If every Ohioan drank one quart of tomato juice a year," he said, "it would mean 5,000 more jobs for Ohio."

REMEMBERING OHIO LEADERS

Dictator of the Northwest

Revolutionary General Arthur St. Clair (right) became governor of the Northwest Territory on October 5, 1787, and "ruled" for 14 years. He was president of the Continental Congress at the time and didn't really want the job. He told Alexander Hamilton he felt like he'd been "… banished to another planet …."

For someone who didn't like his job, St. Clair desperately tried to hang on to it. As early as 1790, he drew up a plan with "creative" boundary lines that would have prevented any part of the territory from acquiring the 60,000 people required for statehood. At the statehood convention in November 1802, he told the delegates their actions were illegal. They wanted statehood; he thought they weren't ready. President Jefferson dismissed St. Clair on November 22, 1802. A ruined man, he returned to Pennsylvania, sold his farm to survive, and died a bitter man in 1818. Although remembered as a "dictator," St. Clair did establish a territorial government under federal authority.

Two gentlemen from Virginia

Two Virginians—Dr. Edward Tiffin, and his brother-in-law, Thomas Worthington—settled in Chillicothe, Ohio, in 1798. Tiffin came with a letter of recommendation written by George Washington to Governor St. Clair. They built beautiful homes like those of Virginia planters. Worthington's estate, Adena, became a popular stop for important people. Thomas Worthington was Governor St. Clair's bitter rival and led delegates to Washington to complain about the governor's anti-statehood tactics. President Jefferson listened and Worthington's mission paved the way for a state constitutional convention. When delegates met in Chillicothe on November 1, 1802, to write the constitution, Edward Tiffin presided. On March 3, 1803, Tiffin was inaugurated as the state's first governor and served from 1803 to 1807. He later became a U.S. senator, served as the first director of the National Land Office, and surveyor-general of the Northwest. Worthington became one of the first two senators from Ohio, and its sixth governor.

No potatoes or creased pants

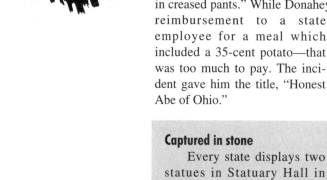

Three-time governor and one-term U.S. Senator Alvin Victor Donahey never minced words. Called "Honest Vic," he set legislative priorities in a simple way in 1923. He divided bills into two stacks—one pile that would do the people good and the other for bills that wouldn't. The bad ones were thrown in the wastebasket. Known as a man of the people, his political slogan was "You can't win a campaign in creased pants." While Donahey was state auditor, he once disallowed reimbursement to a state employee for a meal which included a 35-cent potato—that was too much to pay. The incident gave him the title, "Honest Abe of Ohio."

Captured in stone

Every state displays two statues in Statuary Hall in Washington, D.C., to honor citizens of their choosing. Ohio is represented by the President James A. Garfield and Democratic politician William Allen (right). In 1832, Allen was elected to Congress by just one vote and, at age 71, he became the oldest man to serve as the state's governor in 1874. Both statues were the work of Cincinnati sculptor Charles Niehaus.

THE NATURE OF OHIO

The French called the Ohio River La Belle Rivière or "beautiful river." They could have used "*la belle*" to describe the landscape of the entire state—the gently rolling hills of the Allegheny Plateau in the southeast, the Lake Plains in the north, and the rolling land of the Central Plains, once covered with a carpet of trees.

Ohio's rock layers were laid down over millions of years. Later, the ice and melting water of great glaciers carved the course of the mighty Ohio River and left behind moraines, caves, gorges, and unique rock formations. Today, Kelleys Island glacial grooves are a reminder of the power of those ancient masses of ice.

Natural forces shaped the state's original beauty. And it's still spectacular today, thanks to the efforts of government and private citizens. Wetlands are being restored, forests planted, mining areas reclaimed, and waterways cleaned up. The nature of Ohio is thriving.

- Ancient Treasures
- A Watery Foundation
- Parks and Preserves
- Mother Nature's Wrath
- The Green Canopy
- Wildlife
- Environmental Benefactors
- Hazardous Waste

ANCIENT TREASURES

Rocky times

Glaciers moving down from Canada carried numerous rocks called erratics that were not native to the region. One of those limestone erratics—the Brassfield erratic—lies near Oregonia. The giant 400-million-year-old rock ranges from 5 to 17 feet thick. In the mid-1840s, citizens explained the presence of erratics by claiming they were left behind after the Great Flood described in the Bible.

Underground treasures

Commodore Oliver Hazard Perry discovered a limestone cave on the south side of South Bass Island. Measuring 208 by 165 feet, Perry's Cave was used for ammunition storage before the Battle of Lake Erie, and served as a jail for British prisoners after Perry's victory. Drinking water was pumped from a pool along the north cave wall to the Victory Hotel, at one time the biggest hotel in the world. The hotel burned down in 1919. Perry's Cave isn't open to the public but eight other Ohio caves and caverns are. Two of the most interesting include:

• Ohio Caverns – Near West Liberty, these caverns are often billed as the most colorful in the nation. Orange, red, brown, and yellow mineral deposits provide a striking contrast to the pure white stalactites. Discovered in 1897 when a sinkhole developed, the caverns also boast the largest stalactite in the state—Crystal King (left.) A perfect conical shape, the formation is 5 feet long and approximately 250,000 years old.

• Seneca Caverns – These caverns are in an area southwest of Cleveland known as the "earthquake crack." A huge split in the earth created caverns as long as 250 feet.

Oak Openings

When the last glacier retreated about 12,000 years ago, it left a very unique landscape behind in northwestern Ohio, from southwest Lucas County to Sylvania. When the water level dropped, beaches became ridges of sand where plants and trees grew. In other places, the sand formed dunes and in the wetter areas grasses and plants grew between the dunes. Bur oak trees grew here too, spaced far enough apart so settlers could travel through in their wagons. They named this region Oak Openings for that reason.

Toledo Area Metroparks bought Oak Openings in the 1930s and the state added Maumee State Forest next to it in the 1940s, a grand total of about 6,500 recreational acres. Since most people thought this unsightly area needed a face-lift, thousands of pine trees were planted to get rid of the "sand-blown" look. Today, a more enlightened view protects this place of natural contrasts. Unlike any other area in the state, Oak Openings is a meeting place for plants from every climate in the country. In fact, one-third of all the state's rare plants grow here. But the Karner blue butterfly, endangered elsewhere, perished in the human onslaught.

❧ The Ice Age deposits of Ohio are rich with fossilized animals. Some of the important discoveries include:

Creatures from the past

•The largest skeleton of a giant ground sloth in the world. It was found by Lowell Carter outside Ansonia in Darke County in 1966. Dayton Museum of Natural History (where it is now on display) excavated the skeleton from 1970 to 1972.

• Of some 180 mastodon fossils found in the state, the Ohio Historical Center at Columbus has the largest and most complete. It was discovered on a Clark County farm in 1894.

Teenage DNA whiz

A 17-year-old high-school senior at Bellefontaine's Benjamin Logan High School successfully isolated DNA from a 20-million-year-old plant fossil in February 1995. John Lee is the first high-school student ever to do so—such work is usually left to university graduate students. Beginning in August 1994, Lee worked in the school science lab two nights a week after football practice. The teenager ranks his DNA work among his "best memories from high school, right up there with our football team going 10 and 0 my junior year." His experiment should be highly rewarded at the school science fair!

A groovy place

A glacier moving south and west from Labrador, Canada, carved some very deep furrows in the ancient limestone bedrock of Kelleys Island. The tremendous weight of the mile-thick glacier and the huge boulders dragged with it, cut the long furrows. During the 1870s, large quarrying operations uncovered and destroyed many of the biggest grooves, including the very deep Great Groove. During the 1970s, Richard Goldthwait of Ohio State University and his students excavated the grooves preserved today. Located on a ridge above the north shore of the island, the "mega-grooves" are 400 feet long, 10 to 15 feet deep, and about 30 feet wide. Geologists believe another set of more shallow grooves lies buried next to those that were excavated. There are no plans for their excavation.

A WATERY FOUNDATION

❧ Much of the land near western Lake Erie—about 300,000 acres— used to be marsh and swamp. This region extended south to the Great Black Swamp, a wetland area that was 120 miles long and from 20 to 40 miles wide southwest of the big lake. This area was drained, farmed, and developed until less than 5 percent of the original wetlands remain. Nature may be turning the area into wetland again, however. Scientists have discovered that the entire area near the lake is gradually tilting and that the land southwest of the lake is actually sinking about two feet every century.

Making them wet again

Saving rivers

❀ Ohio established the first state scenic river program in the United States in 1968. Later, recreational and wild rivers were added. The whole purpose of the program is to protect waterways for the future. The "wild" designation means a waterway is free-flowing—its floodplain and forests are basically undeveloped. A "scenic" river is a little less wild. The "recreational" designation is the least scenic or wild. Ohio has some fairly long creeks that are classified as rivers. Waterways, their designations, and the miles protected include:

- Big & Little Darby Creeks Scenic River (82 miles)
- Chagrin Scenic River (49 miles)
- Grand Wild and Scenic River (56 miles). The "wild" section is in Lake County; the "scenic" segment is in Ashtabula County
- Little Beaver Creek Wild & Scenic River (36 miles). The Little Beaver Creek was Ohio's first Wild River and the state's second National Scenic River
- Little Miami Scenic River (105 miles). The first National Scenic River in Ohio
- Maumee Scenic and Recreational River (96 miles)
- Olentangy Scenic River (22 miles)
- Sandusky Scenic River (65 miles)
- Stillwater & Greenville Creek Scenic River (93 miles)
- Upper Cuyahoga Scenic River (25 miles)

Water, water everywhere
Ohio has water everywhere—about one mile of water for each square mile of land. There are 44,000 miles of rivers and streams and over 200,000 acres of water in lakes, ponds, and reservoirs.

That's what friends are for

The Friends of the Crooked River sponsored the first Conserve-A-Curve RiverDay in 1990. They joined with other volunteers to clean up river banks, plant trees, and stencil "Dump No Waste—Drains to Lake" warnings on storm sewers. The Cuyahoga River could have used some concerned friends back on June 22, 1969, when its oily, polluted waters actually caught fire. It was the only river in the nation designated as a fire hazard. The 100-mile-long waterway was dead—not even sludge worms could survive. It had supported 50 species of fish—Native Americans talked about sturgeon the size of dolphins, but by 1970 the river was the butt of jokes. "Anyone who falls into the Cuyahoga does not drown, he decays."

The Cuyahoga, named after a Native-American word meaning "crooked," begins at two springs in northern Geauga County, just 15 miles from Lake Erie where its U-shaped course finally ends. Generations of Ohioans dredged, dammed, and developed the land along the river, changing its shallow, indistinct channel into a major thoroughfare for business. But today, the river is no longer a fire hazard. Since the Clean Water Act of 1972, water-treatment plants and other efforts have brought the river back. Several species of fish have returned, but there's still work to do. No longer the butt of jokes, the Cuyahoga is a model for environmental cleanup.

A really great place

In 1990, The Nature Conservancy compiled a list of a dozen "Last Great Places" worth saving in the world. Ohio's Darby Creek was on that list. Located in Central Ohio, the unimposing 80-mile-long waterway is one of the few clean and healthy Midwest streams still flowing. Major conservation efforts are underway to preserve it—it's the number-two priority for conservation funds in the Midwest region. In the small 556-square-mile watershed there are 34 mammal species, 170 bird species, 80 species of fish, and 40 mollusk species—many of them very rare. Ecologists characterize the stream as "a little piece of what a lot of our country was like 300 years ago." If Darby Creek had been home to four-legged mammals instead of less-noticeable water creatures, it probably would have been a national park years ago.

🍁 Ohio's largest glacial gift, Lake Erie, was reduced to its present size about 25,000 years ago after its overflow became the Ohio River. Known to Native Americans as "sweetwater sea," that sweetness had soured by the early 1970s. The lake was pronounced dead in 1970, choked with pollution and at times resembling "thick pea soup." Mats of algae and scum floated on the surface, beaches were closed, and the whole mess smelled. But the Clean Water Act of 1972 required better wastewater treatment before water reached the lake. And on April 15, 1972, Canadian Prime Minister Pierre Trudeau and President Richard Nixon signed the Great Lakes Water Quality Agreement, promising to clean up the water. Ohio took the lake's protection a step further in 1988 by passing a law that bans the sale of detergents with phosphorus in over 35 Lake Erie watershed regions. Lake Erie is once again a world-class walleye fishery and a great place to enjoy water sports. Citizens are involved in keeping the lake cleaner. Each year volunteers participate in the Coastweeks program, cleaning up beaches and wetlands. In 1992 the program included the first-ever Lake Erie Underwater Cleanup at Put-in-Bay (right). About 180 scuba divers and other volunteers hauled over 1 ton of junk from the harbor waters.

A very big glacial gift

Lake Erie facts
- 4th largest and shallowest Great Lake
- 12th largest freshwater lake in the world
- 241 miles long and 57 miles wide, containing 132 trillion gallons of water
- 28 Ohio communities use Lake Erie as their water source
- Ohio's part of Lake Erie is the only place on the Great Lakes where artificial reefs are being built as habitat for fish. It takes about 25,000 tons of concrete rock or brick pieces to construct one reef.

Buckeye jellyfish

AWESOME

Most of the state's glacial lakes are "small cups of clear water" called kettle hole, pothole, or marl lakes. Some of them are home to a creature you'd expect to find in the oceans but not in freshwater—jellyfish. That's right, freshwater jellyfish! Just look in Portage County's Crystal Lake and you might see the country's only freshwater jellyfish in one of two forms—the medusa with its tentacle-like appendages and the hydroid—a coral-like colony of one to four jellyfish. Sometimes the lakes are teeming with these strange creatures and other times they completely disappear.

The old woman looks good

❦ Estuaries are usually found where a river empties into the ocean, creating a unique habitat where freshwater and salt water mix. But Ohio has an estuary on Lake Erie called Old Woman Creek State Nature Preserve and National Estuarine Research Reserve—the only one on the Great Lakes. Here, freshwater from inland mixes with the freshwater of Lake Erie to make a watery habitat that is chemically different from either. Administered jointly by state and federal governments, these 571 acres of very rare wetland habitat provide a spawning ground for many of Lake Erie's fish species. And 300 kinds of birds, ranging from shorebirds to ducks and geese, find refuge in Ohio's best remaining example of a coastal wetland.

PARKS AND PRESERVES

They're naturals

❦ Some endangered natural lands were bought before the Ohio Natural Areas Act, passed in 1970, provided organization and management for nature preserves and natural areas. The size of each area or preserve isn't important. Allen F. Beck State Nature Preserve in Hocking County covers 2,234 acres, while Bigelow Cemetery Prairie and nearby Smith Cemetery Prairie each cover only 1 acre. Administered by the Ohio Division of Natural Areas and Preserves since 1976, these areas can be found in state forests, state parks—or neither. Many projects are jointly owned and managed by the state and other organizations such as The Nature Conservancy, Toledo Metroparks, and Dayton Power and Light. Today, more than 100 nature preserves protect about 20,000 of the state's most beautiful and unique features. These areas are designed for such low-impact activities as hiking, bird-watching, or photography.

When is a bog a fen?

❦ Cedar Bog in Champaign County was the first land specifically purchased by the state as a nature preserve. But it's not really a bog at all, it's a fen—an unusual wetland fed by underwater mineral springs. Cedar Bog has a climate more like that of a northern Michigan bog—maybe that's how it got its name. July is the only month without any frost.

Edward Thomas, a curator for the Ohio Historical Society, bought the area in 1942 to save it from being drained. He persuaded Governor John Bricker to purchase the land for the state and let the Historical Society manage it. Designated a National Natural Landmark in 1971,

the 400-acre bog once covered 7,000 acres and is home to the endangered massasauga or prairie rattlesnake, the spotted turtle, rare butterflies, 160 species of birds, and 40 species of endangered plants. It hasn't been easy preserving the bog. In 1972, a group of citizens had to stop U.S. Route 68 one mile short of its proposed path next to the bog, to protect their favorite wetland.

At the edge of a ledge

Nelson Kennedy Ledges State Park in Portage County showcases outcroppings of Sharon sandstone that form ledges or rock overhangs on its cliffs. These ledges are usually cooler than the surrounding area and plants uncommon to northeast Ohio—ginseng, rare trailing arbutus, whorled pogonia orchids, and wintergreen—grow here. Although the cliffs and ledges are inviting, you can't climb them at Nelson Kennedy. The only ledges available for rappelling are Whipp's Ledges in Hinckley—you might encounter an unfriendly buzzard there. Administered by Cleveland Metroparks, permits are available to climbers who can prove insurance coverage—$100,000 to cover property damage and $1 million for bodily injury.

A park of superlatives

There are many parks and preserves in southeast Ohio, but none as impressive as Hocking Hills State Park. The caves around the park were well known by 1870, but the first state land wasn't purchased until 1924. Some virgin stands of timber owe their survival to the steep gorge walls that made them inaccessible. Known for its waterfalls and sandstone formations, the park's 10,000 acres are divided into six separate and unique areas. Ash Cave is the largest cave in the state. A popular campsite of Native Americans, mounds of ash were left here by the early campers. Named for an old hermit that lived inside it, Old Man's Cave (left) boasts natural sandstone statues, the Devil's Bathtub and the Sphinx Head. Cedar Falls should be Hemlock Falls—the thick forest nearby is hemlock. The state's favorite waterfall plunges 50 feet to a pool below. Conkle's Hollow, named after W.J. Conkle who carved his name on the gorge walls in 1797, is one of the state's deepest gorges. Its cliffs rise as high as 240 feet. Rock House, set in the side of a cliff, contains large rooms. From 1835 to 1925, this was a popular picnic area with a 16-room hotel nearby. Cantwell Cliffs is located in the most rugged part of the park. Long ago the cliffs' namesake, Framer Cantwell, caught two Native Americans trying to steal his tobacco and locked them in his barn to break them of their habit.

It helped save a river

🍁 Established in December 1974, the 33,000-acre Cuyahoga Valley National Recreation Area was a major factor in the cleanup of the Cuyahoga River. With a charge to "preserve recreational open space necessary to the urban environment," the mostly undeveloped area provides recreational space for nearly 4 million urban residents within 30 miles. Administered by the National Park Service, the National Recreation Area offers more than 12 parks, 2 ski resorts, Hale Farm and Village, 20 miles of old canal towpath trail, and the Cuyahoga Valley Scenic Railroad linking Independence to Akron's Howard Street. It's been called a model for "open space within the urban milieu."

With or without the Feds

The Cuyahoga National Recreation Area sits in the middle of another proposed federal "park"—the Ohio and Erie Canal National Heritage Corridor. This 87-mile corridor would link Cleveland to Zoar by following the Cuyahoga and Tuscarawas rivers and what remains of the Ohio and Erie Canal. The aim is to take visitors back to how things were in 1827 when the canal was in use. Nonprofit groups have been working for 10 years to push for the federal designation, but the bill was unable to make it to the House floor before Congress adjourned in 1994. However, some Ohio communities aren't waiting for the official designation. Akron is already using federal dollars to reopen parts of the canal in its business district that were filled with concrete.

Three-for-one purpose

🍁 The Ottawa National Wildlife Refuge encompasses part of what's left of the original 300,000-acre marsh that used to stretch along Lake Erie. Near Toledo, its nearly 8,000-plus acres contain nesting sites for bald eagles and critical habitat for birds migrating along the Mississippi and Atlantic flyways. Great blue herons live here year-round, with 1,500 pairs nesting on the biggest heronry in the Great Lakes at West Sister Island, an 80-acre refuge managed by Ottawa. This federal wildlife refuge borders the southeast portion of Crane Creek State Park—one of the few nesting sites left on the Great Lakes for the bald eagle. Coupled with the NWR, Crane Creek State Park's 79 acres and 2,600-acre Magee Marsh Wildlife Area make the whole region a birder's paradise.

A state park brief

Ohioans love their state parks. And they visit them more often than the citizens of any other state except California. That's because of the diversity—some parks preserve the state's historical past; others its natural past; and eight are full-service resorts. Today, there are over 75 state parks including:

• Deer Creek State Resort Park is located on federal land. The federal government bought the land and constructed Deer Creek Reservoir to enhance flood control and then leased it all back to the state. President Harding's cabin (left) is in this park. A lottery held every October determines who gets to stay—and pay $735 per week—in the presidential retreat.

- Grand Lake St. Marys State Park was a reservoir for the Miami-Erie Canal, built from 1837 to 1841. Until Hoover Dam was erected, it was the largest man-made lake in the world.
- Headlands Beach State Park boasts the state's longest beach—one mile. It also contains the only state-protected sand dunes.
- Cleveland Lakefront State Park, composed of four parks, is the most heavily used park in the state and the second most heavily visited in the country.

A good deal, and a good deal more

First opened in 1961, Ohio's ReCreation land is a little different than state parks. Spreading across five counties in Southeast Ohio, ReCreation land's 125,000 acres of forests, grassy hills, and over 350 lakes and ponds are located on what was once a strip-mining operation. In a unique partnership, the state and American Electric Power worked together to restore the mined land and stock its lakes with fish. The first 500 Canada geese came from a park in Canada and the flock now numbers several thousand. All you need to enjoy this beautiful scenery is a visitor's permit, which is completely free of charge.

A real original

John Bryan State Park is named after millionaire-eccentric John Bryan who made a fortune as owner of a physician's supply house in Cincinnati. He bought 335 acres along the Little Miami River in 1896, named it Riverside Farm, and built the biggest barn in the world—next to the czar of Russia's. The massive five-story affair—208 feet by 130 feet—was destroyed in 1967. His land was willed to the state on the condition that it would become a "Forestry, Botanic, and Wildlife Reserve Park and Experiment Station" named after him. An atheist, he also stipulated that no religious services could ever be held on the grounds. In May 1923, Bryan's land became one of the state's first parks. Breathtaking Clifton Gorge, whose steep cliffs are habitat to rare plants such as the red baneberry, is found here. You need a permit to even walk through portions of the gorge. An old story tells about one of Daniel Boone's friends, Cornelius Darnell, who jumped across the gorge in the 1780s to get away from his Shawnee captors. That activity is not allowed today.

AWESOME

MOTHER NATURE'S WRATH

Forecasting the weather

🍁 Cincinnati lays claim to the origin of the National Weather Service. While director of the Cincinnati Observatory between 1868 and 1870, New York-native Cleveland Abbe organized several weather-watchers who sent their information by telegraph to Abbe each day. He studied the data and drew the first weather maps, from which he made daily weather forecasts. President Grant decided weather forecasting had merit—at Abbe's constant urging—and in 1870 he formed the U.S. Weather Bureau and put Abbe at the helm. During his lifetime, Abbe wrote more than 300 papers on climate and weather.

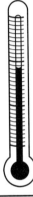

The statistics

Highest temperature – 113°F, Thurman, July 4, 1897, and near Gallipolis, July 21, 1934
Lowest temperature – –39°F, Milligan, February 10, 1899
Most rainfall each year – Chardon, 45.22 inches
Least rainfall each year – Put-in-Bay, 30.96 inches
Most rainfall in short period – 9.54 inches in 8 hours, Sandusky, July 12, 1966
Most snowfall during a single storm – 36 inches in three days, Steubenville, November, 1950
Worst blizzard – January 26, 1978, caused $100 million in damage and 51 deaths
Latest snowfall – June 23, 1902, northern Ohio
Earliest freeze – August, 1942, northeastern Ohio
Longest growing season – Put-in-Bay, 208 days

Too much of a good thing

🍁 With so many rivers and streams, there's always too much water somewhere in the state. Native Americans warned early settlers about founding cities at Dayton and Cincinnati's sites, but what did they know? Plenty! Heavy flooding plagued the state for years, but the 1913 deluge was a giant. Between March 23 and 28, 1913, the Scioto and Miami valleys were devastated. Dayton (left) was hit with the equivalent of 1.5 million gallons of water per second, the same amount of water that passes over Niagara Falls in 30 days. In Columbus, bridges were washed away and 4,000 houses and stores were destroyed. In the end, 200,000 people were homeless, 20,000 houses were destroyed, and damage totaled about $300 million.

Dayton's citizens acted and the city began a study of drainage, storms, and flood control two months after the flood. Six dams were proposed and Governor James Cox of Dayton got the necessary legislation passed. When the big flood of 1937 descended, Dayton wasn't touched, but Cincinnati suffered in "the Black Sunday fire" that burned the city as gas on the water's surface ignited. Congress finally took note and began passing legislation that ultimately became the federal Flood Control Act. Dams, locks, and short canals were built to control flooding.

Twister tales

If you can get through the winter and the floods in Ohio, you've got tornadoes to contend with. The state averages 12 to 14 each year, with 25 percent occurring in June. Two have been especially destructive. On June 28, 1924, the "Lorain tornado" hit Sandusky about 4:30 P.M., veered out over Lake Erie, and then came crashing into Lorain 45 minutes later. Lorain's death count was 78, with 1,200 injured and $11 million in property damage. On April 3, 1974, about 150 tornadoes touched down all the way from Alabama to Ontario, Canada. That day Xenia was hit with a twister that tore through the city for 5 minutes in a half-mile-wide path, causing $100 million in property damage and killing 34.

THE GREEN CANOPY

An awesome forest

Early settlers found 95 percent of Ohio covered with a thick green-tree carpet. And these were big trees—trunk diameters as big as 10 feet weren't unusual. In a little over 80 years—from 1800 to 1883—Ohio's original 24 million acres of forest were down to 4 million. It wasn't just farmers that felled trees. The iron furnaces of the Hanging Rock region needed fuel, lumber companies cut down forests, and the railroads used at least 1 million cords annually by 1860. Today, 7 million acres, or about one-quarter of the state, are forested, with every county claiming at least a patch or two. Lawrence County tops the list with 73 percent of its land forested, while Wood, Madison, and Fayette counties are down around 3 percent. Thanks to reforestation efforts begun years ago, Ohio has tall trees again.

🍁 About 50 acres of virgin forest (white oak, tulip tree, white ash, black gum, beech, sugar maple, and hickory) near Centerville—Dysart Woods—was designated a National Natural Landmark in 1967. Some trees are over 100 feet tall. In 1962, The Nature Conservancy purchased the woods to keep the area from being logged. However, Ohio University rescued the conservation organization, which was unable to pay off the loan, and the university now manages the ancient stand.

Primitive last stand

🍁 In 1955, Ohio decided to formally recognize its big trees. As of 1995, the State Division of Forestry lists 135 state champion trees in its "native and naturalized" species category and 52 on the "ornamental" species list. A number of the champs are growing very well in the state's cemeteries. Cincinnati's Spring Grove Cemetery counts 22 state champion trees; Columbus' Green Lawn Cemetery hosts 9 state champs; and 6 state champs grow at Woodland Cemetery in Dayton. Seven of the state champion trees are also number one for their species nationally—an English oak, a shingle oak, a slippery elm, a swamp cottonwood, a sycamore, a two-winged silver bell, and a yellowwood. Try repeating that list quickly!

We are the champions

A walk on the "wild" side

If you want to take a long walk across the northern United States, try the North Country National Scenic Trail. It begins in New York's Adirondack Mountains and winds all the way to North Dakota—the longest continuous trail in the country. In Ohio, the North Country trail follows a U-shaped path. It also follows portions of the state's "best-kept-secret," the Buckeye Trail. Begun in 1959, this trail's 1,200 miles touch all four corners of Ohio. Marked by spots of blue paint, the footpath winds through national forest, state forests and parks, along old canal towpaths, old railroad beds, and private property. Each 50-mile section, labeled with a different name, is detailed on a waterproof map—does it rain in Ohio? Over 1,000 members of the Buckeye Trail Association in Worthington keep the trail in tiptop shape.

For the love of trees ... and other plants

❧ Mining engineer Albert Holden made his fortune as president of a coal company and managing director of two smelting firms. Before Albert's death in 1913, his sister Roberta convinced him to fund an arboretum in Cleveland. To that end he established a trust fund in memory of his daughter Elizabeth, who died at age 12. Finally, in 1931, a 100-acre site in Kirtland Township was chosen. That original acreage has grown to 3,100 acres with almost 5,000 plant species. Holden Arboretum is now the largest arboretum in the country. The nation's finest botanical library, Corning Library, is also on the grounds.

Ohioan Beman Dawes struck oil in West Virginia, founded the Pure Oil Company, and became a very rich man—rich enough to own five homes. But Daweswood in Licking County was his favorite. He purchased the property to stop loggers from cutting the trees. While living there, he asked some of his famous friends—Orville Wright, Red Grange, Admiral James Byrd, plus about 60 others—to donate trees to help establish an arboretum. It's a practice that continues today—Senator John Glenn and Jesse Owens have donated trees. The 1,000-acre-plus Dawes Arboretum is a living monument to a man who loved nature, and trees in particular. You can even enjoy the garden from the air. Hedges, 2,100 feet long, spell out "Dawes Arboretum" in greenery (above). It's the largest "letter hedge" in the world.

The one and only

❧ The only national forest in Ohio—Wayne National Forest—used to be part of Indiana's Hoosier National Forest, miles away. Until 1993, the Wayne-Hoosier National Forest was administered as one unit from Bedford, Indiana—Wayne National Forest wasn't quite big enough to break away before then. With headquarters in Athens, the Wayne

National Forest now covers 220,000 acres in three separate parcels—the Ironton, Athens, and Marietta units. The federal government first began buying land in 1934, but it wasn't until 1951 that those purchases were officially designated as Wayne National Forest.

A natural evolution

All of Ohio's state forests—and eventually state parks—started with a $10,000 appropriation from the state legislature in 1915. The following year the Division of Forestry bought 1,500 Lawrence County acres for Dean State Forest and 221 Athens County acres for Waterloo State Forest. In 1924, the first state forest-park—Hocking—was purchased, followed by Mohican in 1928. Then came John Bryan, Nelson Ledges, and Hueston Woods.

Things got a little more organized in 1949, when the Department of Natural Resources was created. Areas mainly used for recreation became state parks under the jurisdiction of the Division of Parks. John Bryan, Nelson Ledges, and Hueston Woods became state parks, while the Division of Forestry administered state forests. Today, Ohio's 19 state forest areas cover 177,000 acres.

The Moongate scandal

When the *Apollo* moon mission returned to Earth in 1976, the Ohio Division of Forestry got some sycamore tree seeds that were taken to the moon. The seeds were planted at the Marietta Nursery. One of the tiny seedlings was going to be planted at the forestry office during an impressive ceremony. But when the district forester saw the scrawny, unhealthy-looking sycamore, he decided to replace it with an alternate. After all, who would know? He searched in Shade River State Forest, but didn't find a suitable replacement. While traveling on State Route 50, however, he came to a quick stop after spotting the perfect candidate. He quickly dug up the small tree and sped away. However, another forestry worker saw the dastardly deed and later divulged the shocking truth. To this day no one knows where the original "moon" tree is.

WILDLIFE

The Ohio Fish Commission was created in 1873 by the state legislature to rescue declining fish populations. During the 1930s, the Division of Forestry led reforestation efforts and the wild turkey and white-tailed deer returned. In 1949, what was left of that early organization became the Division of Wildlife in the newly created Department of Natural Resources. In 1975, the Division of Wildlife organized a program for protecting the state's endangered wildlife. Today the division concentrates it efforts on several species, including the paddlefish, pugnose minnow, peregrine falcon, barn owl, common tern, and bald eagle.

Protecting the weak

And then there were none

Passenger pigeons used to blacken the skies of Ohio during the 1700s. In 1774, an eyewitness wrote that "three years ago ... they appeared in such great numbers that the ground under their roosting-place was covered with their dung above a foot high, during one night. The Indians went out, killed them with sticks and came home loaded. At such a time, the noise the pigeons make is such that it is difficult for people near them to hear or understand each other." Pigeons were slaughtered and, a little more than 100 years later, they were extinct. Martha, the world's last passenger pigeon, died September 1, 1914, at the Cincinnati Zoo. The Passenger Pigeon Memorial, located on the zoo's grounds, pays tribute to Martha. She is now displayed, however, at the Smithsonian in Washington, D.C.

Zooming in on zoos

The Cincinnati Zoo, established in 1875, was the second major zoo in the country. Located on 67 acres in the center of the city, *Time* magazine called it the "sexiest zoo in the country" because of its successful captive-breeding program. Since 1970, 37 gorillas have been born, along with half the world's white Bengal tiger population. But the Columbus Zoo has something to brag about, too. Colo (below), the first captive-bred gorilla in the world, was born at the zoo in 1956. This beautiful zoo located on the Scioto River is one of only three zoos in the country to have bonobos or pygmy chimpanzees. Cleveland Zoo has the RainForest, an 80,000-square-foot copper-colored glass building that houses 600 animals representing 118 species. A tropical shower begins every 20 minutes. And let's not forget that the Toledo Zoo has the only hippoquarium in the world.

A peregrine soap

Since 1986, peregrine falcons have been released off the high-rise buildings of Akron, Dayton, Cincinnati, and Columbus as the Division of Wildlife works to establish a breeding population. Each falcon is named and tagged, and its activities are documented by volunteers of the Peregrine Patrol. Cincinnati's Sunrise, a female released in 1992, showed up in Cleveland in March 1994. Szell, a male living in Cleveland, had a fling with Sunrise before he dropped her to mate with Zenith. Jilted, Sunrise flew to an Ohio Edison facility outside Detroit where she got her man, Junior, a son of Toledo's Nellie McClung, Ohio's first nesting female. Meanwhile, farther south in Columbus—on a Rhodes Tower ledge—Aurora and Bandit happily raised their chicks—Nina, Pinta, and Maria. And Dayton's Rachel may have found motherhood too stressful. She raised her two chicks and disappeared.

Extra small migrants

We know that monarch butterflies migrate—they've been tagged and studied for 35 years. But what about dragonflies and damselflies? The mystery might be unlocked in Ohio. Like monarchs, dragonflies travel in huge swarms in one direction resembling migration patterns. Six big migratory swarms were reported in 1993. A naturalist from Akron, Mike Green, documented a huge swarm—probably 500,000 to 1 million dragonflies—that passed over him for 20 minutes on August 29, 1993. He said they "looked like a squadron of bombers all heading due east." Others have reported dragonflies arriving from the south in the spring when wetland ponds are still frozen. The migration theory doesn't seem off-base—dragonflies have been clocked at 35 miles per hour. But no one knows where they go or if they migrate every year.

Endangered Species

There are 116 state endangered animal species and 221 plant species. The animal species include:

Mammals
Indiana bat*
Eastern woodrat
River otter
Bobcat

Birds
American bittern
Least bittern
Yellow-crowned night heron
Bald eagle
Northern harrier
Peregrine falcon
King rail
Sandhill crane
Piping plover
Common tern
Black tern
Barn owl
Yellow-bellied
    sapsucker
Bewick's wren
Winter wren
Sedge wren
Hermit thrush
Loggerhead shrike
Golden-winged warbler
Magnolia warbler
Kirtland's warbler
Northern waterthrush
Canada warbler
Lark sparrow
Dark-eyed junco

Reptiles
Copperbelly water snake
Eastern plains garter snake
Timber rattlesnake

Amphibians
Hellbender
Blue-spotted salamander
Green salamander
Cave salamander
Eastern spadefoot

Fishes
Ohio lamprey
Northern brook
    lamprey
Mountain brook lamprey
Lake sturgeon
Shovelnose sturgeon
Spotted gar
Cisco
Tonguetied minnow
Popeye shiner
Bigeye shiner
Pugnose minnow
Blackchin shiner
Blacknose shiner
Mississippi silvery minnow
Blue sucker
Greater redhorse
Longnose sucker
Blue catfish
Mountain madtom
Northern madtom
Scioto madtom
Pirate perch
Western banded killifish
Channel darter
Spotted darter

Butterflies
Persius dusky wing
Two-spotted skipper
Frosted elfin
Karner blue
Purplish copper
Swamp metalmark
Regar fritillary

Mollusks
Fanshell
Butterfly
Elephant-ear
Purple catspaw
White catspaw
Northern riffleshell
Cracking pearly

Long-solid
Pink mucket
Pocketbook
Yellow sandshell
Eastern pond
Washboard
Hickorynut
Ring pink
White wartyback
Orange-footed pearly
Sheepnose
Clubshell
Ohio pigtoe
Pyramid pigtoe
Rough pigtoe
Fat pocketbook
Rabbitsfoot
Winged maple leaf
Monkeyface
Wartyback
Purple lilliput
Rayed bean
Little spectaclecase

Moths
Unexpected cycnia
Graceful underwing
Pointed sallow
Spartiniphaga inops
Hypocoena enervata
Papaipema silphii
Papaipema beeriana
Lithophane semiusta
Trichoclea artesta
Tricholita notata
Melanchra assimilis
Ufeus plicatus
Ufeus satyricus
Erythroecia hebardi

Beetles
Pseudanophthalmus krameri
Pseudanophthalmus ohioensis
Nicrophorus americanus

*Indicates species is on the Federal Endangered Species List also.

Brave new world?

🍁 Some researchers at Cincinnati Zoo are doing some pretty amazing things. The Carl H. Lindner, Jr., Family Center for Reproduction of Endangered Wildlife (CREW) are working to save endangered species. Sometimes called "Noah's Ark," CREW has labs for embryo sexing, plant-cloning, a tissue culture and greenhouse incubator, and a cryo-preservation lab called the Frozen Zoo and Garden where reproductive cells—sperm, eggs, and embryos—of the world's endangered plants and animals are stored in plastic straws in liquid nitrogen tanks. CREW was recently chosen by the National Cancer Institute to "preserve plants for cancer research."

The Wilds

A 9,000-plus-acre research and breeding facility called The Wilds—shorter for the International Center for the Preservation of Wild Animals—is home to such animals as Cuvier's gazelles, Hartmann's mountain zebras, Przewalski's Asian wild horses, North American red wolf, and the scimitar-horned oryx (right). The state of Ohio, American Electric Power, and eight zoos have joined together to give endangered species safe habitat in this Muskingum County location. It is hoped that the animals bred here will be successfully re-introduced to their natural habitats.

ENVIRONMENTAL BENEFACTORS

A taxing idea

Sixth-grade teacher John Katko of Sheffield School District thinks the hybrid mole salamander is worth saving. And he's put his money where his mouth is by founding FOWL—Friends of Wetlands. Katko thinks the salamander's diminishing numbers indicate that its wetland habitat is also decreasing. FOWL is working to stop further destruction of wetland habitat by publishing a newsletter, monitoring legislation that affects wetlands, and presenting slide shows. But the group's long-range goals are much more ambitious. They want to restore Lake Erie's coastal marshes and push the legislature to use a new kind of tax—the "habit tax"—so that developers would have to pay more for undeveloped wetland sites. Maybe they'd think twice or look somewhere else.

Ahead of their time

🍁 Born in 1889, Dr. Emma Lucy Braun was a popular botany teacher at the University of Cincinnati. Respected by her peers, she became the first and only woman president of the Ecological Society of America in

1950. Dedicated to studying and saving the state's remaining prairie segments, she sought out natural areas that needed preserving—especially in Adams County. It was Braun's idea to combine all the natural prairies in Adams County into an Edge of Appalachia National Park. Today, her idea is called the Edge of Appalachia Preserve System— eight reserves in Adams County, covering 11,000 acres. But Lucy wasn't the only studious and influential Braun. Her sister, zoologist Annette Braun, was the first female to receive a Ph.D. from Cincinnati University.

Conservation Hall of Fame

The last inductee into the Ohio Conservation Hall of Fame was Richard Moseley in 1994. A naturalist with the State Parks Division, he founded the Division of Natural Areas and Preserves, now recognized as one of the best programs in the country. He directed the purchase of the state's first nature preserve in 1971, 133-acre Fowler Woods in Richland County. He also initiated the state's Scenic River Program. As of 1995, 118 Buckeyes have been inducted into the Ohio Conservation Hall of Fame.

The apple man

Massachusetts-born John Chapman was one of the first inductees in the Ohio Conservation Hall of Fame when it was established in 1966. You probably know him by the name of Johnny Appleseed. Some say it was a call from God that lured Chapman to Ohio; others say he heard all Ohio's apple trees were dying and decided to singlehandedly remedy the situation. In any event, he gathered appleseed from Pittsburgh's cider presses and arrived in Ohio in the early 1800s. Traveling throughout the state for more than 30 years, he planted apple tree nurseries anywhere there was a clearing. Although almost every county has Johnny Appleseed stories, he was most familiar to the folks in Ashland, Knox, and Richland counties. But Chapman didn't spend all his time planting seeds. He saved the city of Mansfield from a Native-American raid during the War of 1812 by running 30 miles to Mt. Vernon to get troops.

A simple Christian man who carried no rifle and ate no meat, he eventually abandoned traditional clothing, believing it was an evil "indulgence." Someone once reported seeing him with a kettle on his head and a coffee sack for clothing. By the late 1830s, Chapman decided Ohio was too crowded for him. He moved to Indiana, planting seeds along the way, and died near Fort Wayne, Indiana.

HAZARDOUS WASTE

A "tiring" dilemma 🍁 Have you ever wondered where your old tires go after you buy new ones? They could end up near Sycamore at the Kirby Tire Recycling Company, the largest scrap-tire pile in the nation. Approximately 60 million to 80 million old tires—and counting—sit in mountains of trouble waiting to happen. The Ohio EPA is trying to get regulations passed that would stop companies such as Kirby from stockpiling scrapped tires. But the problem is a tricky one. Recyclers can only use about 40 percent of the old tires every year. While that percentage has been increasing, it's not going up fast enough. The Goodyear Tire and Rubber Company says that the whole dilemma should be solved by the year 2000 as uses for old tires—in crash barriers, artificial reefs, and road embankments—become more acceptable. Some experts think tires should be shredded into "crumb rubber" and used in asphalt. A federal mandate requiring that practice became law in 1991 but most states simply ignored it. Ohio tried the stuff on nine road projects but after five months the crumb rubber asphalt simply fell apart on one highway and had to be removed. The state didn't want any more to do with the crumbly stuff and gave it up in 1994.

Superfund sites

The federal government lists 34 superfund sites on the National Priority List (below). Ohio's Environmental Protection Agency has a list of more than 1,000 hazardous waste sites and, as of February 1995, is overseeing the cleanup of 95 of those sites.

Alsco Anaconda, Tuscarawas County
Arcanum Iron & Metal, Darke County
Big D Campground, Ashtabula County
Bowers Landfill, Pickaway County
Buckeye Reclamation, Belmont County
Chem-Dyne, Butler County
Coshocton City Landfill, Coshocton County
Fields Brook, Ashtabula County
Fultz Landfill, Guernsey County
G.E. Coshocton Plant, Coshocton County
Industrial Excess Landfill, Stark County
Ironton Coke, Lawrence County
Miami County Incinerator, Miami County
Nease Chemical, Columbiana County
New Lyme Landfill, Ashtabula County
Old Mill Rock Creek, Ashtabula County
Ormet, Monroe County

Poplar Oil-Laskin, Ashtabula County
Powell Road Landfill, Montgomery County
Pristine, Hamilton County
Republic Steel Quarry, Lorain County
Cardinton Road, Montgomery County
E.H. Schilling Landfill, Lawrence County
Skinner Landfill, Butler County
South Point Ethanol, Lawrence County
Summit National, Portage County
TRW, Stark County
United Scrap Lead, Miami County
VanDale Junkyard, Washington County
Zanesville Well Field, Muskingum County
Wright Patterson AFB, Greene County
Reilly Tar, Tuscarawas County
U.S. DOE FMPC, Hamilton County
U.S. DOE /Mound, Montgomery County

BUCKEYE CHRONICLE

When the Treaty of Greenville was signed in 1795, Ohio's Native American "menace" was brought under control and white settlement acclerated. Future president and Ohio resident William Henry Harrison made the West affordable for ordinary folks in 1800 when the Harrison Land Law passed. Settlers could buy 320 acres of land on a four-year installment plan at $2 per acre. Four years later, the terms were even better—160 acres for $80 down and three annual installments of $80. No wonder "the old America [seemed] to be breaking up and moving West," as one historian wrote in 1817.

By 1850, ranking third in population, Ohio was home to Yankees from New England and Virginians and Kentuckians from the South. Later, the state's growing influence spread across the land. Congressmen, senators, abolitionists, vice presidents, cabinet members, and presidents came from Buckeye origins. Activists for prohibition, civil rights, and women's rights used their voices to sway the nation. Military heroes served with distinction. Author Sherwood Anderson summed up his native state's performance in some simple words—"I'll say we've done well."

- Native Ohio
- Competing Interests
- Fighting for the Land
- Settling Ohio
- A State and Nation Divided
- The Ohio Presidents
- Women and Minorities
- Serving the Nation
- Military Heroes

NATIVE OHIO

Mounds of mounds

By the time early Europeans entered Ohio country, its first inhabitants had disappeared. Thaddeus Harris of the Massachusetts Historical Society came to Ohio in 1803 and wrote about the earthen structures these people left behind. "You cannot ride 20 miles in any direction without finding some of the mounds, or vestiges of the ramparts." Since Harris's account, over 5,000 ancient earthen mounds have been found.

The mound builders

The mounds were built from 100 B.C. to A.D. 900 by people descended from ancestors who crossed the Bering Strait 12,000 to 15,000 years ago.

The most primitive culture is called Fort Ancient—after a prehistoric earthen fort in Warren County on the Little Miami River. Probably a defensive structure, it encloses 100 acres with walls from 6 to 20 feet high. Fort Ancient is now a state park.

The Adena culture (800 B.C. to A.D. 100) is characterized by large conical burial mounds. Named for a mound near Adena, Thomas Worthington's estate, these people lived near the Miami and Scioto rivers.

The most advanced culture is called Hopewell (100 B.C. to A.D. 500), named after the mounds on Captain M.C. Hopewell's property near Chillicothe. These people probably traded extensively with other groups, since pearls and other materials not native to the region have been found. Hopewell Mound City Group National Monument near Chillicothe contains 23 mounds on 67 acres.

In the southwest corner of Adams County, the world's biggest serpent effigy mound winds along for 1,330 feet. Twenty feet wide and up to four feet high, the large stone and earthen serpent looks as if it's eating a meal. The mound probably had some religious purpose in the Adena Culture.

People by the lake

Ohio's first Native American inhabitants were probably the Erie, who lived along the shore of Lake Erie. But the Iroquois Confederacy—Mohawk, Oneida, Onondaga, Cayuga, and Seneca peoples—destroyed the Erie in 1655. An early history details a battle so vicious that blood "in some places was knee deep." Following the bloodbath, the region was relatively uninhabited for 50 years until other Native Americans, forced to find safer places, entered Ohio.

Native Americans in Ohio

The Native American population never reached more than 45,000 in Ohio Country.

- Miami – The dominant Ohio group, they came from Canada and lived in western and southwestern Ohio. Pickawillany near present-day Piqua was their main settlement.
- Shawnee – Pushed out of Tennessee by the Cherokee, they were the most resistant to white settlement. Although the Shawnee never mustered more than 300 warriors, they defeated whites 20 times. They lived in central Ohio southward along the Scioto River Valley.
- Ottawa – From the Algonquin family, they came from the Georgia Bay region of Canada and settled in northwest Ohio along the Maumee River.
- Wyandot – Of Iroquoian stock, they were pushed out of eastern Canada by the Iroquois and lived in what are now Marion, Crawford, and Wyandot counties.
- Tuscarora – Part of the Six-Nation Iroquois Confederacy, they moved from New York to the northeastern Muskingum River Valley.
- Seneca – Also called *Mingo*, meaning "treacherous." They lived in eastern Ohio and in the Upper Scioto and Sandusky valleys, with the main settlement at Logstown. They were more nomadic than other Native Americans.
- Delaware – Moved into Ohio to escape Iroquois and Dutch and Swedish settlers. They lived in the Muskingum River Valley with settlements near Coshocton, Marietta, and Delaware.

Spouse swapping

Ohio Land Company agent Christopher Gist detailed a peculiar Shawnee festival in 1751. According to Gist, near Chillicothe, a proclamation by a Shawnee chief dissolved all marriages. After eating all day for three days and dancing all night for two nights, the women chose new mates. About 100 men danced alone around the fires and through the long council houses. The women, forming a stationary line, began singing, "I am not afraid of my husband, I will choose the man I please." As the men danced past them, each woman stepped in, grabbed the man she wanted, and began dancing also. When all the women had husbands, the party was over and the new couples retired to consummate their "marriages." No messy divorce or custody battles were reported!

And then there were none

After the Revolutionary War and the War of 1812, the government continually broke promises made to Native Americans. By 1817, all the Native Americans had left were several reservations. And even those were taken from the Delaware in 1829, from the Mingo in 1831, and from the Wyandot in 1842.

COMPETING INTERESTS

The first Frenchmen

As early as 1615, Etienne Brulé, Champlain's French-Canadian guide, visited the site of present-day Toledo. He found the Erie living in the forests and swamplands at the mouth of the Maumee River. In 1662, Father Lalemant of Montreal wrote that "… if we believe our Iroquois who have returned thence … it is a country which enjoys none of the severity of our winter … villages are situated along a Beautiful River, which serves to carry people down to the Great Lake [for so they call the sea], where they trade with Europeans …." The French assumed these Europeans were Spaniards at the mouth of the Mississippi.

In the winter of 1668-1669, the governor of New France gave René Robert Cavelier, sieur de La Salle (left), permission to go exploring. Some say La Salle saw the Ohio River in 1669—others say no. Apparently La Salle never recorded anything either way—his records have a two-year gap. In any event, the Seneca had told the Frenchman about a great river to the south. French historian Pierre Margry supplied the main evidence in support of La Salle's discovery. And the French Crown based its claims to the Ohio River on La Salle anyway. In 1671, France officially claimed all the land north and west of the Ohio River.

Enter the English

As early as 1648, the English were talking about a river in the West. An English fur trader, Abraham Woods, may have traveled on the tributaries of the Ohio River between 1654 and 1664. By 1669, the English had seen the Ohio River for sure. As long as the French were busy in New France and the English with their colonists along the Atlantic, everything was all right. But things have a way of changing.

The Iroquois sell Ohio

Representatives of the colonies of Virginia, Maryland, Pennsylvania, and New York met with delegates of the Iroquois at Lancaster, Pennsylvania, in 1744. After the colonists plied them with liquor, the Iroquois sold the land "to the west" of their present borders (even though they probably didn't have the right to). This transaction was the basis on which England—and later the United States—claimed the land near the upper Ohio River. The Miami, Shawnee, and Delaware met in Logstown in June 1752, and ratified what the Iroquois had done earlier—again with the help of a large quantity of liquid refreshment. This transaction further strengthened English claims to Ohio country.

Colonial claims

In 1748, the Ohio Land Company of Virginia was organized with England's blessing to colonize 500,000 acres on the banks of the Ohio. Rather like a chess game, the English were baiting the French "…by taking possession of that country southward of the Lakes to which the

French have no right." The English king wanted to encourage trade and test the French—would they fight for the land? Christopher Gist, agent for the Ohio Land Company, left for Ohio in October 1750. When the governor of Pennsylvania heard what Virginia was up to, he decided to send George Croghan west right away. Both colonies claimed the land by right of their colonial charters. At the mouth of the Muskingum River, Gist stopped at Croghan's trading post, only to discover that a Frenchman named Celoron was moving through Ohio too. Gist and Croghan traveled together, reminding Native Americans to "... fear the French, trust the British, and come to a council at Logstown ..."

Last ditch effort

New France (Canada) sent Pierre Joseph Celoron, sieur de Blainville, to Ohio to remind everyone just whose land it was. Ordered to bury lead plates along the Ohio River inscribed with the arms of France, Celoron left Canada with 250 unruly men in June 1749. He buried at least six plates, the last one at the mouth of the Great Miami River. He knew his efforts were futile. Native Americans did lower the English flag when he passed through and gave him empty promises. But they were tied to the British—for the moment—who offered them more money for their furs.

The final round

The French and Indian War (1754-1763) was the last in a series of four conflicts between the French and British. Things looked dismal for the British when General Braddock was ambushed and defeated at Fort Duquesne in 1755. Native Americans decided the French looked more like winners and sided with them. When William Pitt came to power in England in 1756, everything changed. The rejuvenated British captured fort after fort, soundly defeating the French at the decisive Battle of Quebec. France lost Canada and all claims east of the Mississippi by treaty in 1763. They were left with two tiny islands off Newfoundland.

But the French didn't quite give up. They convinced Chief Pontiac that he could drive the English out. Called Pontiac's Conspiracy, the fighting ended when the French didn't come to Pontiac's aid at Detroit. The chief signed a treaty in 1765 and returned home to the Maumee River.

FIGHTING FOR THE LAND

A Christian group called the Unity of the Brethren, or Moravians, came to Ohio to convert and educate the natives, and build utopian communities. In 1761, Moravian Christian Frederick Post received permission to build a cabin about 1-1/2 miles southwest of present-day Bolivar. He was the first white man who wasn't a trader to build a cabin in Ohio. Unfortunately, the future Moravian settlements were established in areas where they could never survive peacefully.

Invited to settle

Christian converts

Delaware Chief White Eyes invited Moravian David Zeisberger to bring his group of Christian Indians to Ohio from Pennsylvania. They founded Schoenbrunn in the Tuscarawas Valley in August 1772. Later that year another group of Christian Indians founded Gnadenhutten. Unfortunately, the Moravians were pacifists caught in the middle of the Revolutionary War. The British were on the west, the Americans on the east, and hostile Native Americans all around.

As tensions grew, Schoenbrunn was abandoned in 1777. Gnadenhutten hung on until 1781, when a group of Delaware forced the Moravians to move to the Sandusky plains. About 150 Moravians returned in February 1782 to glean corn from their old fields. An expedition under American Captain David Williamson arrived at the same time. His rowdy posse of backwoodsmen erroneously accused the Moravians of raiding American settlements. They were disarmed and locked in two cabins. After drinking all night, the posse slaughtered 34 children and 62 adults. For the next 16 years the Gnadenhutten survivors were transients until a repentant Congress granted them 12,000 acres of Ohio land in 1797. Sadly, the new settlements failed and the land was sold in 1823 for $6,600. Today, a marble monument commemorates the bloody massacre at Gnadenhutten (above). The Schoenbrunn site was rediscovered in 1923 and restored. During the Ohio Bicentennial, a play written by Paul Green called *Trumpet in the Land,* was staged to honor the Moravians.

Winning the Northwest

Virginian George Rogers Clark (left) settled in Kentucky and wanted to make sure his new home didn't suffer the same kind of endless fighting that Ohio had experienced. He decided the best way to do that was to capture all the British forts north of the Ohio River and send the English home. With the blessing of Virginia Governor Patrick Henry, Clark raised an army of 350 backwoodsmen. They arrived at the Falls of the Ohio River and established a base in June 1778. Over the next five years, Clark won the Northwest Territory for the United States. Jefferson later tried to persuade Clark to head west in 1803 and explore a route to the Pacific. He declined, but his younger brother, William, and Meriwether Lewis accepted Jefferson's offer 20 years later.

Revolutionary heroine

It was September 11, 1782, and Native Americans and British were advancing toward Fort Henry. The gunpowder was soon gone inside the fort and Ebenezer Zane's 14-year-old daughter Elizabeth volunteered to get more. The Native Americans were so surprised to see a young girl dash out of the fort, they didn't fire a shot! Back at her family's cabin, she filled a tablecloth with gunpowder and tied it to her waist. Dragging the heavy bundle, she hurried back to the fort. Elizabeth Zane is honored as the youngest heroine of the Revolutionary War. Zane Gray immortalized his great-great aunt in his first novel, *Betty Zane*, self-published in 1903, and Martins Ferry honors the brave girl with its annual Betty Zane Frontier Days celebration.

The decisive battle

The Northwest Ordinance didn't quell fear about the restless Native Americans. The task of clearing out the "menace" was finally given to Revolutionary War General "Mad" Anthony Wayne, who established Fort Greene Ville in 1793. The next spring he led his troops down the Maumee River toward Lake Erie. Coming to place a called Fallen Timbers—where a tornado had toppled trees—his soldiers hid and waited. On August 20, 1794, in less than an hour, Native American forces were soundly defeated. But it wasn't until August 3, 1795—after 50 days of feasts, ceremonies, and begging—that Native Americans signed the Treaty of Greenville. They agreed to give up claim to all of Ohio except the northwest quarter in exchange for $20,000 in merchandise and an annual payment of $9,500. What they didn't give up, they agreed could be sold to the United States. So rapid was the resulting influx of settlers that eight years later Ohio was a state. However, Shawnee Chief Tecumseh wasn't at the peace table.

The greatest chief of all

The Shawnee called him *Tikamthi* ("Crouching Panther"); whites called him Tecumseh—the greatest Native-American leader in the Northwest. After his brother was killed in the Battle of Fallen Timbers, Tecumseh refused to sign the Treaty of Greenville and spent the rest of his life trying to unite his people to stop white settlement.

The British encouraged Tecumseh to establish Prophet's Town in 1805 on the white man's side of the Greenville Treaty line. When the town's population swelled to 800, nervous whites urged state officials to do something. And they did. Prophet's Town was removed to a site on the Tippecanoe River in Indiana. Tecumseh continued to demand the return of Native-American land from Governor William Henry Harrison. But Harrison continued making treaties for land. As tensions mounted, Harrison marched toward Tippecanoe—attacking and destroying Prophet's Town in November 1811. Tecumseh was gone at the time but he had earlier issued a warning—he would shake the ground in the middle of December. On December 16, 1811, the New Madrid earthquake did just that, giving many Native Americans the push they needed to join Tecumseh. The great chief—dressed in a British uniform—was killed in the Battle of the Thames during the War of 1812, ending all hopes of Native-American resurgence.

Chiefs remembered

- Shawnee Chief Cornstalk led a rebellion called Lord Dunmore's War. He made peace with Virginia Governor Lord Dunmore in 1774, giving up land south of the Ohio River. He and his son were murdered by Americans in 1777, an offense that was never forgotten.
- Miami Chief Little Turtle attacked Governor St. Clair's forces on November 3, 1791. The governor lost 900 men and his reputation as a result of this surprise attack.
- Shawnee Chief Blue Jacket was actually a white man—Marmaduke Swearingen of Pennsylvania—who was kidnapped while wearing a blue shirt, hence the name Blue Jacket—and brought to Ohio as a teenager. He married the chief's daughter and became a chief himself. He gave up the fight against the whites for a $300-per-year pension and became an officer in General Wayne's army.

The enemy was his

The War of 1812 came to Ohio on Lake Erie. Oliver Hazard Perry, a 28-year-old Navy commander, was given command of a fleet of nine ships. He navigated through a British blockade, sailed into western Lake Erie, and dropped anchor at Put-in-Bay on South Bass Island where he waited for the British. Outgunned, the Americans fought so bravely that the British were forced to surrender. On September 10, 1813, Perry sent a message to General Harrison: "…We have met the enemy; and they are ours! 2 ships, 2 brigs, 1 schooner, and 1 sloop …." William Henry Harrison's victory at the Battle of the Thames was assured and the Northwest was firmly United States territory. Today, Perry's Victory and International Peace Memorial (left) at Put-in-Bay honors Commodore Perry. Dedicated September 10, 1913, the granite shaft rises 352 feet.

SETTLING OHIO

It started at the Bunch of Grapes

The Bunch of Grapes tavern in Boston was the gathering place for a group of Revolutionary War veterans in January 1786. General Rufus Putnam (left) and Benjamin Tupper organized the group into the Ohio Company of Associates. The men pooled their land warrants and bought 1 million acres of land in southeastern Ohio. Congress approved the land deal on October 27, 1787. Forty men left Massachusetts in December 1787 led by Putnam. They arrived at the mouth of the Muskingum River on April 17, 1788, and quickly set about building a fort on a site overlooking the river. The fort was named *Campus Martius*, Latin for "field of Mars." Settlers built a town—originally called Muskingum—near the fort. The territory's leaders renamed Ohio's first American settlement Marietta, for France's Queen Marie Antoinette. In 1800, Marietta became the first incorporated city in Ohio. By that time, its frame and brick houses made it look like a New England village.

Sucked into a crazy scheme

Irish aristocrat Harman Blennerhasset and his beauitful 19-year-old bride bought 170 acres on an island near Marietta in 1798. They built a beautiful $40,000 mansion that attracted the rich and famous. But one visitor who came by in 1805—former Vice President Aaron Burr—brought big trouble. Burr had some fantastic scheme for establishing an empire in the Southwest and Blennerhasset joined him by contributing money for military supplies. Local citizens contacted officials in Washington when they noticed barges being built. On November 27, 1806, President Jefferson ordered the arrest of everyone involved. Burr and Blennerhasset were caught at Nashville and ultimately tried and acquitted. Nothing but bad luck followed the Irishman the rest of his life. His island paradise was vandalized by drunk militiamen, battered by floods, and finally burned to the ground in 1811. Blannerhasset returned to the Isle of Guernsey where he died. His wife came to the United States in 1842 to petition Congress for compensation of her destroyed property but she died in New York before accomplishing her mission.

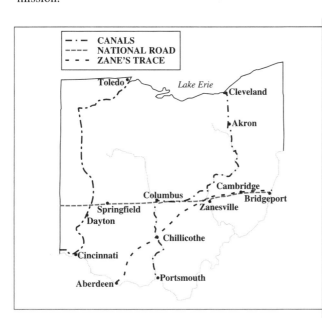

Map legend:
- – · – CANALS
- – – – NATIONAL ROAD
- – – – ZANE'S TRACE

Toledo · Lake Erie · Cleveland
Akron
Cambridge
Columbus · Bridgeport
Springfield · Zanesville
Dayton
Chillicothe
Cincinnati
Aberdeen · Portsmouth

Routes to settlement

The easiest way to enter Ohio was to float down the Ohio River—and many did. Travel was almost impossible on land. Congress authorized Ebenezer Zane to build a road from Wheeling, West Virginia, to Limestone (present-day Maysville, Kentucky) in 1796. Completed in 1798, the narrow, rough road moved through St. Clairsville, Cambridge, Zanesville, Chillicothe, and Aberdeen. So many settlers used Zane's Trace that huge ruts "deep enough to bury a horse" were carved in the land—probably the first major potholes in Ohio.

The first superhighway

In 1806, a more ambitious federal road-building project was started. The Cumberland or National Road, with its eastern terminus in Cumberland, Maryland, stretched west to Wheeling, West Virginia, by 1818. It reached Zanesville in 1826, Columbus in 1833, and Springfield in 1838. The National Road was the first "improved" road in Ohio and the migration route west between 1830 and 1860. Taverns and settlements popped up to service passengers. Stage companies, with such names as Oyster, June Bug, and Shake Gut, carried people in coaches dubbed the Henry Clay, Queen Victoria, or Rough and Ready. Many of these brightly painted vehicles were traveling works of art, with silk-covered seats and portraits of famous people.

Birth of the toll

Ohio created tollgates along the National Road every 20 miles—a distance that was later shortened to 10 miles. The amount of the toll was based on how much damage vehicles and animals caused. For example, it cost half as much to move cattle as hogs, but was more expensive to move hogs than sheep. And the narrower a vehicle's wheels, the more a traveler paid (narrow wheels cut deeper into the  roadbed). By 1837, the toll for a horse was three cents while a stagecoach passed for a quarter. The road was never self-sustaining and in 1876 Ohio gave county commissioners responsibility for the road segments that passed through their jurisdictions. They were also directed that no tolls could be levied between the State Capitol and Ohio Central Lunatic Asylum!

Canals and railroads

Ohio copied New York's canal-building ventures. On July 4, 1825, New York Governor DeWitt Clinton broke ground with Ohio Governor Jeremiah Morrow at Licking Summit for the Ohio and Erie Canal. By December 1, 1832, the 308-mile canal from Cleveland to Portsmouth opened, connecting the Ohio River with Lake Erie. The Miami and Erie Canal was started at Hamilton several days later. This canal boosted settlement in northern Ohio. Opened on June 17, 1845, the canal ran from Toledo to Cincinnati. Ultimately about 1,000 miles of canals crisscrossed the state, moving immigrants and cargo. When the Pittsburgh, Fort Wayne, and Chicago Railroad (later Pennsylvania Railroad) was built across the same territory serviced by the Ohio and Erie Canal, the end of an era was at hand. As 1860 approached, about 2,300 miles of railroad lines were doing the work of the canals—quicker and cheaper.

A STATE AND NATION DIVIDED

They kept the idea alive

He was a slight, almost deaf man with a mighty message! Quaker Benjamin Lundy of St. Clairsville, publisher of *The Genius of Universal Emancipation* in Mount Pleasant, is credited with keeping abolitionist ideas alive during the 1820s. Eventually his views of the evil "slavocracy" became widespread. Presbyterian minister John Rankin of Ripley used the newspaper to publicize his abolitionist stand. Both Rankin and Lundy have been called the "fathers of the new abolitionism."

A disappearing fugitive

Before 1835, the routes to freedom for runaway slaves were known as the Underground Road. Although there are several stories about the origin of the name, the most widely accepted one came from the mouth of a frustrated Kentucky slaveowner in 1831. His slave crossed the Ohio River near Ripley with his master right behind him. When the slave "disappeared," the owner declared, "That [slave] must have gone off on an underground road." Soon the entire system was known as the "underground road." It later became "railroad" with "conductors" and "stations" along established routes (see map on p. 49).

Center of influence

Southeastern Ohio became a magnet for Quakers, many of them unable to continue living in North Carolina because they thought slavery was morally wrong. One of the most influential abolitionist strongholds—and a popular stop on the Underground Railroad—Mt. Pleasant was founded in the early 1800s. *The Philanthropist*—first abolitionist newspaper in the country—was published here by Charles Osborn from 1817 to 1818. In 1837, the first abolitionist convention in Ohio met in Mt. Pleasant, and the Free Labor Store, which wouldn't sell products made by slave labor, opened in 1848.

Traveling on the U.G.R.R.

By 1840, Ohio had more Underground Railroad stations than any other state. On the northern bank of the Ohio River there were "23 ports of entry." Up to 3,000 miles of "track" honeycombed northward to Lake Erie (below) where fugitives found safe passage to Canada. Trumbull County had 53 miles of "road," more than any other Ohio County. Because no records were kept, most people estimate that 40,000 to 80,000 slaves may have escaped by using the Underground Railroad—costing slave owners $3 million. While the actual number of fugitives wasn't high compared to the total slave population, the problem was concentrated in the three northern border slave states. Pressure from these states brought about the passage of the Fugitive Slave Act of 1850, with its harsh penalties for those who aided runaways.

John Rankin's house on a hill near Ripley was a welcome sight for runaways. Legend has it that the abolitionist left a lantern in his window if runaway slaves could safely stop. Rankin supposedly gave refuge to the original "Eliza," a character in Harriet Beecher Stowe's *Uncle Tom's Cabin*.

Myths of the road

Although white abolitionists played a significant role in organizing activities along the railroad, it was usually freed slaves and other runaways who hid fugitives. Abolitionist James Birney remarked in 1837: "Such matters are almost uniformly managed by the colored people. I know nothing of [the fugitives] generally till they are passed." There was no underground tunnel system. Most runaways were hidden aboveground in farm outbuildings. And some weren't hidden at all. Every conductor's activities weren't secret. Quaker Levi Coffin, the wealthy Cincinnati merchant dubbed "President of the Underground Railroad," once invited some leading citizens to his house to view a "curiosity from the South." Upon their arrival, Coffin brought two well-dressed runaways into the room.

A Buckeye snake

Ohio wasn't strictly the territory of abolitionists. While many people didn't endorse slavery, they weren't openly critical—the thought of civil war was unthinkable. Called Peace Democrats, their opponents nicknamed them Copperheads, after the poisonous snake. One of Ohio's most powerful Copperheads was Clement Vallandigham, born in New Lisbon in 1820. As a newspaperman in Dayton, he was elected to Congress in 1858. Uncompromisingly against civil war and for peace, Vallandigham called for the impeachment of Lincoln. Unable to win another Congressional term (his opponents had gerrymandered his district just to be sure he didn't), he set his sights on the governorship in 1863. Things weren't going well for the Union then and it looked as if Vallandigham might become governor—much to the chagrin of President Lincoln.

Then General Ambrose Burnside issued his famous General Order No. 38 from Cincinnati in April 1863, which stated that anyone speaking sympathetically about the enemy would be arrested and tried as a traitor. In front of 20,000 enthusiastic supporters, Vallandigham said he "despised the document." He was arrested, tried, found guilty, and imprisoned at Fort Warren in Boston Harbor. His treatment caused an uproar and Lincoln banished Vallandigham to the Confederate states instead. But the rebels didn't want him either. He escaped to Canada—still a candidate for governor. On election day, Vallandigham won in 18 counties, but lost the race. Lincoln sent a telegram to the victor John Brough which read "Glory to God in the Highest. Ohio has saved the Union." In 1871, Vallandigham accidentally shot himself and died at the Golden Lamb Inn in Lebanon.

The only battle

In July 1863, about 3,000 Confederate soldiers under the command of General John Morgan crossed the Ohio River into Indiana. Turning east, they headed for Cincinnati and then raced across southern Ohio. All along the way, Morgan raided the countryside while looking for a good spot to ford the Ohio River and head south. Near Portland, 700 of Morgan's men were captured and Morgan was caught south of Lisbon. There was really little military value to Morgan's raid. The only actual damage was to civilian property. But the fear that Morgan caused had disastrous consequences. When Chillicothe residents heard Morgan was coming, they posted guards at the bridge over Paint Creek. Mistaking local militiamen for Morgan's men, they set fire to the bridge and destroyed it. Morgan never showed up, but it's unlikely that the lack of a bridge would have stopped him if he had. It was summer and Paint Creek was just one foot deep!

Booth's Buckeye connection

The Union leased Johnson's Island north of Sandusky for a prison camp in 1861. Near the end of the war, 15,000 rebels were held captive there. Confederate sympathizers devised a risky plan to free them. They hijacked two steamboats, the *Philo Parsons* and the *Island Queen*, in September 1864, freed the passengers, and told them to stay quiet for 24 hours. Scuttling the *Island Queen*, the conspirators steamed toward Johnson Island where the U.S.S. *Michigan*—the only Union warship on the Great Lakes during the war—was anchored in the bay. When the *Philo Parsons* arrived, rebel sympathizers waited anxiously for a signal from the *Michigan* that never came. Charles Cole, the brains behind the scheme, was supposed to be on the *Michigan* cooking dinner for the Union crew, complete with drugged wine. But his plot was discovered, he was arrested, and sentenced to death. (Cole later escaped and settled in Texas.) But another conspirator, John Yeats Beall—a good friend of John Wilkes Booth—wasn't as lucky. Beall was hanged in February 1865 for his part in the scheme. Booth tried several times to secure the release of his friend. Some people think Booth never got over his friend's death, which further embittered him toward the Union and led him to assassinate Lincoln less than two months later.

Known as a "big jolly boy" and a prankster, New Rumley-native George Armstrong Custer graduated at the bottom of his West Point class. During the Civil War he is remembered for chasing Lee's army out of Richmond in April 1865. The tenacious fighting of his troops broke the rebels' resistance and ended the war. The Confederate truce flag was brought to Custer on April 9, and later given to him permanently along with the table Grant had used to write the terms of surrender. General Sheridan said, "I know of no one whose efforts have contributed more to this happy result than those of Custer." This was the same Custer who met his death along with all his men—which included his two brothers Tom and Boston—at the Battle of Little Big Horn on June 25, 1876.

He ended the war

THE OHIO PRESIDENTS

The lone Whig

Virginia-born Whig William Henry Harrison served as president for 32 days (the shortest term of any president), from March 4, 1841, to April 4, 1841—and he was sick with pneumonia the whole time. Elected at age 68, he unwisely delivered the longest inaugural speech in history (1 hour and 45 minutes) in very cold weather without wearing a coat. His wife never even made it to the White House— she wasn't planning to arrive in Washington until May. Harrison was the first chief executive to die in office. Ironically, the election of 1840 was the first and last time he cast his vote in an election.

Hard cider and log cabins

Harrison's campaign manager was editor Horace Greeley. A Baltimore editor made fun of the "simple" Harrison by writing that Harrison would be content to sit on the porch of a log cabin, drink hard cider, and collect a pension. Greeley used the criticism to tie Harrison to the frontier, as an asset. (It's true that Harrison lived in a log cabin but by the time he ran for president, it was a 16-room "cabin" in North Bend.) Greeley had campaign workers build log cabins all over the country to symbolize their "man of the people"—and it worked. Van Buren looked like an aristocratic fop. The campaign also coined the now-famous slogan "Tippecanoe and Tyler, too" reminding voters it was Harrison who made the frontier safe for settlement at the Battle of Tippecanoe.

The war hero

Born in Point Pleasant, Ohio, on April 27, 1822, the first native-born Buckeye president was General Ulysses S. Grant. Ulysses' father thought an appointment to West Point might spark his oldest son's ambition, but Grant hated the place. Leaving the military shortly after the Mexican War (1846-1848), Grant went to Galena, Illinois, and clerked in his father's store. When the Civil War began in 1861, he offered his services to General McClellan at Cincinnati but McClellan didn't have time to see the young store clerk. Eight months later, Grant was in command of the Union forces.

Easily elected as president for two terms, Grant served from 1869 to 1877. Although he was an honest man personally, his appointees weren't and his administration was marked by corruption. Out of office, he settled in New York and tried his hand at investment banking, but a partner left him deep in debt. At the suggestion of Mark Twain, the former president, ill with throat cancer, wrote his memoirs for an advance and a 20 percent royalty. He began writing in February 1884, and finished in July 1885, one week before his death. A best-selling book, his memoirs earned about $500,000. He died at Mount McGregor, New York on July 23, 1885.

An honest man and a dishonest election

Rutherford Birchard Hayes was born in Delaware, Ohio, on October 4, 1822, two months after his father died. His uncle, Sardis Birchard, took the family in and provided the young boy with every advantage. Hayes graduated from Kenyon College as valedictorian, went to Harvard Law School, and was admitted to the bar in 1845. He was nominated for the presidency in 1876, while serving his third term as Ohio's governor. In what has been touted as a "dishonest" election, Hayes beat Samuel Tilden by one electoral vote, 185 to 184. The electoral votes of three states—Louisiana, Florida, and South Carolina—were contested. Tilden needed only one electoral vote—Hayes needed all of them. In January 1877, Congress established an Electoral Commission composed of eight Republicans and seven Democrats. Naturally Hayes won, when the Republicans promised to end Reconstruction and withdraw troops from the South. Hayes' election was made official on March 2, 1877, when he took the oath of office in a private ceremony. Since Hayes was a devout Christian, he refused to break the Sabbath by taking the oath when it was normally scheduled. On Monday, March 4, the first president sworn in twice for the same term, received the oath in a public ceremony. Serving just one term as he had promised, Hayes retired to Spiegel Grove, his estate near Fremont, and died on January 17, 1893.

The reluctant office-seeker

A native of Orange, James A. Garfield was elected to the House of Representatives in 1861, while serving in the Union Army. He held the congressional post 18 years, but he didn't want the job at first. Lincoln had to persuade Garfield to resign from the Army and go to Washington. In 1880, on the 36th ballot, Garfield—who wasn't a candidate for the presidency—was nominated by the Republican convention. He'd been trying to help fellow Ohioan John Sherman win the presidential bid. Garfield was president just 200 days—from March 4, 1881, to September 19, 1881. He was shot by an angry office-seeker on July 2, 1881. Alexander Graham Bell was summoned to the White House to locate the bullet in Garfield's body with his "induction balance electrical" machine. Bell's invention failed and Garfield died on September 19 after infection set in.

In grandpa's footsteps

When Benjamin Harrison was seven, his grandfather, William Henry Harrison, was elected president. After studying law in a Cincinnati law office, Benjamin passed the bar and got his first job in Indianapolis, Indiana, as a court crier—which meant he shouted "Oh yes! Oh, yes! Oh, yes! Court is now convened." When the Civil War began, Harrison didn't enlist—he had no military experience and the pay was bad. A talented speaker, he was asked to convince others to volunteer, but he said he couldn't persuade others to serve when he wouldn't. When he was offered an officer's commission and $80 a month, he bought a military tactics book, a uniform, and rode off to battle.

Harrison was the Republicans' compromise presidential candidate in 1888. Although he didn't win the popular vote, he was elected with 233 to 168 electoral votes. Congress appropriated its first billion-dollar budget and passed the Sherman Anti-trust Act (authored by Ohio Senator John Sherman) during his term. Harrison lost his bid for a second term to Democrat Grover Cleveland. Returning to Indianapolis, he died, March 13, 1901. Electricity was installed in the White House during Harrison's tenure but Harrison's servants were too afraid of it to flip a switch!

Hanna's man

William McKinley was born in 1843 in Niles. A lawyer in Canton after the Civil War, he was elected to Congress for the first time in 1876. Known as a businessman's politician, McKinley had close ties to powerful Cleveland entrepreneur Mark Hanna, who supported him for Ohio governor and president. McKinley is remembered as the president who made the United States a world power. He presided over the 1898 war with Cuba, the Open Door policy with China, and the annexation of Hawaii. Shot by anarchist Leon Czolgosz in Buffalo, New York, McKinley was the last president who had served in the Civil War. Devoted to his invalid wife, Ida, his last words were about her when he died on September 14, 1901. Ida moved back to Canton where she visited her husband's grave every day.

Big man—big job

Cincinnati-native William Howard Taft was the only man to serve as president and chief justice of the Supreme Court. He was also the most portly chief executive, weighing in at 332 pounds. His girth

required the installation of a custom-built bathtub in the White House. But his wife Nellie affectionately called him "sleeping beauty"! Supposedly, Taft never liked politics—once saying that "politics makes me sick"—but he served the public all his life, beginning as prosecuting attorney in Hamilton County. Taft's lifelong dream was to serve on the Supreme Court, a position he turned down three times when he was governor of the Philippines. For a man who wasn't much of an innovator, we can thank President Taft for the idea of a constitutional amendment for the income tax. Taft was defeated for a second term when his former good friend Theodore Roosevelt ran on the Bull Moose Party ticket (Roosevelt thought Taft had abandoned progressive policies). Woodrow Wilson beat both of them. When President Harding appointed Taft chief justice, he said that he didn't "… remember that I was ever president." Taft retired from the Supreme Court 33 days before his death on March 8, 1930.

All in the family

Born September 8, 1889, Robert A. Taft, son of William Howard Taft, was Ohio's Republican senator from 1939 to 1953. He sponsored the Taft-Hartley Labor Relations Act in 1947—the law that forces people back to work if it's in the nation's interest. Known as "Mr. Republican," he also sought the presidential nomination three times. If Eisenhower hadn't come on the scene, another Taft probably would have entered the White House in 1952.

AWESOME

Warren Harding invested in the bankrupt *Marion Star* in 1884, when he was 19. Along with his wife, he made the paper successful and invested in other town businesses. Before the television age, a dead-locked Republican Party thought Harding, who "looked like a president," would be a good nominee. Women could vote for the first time in the 1920 national election, so party regulars thought the best-looking candidate would receive the female vote. Although Harding promised good government, his administration was riddled with corruption. When news of the Teapot Dome scandal (p. 158) broke, Harding was returning from a trip to Alaska. He collapsed and was taken to the Palace Hotel in San Francisco where he died on August 2, 1921. Some thought his wife poisoned him. During Harding's term, the immigration quota system was adopted.

He looked like a president

Love in a White House closet

Harding's personal life wasn't without controversy either. Unhappy in marriage, a number of extramarital affairs were reported. The most famous story involved Nan Britton from Marion. She alleged in her book, *The President's Daughter*, that Harding fathered her child and gave her $150 in child support every week. She detailed love trysts in a tiny White House coat closet. When Harding died, Nan asked for $50,000 from his estate, which was denied, so she wrote her tell-all memoirs. The book earned twice the amount she'd requested from the Hardings. She used a portion of the proceeds to establish an organization—the Elizabeth Ann Guild—to help unwed pregnant women.

AWESOME

Ohioans in the Cabinet

President	Secretary of the Treasury	Appointed
Harrison, W.	W.H.Thomas Ewing	1841
Fillmore	Thomas Corwin	1850
Tyler	Thomas Ewing	1841
Lincoln	Salmon P. Chase	1861
Hayes	John Sherman	1877
Harrison, B.	Charles Foster	1891
Eisenhower	George M. Humphrey	1953

Secretary of War

President		Appointed
Jackson	Lewis Cass	1831
Lincoln	Edwin Stanton	1862
Grant	William T. Sherman	1869
Grant	Alphonso Taft	1876
Harrison, B.	Stephen B. Elkins	1891
McKinley	Russell Alger	1897
Roosevelt, T.	William H. Taft	1904
Wilson	Newton D. Baker	1916

Attorney General

President		Appointed
Buchanan	Edwin M. Stanton	1860
Johnson, A.	Henry Stanbery	1866
Grant	Alphonso Taft	1876
Cleveland	Judson Harmon	1895
Harding	Harry M. Daugherty	1921
Nixon	William B. Saxbe	1974
Ford	William B. Saxbe	1974

President	Secretary of the Interior	Appointed
Taylor	Thomas Ewing	1849
Grant	Jacob D. Cox	1869
Grant	Columbus Delano	1870
Harrison, B.	John Noble	1889
Roosevelt, T.	James A. Garfield	1907

Secretary of Defense

President		Appointed
Eisenhower	Charles E. Wilson	1953
Eisenhower	Neil H. McElroy	1957

Secretary of Labor

President		Appointed
Truman	Charles Sawyer	1948
Reagan	C. William Verity, Jr.	1987

Secretary of Health, Education and Welfare

President		Appointed
Eisenhower	Arthur S. Flemming	1958
Kennedy	Anthony Celebrezze	1962

Secretary of Housing and Urban Development

President		Appointed
Nixon	James T. Lynn	1973

Secretary of Commerce

President		Appointed
Truman	Charles Sawyer	1948

A Buckeye year 🚂 Democrats finally nominated an Ohioan to run for the presidency in 1920. James Cox who, like Harding, had been a governor, congressman, and newspaperman, was crushed by the Republican landslide—as was fellow Buckeye Max S. Hayes who ran for vice president on the Farmer-Labor Party ticket the same year.

WOMEN AND MINORITIES

The presidents' ladies 🚂 Several Buckeye First Ladies influenced movements of their day or established traditions that continue today.

- Lucy Webb Hayes – An active temperance supporter and the first president's wife with a college education, she was known as "Lemonade Lucy" when she banned liquor from the White House. She was called the nation's "First Lady" by reporter Mary Clemmer Ames. After Mrs. Hayes' tenure, every president's wife was First Lady—it was easier to use than the previous title, "Presidentress."
- Caroline Lavinia Scott Harrison (wife of Benjamin Harrison) – She raised money for the Johns Hopkins University Medical School on the condition that women would be admitted. She also presided over the first renovation of the White House. With a $35,000 budget, she rid that stately home of rodents and insects, and fixed the plumbing.
- Helen Herron Taft (nicknamed "Nellie") – She received cherry trees from the Japanese government and planted the first 300 at the Tidal Basin on March 27, 1912. Buried at Arlington National Cemetery in 1943, she was the first First Lady interred there.

Feminist fatale

Gloria Steinem was born in 1934 in Toledo. Her parents divorced in 1946, sending Gloria and her mother to the slums of east Toledo. Gloria had dreams of becoming a dancer, but she had to take care of her mother who couldn't work because of depression. Entering Smith College in 1952, Gloria graduated cum laude and moved to New York City in 1960, determined to be a journalist. In 1963, she used her personal experience as a Playboy bunny in Manhattan to write an article, "I Was a Playboy Bunny." Soon she was writing for *McCall's*, *Cosmopolitan*, and *Vogue*. In 1968 Steinem became an active feminist after attending a Redstockings meeting—a radical feminist group. She listened to the women share their stories about illegal abortions and her life was changed forever. (Steinem had undergone an abortion herself after college.) In 1971 she joined Congresswomen Bella Abzug and Shirley Chisholm, and Betty Friedan to organize the National Women's Political Caucus. In 1972, she started *Ms.* magazine which she sold in 1987 to pursue writing and lecturing.

- Victoria Woodhull was the first woman to run for president on the Equal Rights Party ticket. She was nominated by Judge David Carter of Cincinnati (who had helped nominate Lincoln in 1860). Frederick Douglass declined the offer as her vice presidential running mate.
- One of Oberlin's first college graduates, Betsey Mix Cowles, was president of the first Women's Rights Convention held in Salem on April 19 and 20, 1850.
- Oberlin-native Mary M. Talbert was an activist for African-American freedom and women's rights all over the world. Talbert headed the effort to restore the Frederick Douglass home and was awarded a Spingarn Medal in 1922.
- Akron-native Eleanor Smeal was forced to stay in bed for a year in 1969 because of a back problem. Unable to find suitable day care for her children, she and her husband took up the feminist banner. In 1977, she was elected president of NOW (National Organization of Women), and in 1991 she organized the Fund for the Feminist Majority.
- Although born in St. Louis, Faye Wattleton, former head of Planned Parenthood, graduated from Ohio State University in 1959 with a degree in nursing, later became director of Dayton Planned Parenthood, and in 1978 was appointed president of Planned Parenthood Federation of America.

All in the family

Ohio's first elected congresswoman, Frances Payne Bolton, was also the first congresswoman to represent the United States in the United Nations General Assembly. Her grandfather Henry B. Payne started the family's political tradition as a U.S. senator. After the death of her husband, Representative Chester Castle Bolton, in 1939, Frances was appointed to serve the remainder of his term. (Once dubbed the "richest man in Congress," Chester Bolton was the son of Republican boss Mark Hanna's partner and became wealthy from the steel business.) Mrs. Bolton was elected in her own right in 1940. A nurse by education, Bolton tried to advance nursing as a profession. The Army School of Nursing and a Cadet Nurse Corps were created due to her efforts. When her son—Oliver Payne Bolton—was elected to Congress in 1952, the two were the first mother-and-son team to serve in the same Congress.

Other Women in the House
(year first elected)
Mary Rose Oakar, 1976
Jean Spencer Ashbrook, 1982
Marcy Kaptur, 1982
Deborah Pryce (above), 1992

Leading the way

- The first African-American member of Ohio's General Assembly was a Republican attorney from Hamilton County—George Washington Williams, elected in 1880.
- The first African-American member of Ohio's Senate was also a Republican attorney, John Patterson Green, from Cuyahoga County, elected in 1892.
- Carl B. Stokes (left) was elected in 1967 as the first African-American mayor of a major city (Cleveland). (As of 1995, Stokes was Ambassador to the Seychelles—a long way from Cleveland.) But Stokes wasn't the first African American to lead an Ohio city. That was Robert Henry, elected mayor of Springfield in 1965.
- Cleveland's Louis Stokes, brother of Carl, was the first African-American congressman from Ohio. He began serving in 1968.
- John M. Langston was elected clerk of Brownhelm Township in 1855, the first African American to win any elective office in the United States.
- Ohio's first elected African-American judge was Cleveland's Perry Jackson in 1945. He had previously been the state's first appointed African-American judge in 1940.
- When Ellen Craig was elected mayor of Urbancrest in 1971 she was the first African-American female elected as a mayor in the state. But the first female elected to any public office was Catherine Avery who won a seat on Cleveland's Board of Education in 1896.
- An aspiring musician, Florence Ellinwood Allen was elected judge of the Cuyahoga County Common Pleas Court in 1920—the first woman elected to the bench in the nation. In 1921, she was the first female judge to sentence a defendant to death. And in 1922, she became the first female justice of Ohio's Supreme Court.
- In 1922, Warren-native Genevieve Rose Cline was the first woman appointed as a federal judge. Cline was confirmed on May 25, 1928, and served 25 years on the United States Customs Court in New York City.
- In 1971, Defiance-native Alene B. Duerk became a Navy Rear Admiral—the first American woman to earn that rank.

SERVING THE NATION

A Fuller Brush man

Self-made millionaire Howard Metzenbaum was the grandson of a Hungarian Jew who settled in Cleveland. As a Fuller Brush salesman, Metzenbaum earned enough to pay for his education at Ohio State University. In 1941, he received his law degree and started a practice in Cleveland with Sidney Moss. In 1942, he was elected to the Ohio House of Representatives, the youngest man elected up to that time.

Always a liberal, his political career advanced until he beat John Glenn in 1970 to become Democratic candidate for the United States Senate. Although he lost that election to Robert Taft, Jr., he was appointed by Governor John Gilligan to serve the remainder of William Saxbe's term in 1973. Metzenbaum won on his own in 1976, and served until retiring in 1994.

Supreme Court Justices born in Ohio

William B. Woods	1880-1887
Stanley Matthews	1881-1889
William R. Day	1903-1922
John H. Clarke	1916-1922
William Howard Taft*	1921-1930

* Indicates Chief Justice

Man with a mouth

It's a good thing Ohio's William Saxbe wasn't a public relations man. Born in Mechanicsburg, he once thought of becoming a minister, but studied law instead. Elected senator in 1969, he once called labor leader George Meany "a crotchety and rude old man" and Vice President Agnew a "witch hunter." Nixon aides John Ehrlichman and Bob Haldeman were dubbed "Nazis." After Elliot Richardson resigned as attorney general, President Nixon appointed Saxbe to serve in the post. As the Watergate investigation and impeachment proceedings progressed, Saxbe refused to be the president's lawyer. After serving in the Ford administration, Saxbe went back to his Ohio farm and his law practice. He never entered politics again.

MILITARY HEROES

The son of former slaves, Charles Young came to Ripley with his parents when he was 14 months old. In 1884, he entered West Point, graduating in 1889. In 1916, he was awarded a Spingarn Medal for his work in Liberia and also promoted to lieutenant colonel in charge of the Tenth Cavalry Regiment. But that promotion put him in command of white junior officers and white enlisted men—which meant trouble. In 1917, government officials decided to give Young command of a "colored" unit in Ohio instead. Later—supposedly physically unfit for duty—he was forced to retire. But Young proved his physical status was fine when he traveled from Ohio to Washington, D.C., on foot and by horse in 16 days in June 1918. The government had no choice but to reactivate Young. He was buried in Arlington National Cemetery on June 1, 1923, almost 18 months after his death.

He walked a long lonely road

Train to honor   Sixteen Ohio soldiers were involved in the Great Locomotive Chase of April 1862. Twenty-two volunteers, along with Union spy James Andrews, hijacked a Confederate train in Atlanta and headed north, destroying track, trying to set fire to bridges (they were too wet to burn), and cutting telegraph lines. The Union hijackers ran out of steam about 90 miles from Atlanta where they were arrested. Some escaped while others were hanged or imprisoned. Six of these soldiers were awarded the first Medals of Honor ever given on March 25, 1863. Secretary of War Edwin Stanton of Steubenville pinned the first medal on 19-year-old Private Jacob Parrot of Fairfield County. The other five Buckeye recipients that day were William Bensinger of Wayne County, Robert Buffum (home unknown), Elihu Mason of Wood County, William Pittinger of Jefferson County, and William Reddick (home unknown). The rest of the Buckeye volunteers received Medals of Honor later in 1863. Walt Disney used this story as the basis for the movie *The Great Locomotive Chase*.

Medal of Honor

The Medal of Honor —the United States highest award for bravery in combat—was awarded to 1,520 Civil War soldiers. President Truman once said, "I'd rather have this medal than be president." The criteria for receiving the medal include clear risk of life, voluntary action beyond the call of duty, and two eyewitnesses.

New Rumley-native Thomas Ward Custer, brother of George A. Custer, received the Medal of Honor twice—both times for bravery during the Civil War. Custer was the first of 18 soldiers ever to receive the honor two times. The list below includes honorees and their birthplaces.

World War I
Albert E. Baesel, Berea*
Patrick McGunigal, Hubbard
Edward V. Rickenbacker, Columbus

World War II
Sylvester Antolak, St. Clairsville*
Edward A. Bennett, Middleport
Charles J. Berry, Lorain*
Herbert F. Christian, Byersville*
Joseph J. Cicchetti, Waynesburg*
Emile Deleau, Jr., Lansing*
Harold G. Epperson, Akron*
William A. Foster, Cleveland
Donald A. Gary, Findlay
Lewis Hall, Bloom*
Joe R. Hastings, Malvern*
Patrick Kessler, Middletown*
Isaac Kidd, Cleveland*
Harry Martin, Bucyrus*

Williams E. Metzger, Jr., Lima*
Frank J. Petrarca, Cleveland*
Robert R. Scott, Massillon*
Tony Stein, Dayton*
John R. Towle, Cleveland*
James R. Ward, Springfield*
Howard Woodford, Barberton*
Rodger Young, Tiffin*

Vietnam War
Sammy L. Davis, Dayton
Douglas E. Dickey, Greenville*
Frank A. Herda, Cleveland
Joseph G. LaPointe, Jr., Dayton*
Donald R. Long, Blackfork*
Melvin Earl Newlin, Wellsville*
Gordon R. Roberts, Middletown
Brian M. Thacker, Columbus

* Indicates awarded posthumously

ALL OVER OHIO

Author John Gunther once wrote that Ohio is nothing more than " ... a giant carpet of agriculture studded by great cities." In fact, you can't travel in any direction for any length of time and not pass through a city, town, or village. Each place has its own unique history and heritage. Potters, lawyers, farmers, wigmakers, laborers, oilmen, winemakers, and ministers—people from every walk of life with big dreams—founded settlements.

During the 1970s many Ohio cities and towns lost their industrial base—and, for a time, dreams were dashed. But the cities and towns of the so-called Rust Belt era are on their way back. Let's visit a few and catch a glimpse of the indomitable Buckeye spirit.

- The Big Three
- Around Lake Erie
- Along the Ohio River
- The Name Game
- City Hall
- Famous Natives
- Claims to Fame
- Monuments and Museums
- That Calls for a Celebration
- On the Road
- A City Scrapbook

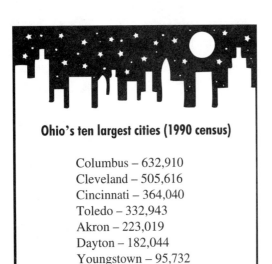

Ohio's ten largest cities (1990 census)

Columbus – 632,910
Cleveland – 505,616
Cincinnati – 364,040
Toledo – 332,943
Akron – 223,019
Dayton – 182,044
Youngstown – 95,732
Parma – 87,876
Canton – 84,161
Lorain – 71,245

THE BIG THREE

A bad record keeper

A New Jersey Supreme Court judge and Revolutionary War veteran, John Cleves Symmes, organized a land company and was granted 1 million acres between the Little Miami and Great Miami rivers for a down payment, with the remainder to be paid in installments. Advertising that the title to these lands "…will be clear and certain, and no possible doubts can arise…" Symmes lured many Yankees to Ohio. Three early settlements were founded. Symmes started North Bend in 1789, several miles from present-day Cincinnati. His friend, Benjamin Stites, founded Columbia in 1788. The town failed and the Cincinnati airport now occupies the site. Israel Ludlow founded Losantiville in 1788, which became Cincinnati. Unfortunately Symmes was a very bad record keeper and businessman—he sold land that wasn't his. His holdings were finally seized by the courts to satisfy debts and claims against him. He died poor in North Bend—a long way from the prominence he once enjoyed. As secretary of the Northwest Territory, Symmes had enough influence to get his son-in-law, William Henry Harrison, appointed as the delegate to Congress.

What's in a name?

Cincinnati was named by Governor Arthur St. Clair in 1790 for the Society of Cincinnati, an organization that honored Revolutionary War officers. (Cincinnati was a military hero of early Rome.) The new name replaced Losantiville, which was more descriptive geographically. The *L* stood for Licking Creek, *os* was Latin for "mouth," *anti* was Greek for "opposite," and *ville* was a suffix meaning town. Put them altogether and *Losantiville* meant "town opposite the mouth of Licking Creek."

From Porkopolis to Queen

As one of three U.S. cities with a population of 100,000 by 1860, Cincinnati was influential and inspired several nicknames. It was called "Porkopolis" because the world's largest hog market was located at Fountain Square during the 1840s and 1850s. A sculpture at Bicentennial Commons at Sawyer Point known as the "Flying Pigs" commemorates the swines' past prominence. "Queen City" is a more endearing moniker popularized by poet Henry Wadsworth Longfellow after he sampled the newly introduced Catawba wine on a visit to Cincinnati in 1858. He wrote

And this song of the Vine,
This greeting of mine
The winds and the birds shall deliver,
To the Queen of the West
In her garlands dressed
On the banks of the Beautiful River.

You might also hear Cincinnati called "Blue Chip City" because the economy is so "steady, dependable [and] well-planned." And since Cincinnati was listed in the *1993 Places Rated Almanac* as the number-one place to live in the country, some folks have coined a new name—"Cincinnati USA."

Seven hills

The city grew up on the slopes of what locals call the Seven Hills. But no one is quite sure which seven hills those are. *We Live in Cincinnati* (1961) lists them as Mt. Adams, Walnut Hills, College Hill, Fairview Heights, Vine Street Hill, Auburn, and Fairmont. One of the most beautiful neighborhoods is Mt. Adams, which Nicholas Longworth purchased

The Cincinnati skyline with the *Delta Queen* steamboat in the foreground

in 1830. It was here that he planted the Catawba grapevines whose fruit produced the wine that so pleased Longfellow. The yield was so large that Longworth called his vineyard a "Garden of Eden." He donated four acres of land for an observatory that was dedicated by President John Quincy Adams in 1834—that's where the hill got its name. When the grapevines were destroyed by disease, Longworth's son gave the land to the city. Today, it's Eden Park—named after Longworth's early appellation—site of the Cincinnati Art Museum, the Krohn Conservatory, and the Rookwood Building where the famous pottery of the same name was made. The first National Arbor Day was celebrated here in 1882. Children planted trees to honor the presidents of the United States. Since that time the nation's chief executives have been asked to choose their favorite trees for planting in President's Grove. Of all the trees in that grove, Nixon's bald cypress has been the only one to die.

> **Did you know?**
> One of the largest prison camps of the Civil War was Columbus's Camp Chase. Now near Sullivant Avenue, the camp housed 9,000 soldiers. About 2,000 Confederates died while incarcerated.

Taking inventory

An audit of Cincinnati's public property released in November 1994 listed 335 miles of railway to Chattanooga, Tennessee; University Hospital, which is leased to the University of Cincinnati until 2008 for $1 per year; and the rights to "Guns 'N' Hoses," a cable-access television show in which callers talk with police officers and firefighters.

A ship of honor
🏠 Columbus honored its namesake—Christopher Columbus—during its 1992 bicentennial celebration. Since it's the largest city in the world named after the explorer, citizens decided a replica of Columbus's flagship—the *Santa Maria*—would be a fitting addition to the city's landscape. Costumed guides lead visitors through the ship, now moored on the Scioto River at Battelle Park. It was built in Pennsylvania from historically accurate plans reproduced by José-Maria Martinez Hidalgo of Spain. Christened on October 11, 1992, the *Santa Maria*'s vital statistics include:

Length – 98 feet

Height – 89 feet from bottom of hull to top of main mast

Weight – 135 tons with ballast

Sails – 2,700 square feet

Amount of lumber used – 44,000 board feet of cedar for the hull; 22,000 board feet of fir for deck, and one Douglas fir tree for the 65-foot main mast.

A 21st-century name
🏠 Columbus was called "Buggy City" in the late 1800s because about 20 local companies manufactured buggies there. It was "Arch City" at the end of the 19th century. During a convention of 250,000 Union veterans, lighted arches stretched across High Street in their honor. The city left them up for a long time after the veterans left. In 1959 Columbus was proclaimed an "All-American" city. And now the United Nations has chosen Columbus as one of 16 "Trade Point Centers" in the world. Called "Infoport," the city is using modern technology to break down trade barriers for small and medium-sized businesses and governments all over the world.

A different heritage
🏠 Unlike Cleveland or Cincinnati, Columbus experienced only one large immigrant influx—and that was from Germany during the 1840s. Its early settlers were mostly non-slave-owning, independent farmers from Kentucky and Virginia. And so many people came from Appalachia that an old joke pokes fun at "the mountain people [who were] products of the three R's—reading, 'riting, and Route 23"—the main highway from West Virginia. Because the city lacks the ethnic heritage of the state's other large cities, Columbus has sometimes been called (much to its chagrin), "White Bread, Ohio."

German Village

The German Village Society, founded in 1960, has restored the German district just south of downtown Columbus. Called German Village, the restoration project is the largest and most successful project of its kind—a model for the nation. During the 1800s, about one-third of the city's population was made up of German people who lived near their breweries in German Village. Today, ten restored homes and gardens, parks, shops, restaurants, and galleries celebrate this history. The annual Oktoberfest is like no other in the country.

A slow start

Connecticut lawyer Moses Cleaveland (left) knew his home state's financial condition was bad. So he took $32,000 of his own money and organized the Connecticut Land Company. The state eagerly agreed to sell his syndicate all the Western Reserve, except the Fire Lands, for $1.2 million in 1795. On July 22, 1796, Cleaveland and his party of 50 reached the mouth of the Cuyahoga River. The future city site in New Connecticut was surveyed and named in his honor. Cleaveland returned to his lucrative law practice in October and never came back to his namesake. The town site wasn't an inviting place. The few people who remained on the site suffered from insect bites, dysentery, and the ague—and soon left.

Lorenzo Carter arrived in 1799. In 1800 he presided over a population of seven. His house was the center of Cleaveland and the site of the first wedding, the first school—and the first jail. In 1804 Carter launched the city's first boat, which he built himself—the 30-ton *Zephyr*. In 1818, the *Walk-in-the-Water*, the first steamboat on Lake Erie, stopped in Cleaveland Harbor. Both boats were a harbinger of things to come. With the completion of the Erie Canal in 1832, the city became a boom town that would later emerge as the industrial and financial capital of the state.

The name was too long

On July 1, 1832, the editor of a new paper, the *Cleaveland Gazette and Commercial Register*, dropped the "a" in Cleaveland because the paper's name wouldn't fit on the masthead. Cleveland was born and Cleaveland abandoned.

Did you know?

Moses Cleaveland declared that Cleaveland would one day be as large as Wyndham, Connecticut. The Cleveland metropolitan area now boasts a population of about 2.89 million. Wyndham counts 21,960 people.

The comeback city

 Industry almost ruined Cleveland. By the 1960s and 1970s, it was heavily polluted, racially unstable, and bankrupt. Known as "the mistake by the lake" then, the city dug in, cleaned up its act, and came back. Now called "Comeback City," Cleveland is a model for other large metropolitan areas. Celebrating its bicentennial in 1996, some of the city's well-earned accomplishments include:

• Cleveland is the only city in the country awarded five All-America City titles.
• About $3.5 billion has been invested in downtown development, with one-fourth of that in Public Square.
• A new $300-million development called North Coast Harbor includes the Rock and Roll Hall of Fame and Museum, the Great Lakes Science Center, and a park.

• Opened in 1994, the $362-million Gateway sports complex is now the home of the Cleveland Cavaliers and the Cleveland Indians.

The Flats

In 1976 the Flats Oxbow Association was organized to breathe new life into Cleveland's decaying industrial district. The name "Flats" came from the flat land on both sides of the Cuyahoga River where Moses Cleaveland came ashore in 1796. John D. Rockefeller built his first office and later his oil trust headquarters in the Flats. Today, in a unique partnership with industry, the Flats is home to more than 50 entertainment venues, an amphitheater, and a waterfront boardwalk. LTV Steel operates the largest cold-rolled steel mill in the country in the Flats, and the salt mines on Whiskey Island are still in operation. Old buildings such as the Powerhouse (above)—originally built by Mark Hanna to provide power for streetcars—is now an entertainment venue. A replica of Lorenzo Carter's log cabin stands in Heritage Park I. Flatsfest, a river festival held each July to celebrate the area's comeback, features water ballet, rowing championships, a sailing regatta, and a boat parade.

Heard around town

Could George Stephanopoulos, President Clinton's aide, be the next senator from Ohio? Rumor has it that John Glenn won't run again—he'll be 75 when his term expires in 1998. Stephanopoulos is a Cleveland native who some say has the two prerequisites required for election—name recognition and good looks.

What's a pierogi?

 A pierogi is a lot like ravioli except the pastry shell is filled with mashed potatoes and fried in butter and onions. Cleveland has been called the "Pierogi Capital of the World" since more than 10 percent of its residents trace their roots to Poland. Known as the Gateway City, Cleveland welcomed Germans, Irish, Welsh, French, Slovenians, African Americans, Lithuanians, Hungarians, Czechs, Russians, Romanians, Scots, Bohemians, Jews, Poles, Hungarians, Italians, and Russians—in all, at least 70 different ethnic groups are found in the metropolitan area. At one time the community of Buckeye was the largest Hungarian enclave in the world outside Budapest.

When 52-story Terminal Tower opened in June 1929, it was the state's tallest building. The Public Square landmark was renovated in 1990. Now called The Avenue at Tower City Center, theaters, restaurants, and shops lure visitors.

AROUND LAKE ERIE

A real melting pot

Nathan Perry and Mr. and Mrs. Azariah Beebe built a trading post at the mouth of the Black River in 1807. In 1836 the town was incorporated as Charleston. The Cleveland, Lorain and Wheeling Railroad brought new life to the little village and it was re-chartered in 1876 as Lorain. With a railroad and a port, Lorain became a steel town. In 1894, Tom L. Johnson moved his plant from Pennsylvania and workers came running. When United States Steel bought the plant, a wave of immigrants—Poles, Slovaks, Hungarians, and Italians—came to relieve the labor shortage. The immigrants were so well assimilated into the population that a newspaper feature editor who came to write a story couldn't tell where the foreigners lived. When he asked his host to see the foreign district, he was told, "We have been in it for the last 15 minutes." Lorain still welcomes foreigners. The United States Steel Plant is now called USS/Kobe—the Japanese bought into the operation in the early 1990s.

Sister city

According to a report by the zoology department at The Ohio State University, Lake Erie may have sea "monsters." At least 125 sightings of aquatic creatures 35 feet long and weighing up to 2 tons have been recorded. The Lake Erie town of Huron has applied to become the sister city to Inverness, Scotland—home of the world-famous Loch Ness sea monster.

Drinking room

If you like having plenty of room at a bar, go to South Bass Island. The Beer Barrel Saloon boasts the longest bar on the planet at almost 406 feet.

Down with the law

🏠 Moses Cleaveland liked to use family names for geographic features, so when he and his surveying party camped near present-day Ashtabula in 1796, he suggested the river should be named "Mary Esther," after his daughter. Everyone agreed—after drinking several gallons of wine, but later came to their senses. The river, and later the town, was named Ashtabula instead, after an Algonquin word meaning "the river of many fish." A farming and fishing center, Ashtabula's citizens were staunch abolitionists and the town became an important stop on the Underground Railroad. An article in the December 21, 1850, issue of the *Ashtabula Sentinel* detailed stand against slavery and the Fugitive Slave Law of 1850.

"Resolved, That Herod made a law in regard to male children; King Darius made a law in regard to Daniel; … and meanest of all, Congress made a law in reference to fugitive slaves … Cursed be said law! … we will not aid in catching the fugitive but will feed and protect him…."

The town's residents claimed that not one runaway slave was ever recaptured within Ashtabula.

It's easy to pronounce

🏠 General Anthony Wayne ordered a stockade built on the site of Toledo. Known as Fort Industry, it was abandoned at the beginning of the War of 1812. In 1817, a group of Cincinnati investors bought some land in the same area and named their first settlement Port Lawrence. In 1833, Port Lawrence and Vistula voted to become one city named Toledo. There are many stories about the origin of the town's name. Some say New York author Washington Irving was traveling through Spain at the time and told his brother—a local resident—that Toledo would be a fitting name. But the most credible origin is from local businessman Willard J. Daniels who said Toledo was "easy to pronounce, is pleasant in sound, and there is no other city of that name on the American continent." There are connections to Spain, however. The Spanish government awarded the city's oldest newspaper, the *Toledo Blade*, its royal coat of arms. And in 1931 the University of Toledo was given permission to use the arms of King Ferdinand and Queen Isabella.

USS *Toledo*

🏠 Toledo has been a friend of the U.S. Navy for many years. The first Navy vessel to bear the city's name was a heavy cruiser, the USS *Toledo*—now out of commission. On February 25, 1995, the city was honored a second time when a 362-foot-long nuclear submarine was christened the USS *Toledo* at the Norfolk Naval Station in Virginia. Through the work of the Toledo Council of the Navy League of the United States, the crews of Navy ships that dock at Toledo have been cared for very well. For the new USS *Toledo*, the organization supplied a gift for every crew member, as well as gifts for the crew to present to city officials wherever they travel. The organization also started a scholarship fund for crew members to use when their service is finished.

ALONG THE OHIO RIVER

Making pots

East Liverpool was founded by Irishman Thomas Faucet in 1798. It was called Faucet's Town until the population of English immigrants from the pottery city of Liverpool, England, became so numerous that the name was changed in 1860 to East Liverpool. In 1838, James Bonnet, a 23-year-old potter, came to town and noticed that the clay deposits were good for making pottery. He built a plant with four local citizens and made $250 profit the first year. By the 1930s, 62 pottery manufacturers employed 10,000 people and East Liverpool was the "crockery capital of the world." Today, two large companies survive along with the Museum of Ceramics.

🏠 Nearly 11,000 steam-powered boats plied the waters of the Ohio River during the 1800s. Today only 6 large working steamboats survive—all of them based in New Orleans—the *Delta Queen*, the *Mississippi Queen*, the *Natchez*, the *Belle of Louisville*, the *Julia Belle Swain*, and the newest, the *American Queen*, built at a cost of $60 million and launched on June 27, 1995. Captain Frederick Way was responsible for piloting the *Delta Queen* from San Francisco to the Ohio River after World War II. Each year the Sons and Daughters of the Pioneer River Men sponsor the Ohio River Sternwheel Festival at Marietta to commemorate the Golden Age of steamboating on the Ohio River. From 15 to 38 steamboats dock at Marietta, including the *Delta Queen*.

The Golden Age of steamboating

🏠 What were 600 Frenchmen from the *bourgeoisie* doing in the Ohio wilderness in 1795? These were people not trained in wilderness survival—wigmakers, perfume distillers, jewelers, hairdressers, watchmakers, glassblowers, coach makers—people used to the good life. Worried that the impending revolution in France would threaten their lives and livelihood, they bought (or so they thought) 150,000 acres at the Paris office of the Scioto Land Company. Maps showed a town called Gallipolis (City of Gauls) located in a virtual Garden of Eden. But the French were duped—all they had purchased was the right to buy the land. Furthermore, the Scioto Company didn't meet any of its payments to the federal government and a survey revealed that Gallipolis was actually in territory owned by the Ohio Company of Associates. When the first group of Frenchmen arrived in Alexandria, Virginia, they made the journey to "their" town anyway, arriving on October 17, 1790. All they found were 80 log cabins—and a few cows. Some of the immigrants left for eastern cities or French settlements on the lower Ohio or Mississippi rivers. In 1795, the federal government redressed the wrong by awarding the Frenchmen 24,000 acres along the Ohio in what is now Scioto County.

Land scam dupes French

THE NAME GAME

Oops! Wrong river

Moses Cleaveland and his party thought they were following the Cuyahoga River. When they realized they weren't, they were so embarrassed that they named the falls where they stopped Chagrin Falls—now a quiet little town on the Chagrin River.

Adapted from the original

Some town names adapted from Native American words include:
Wyoming– Native American meaning "pleasant valley"
Wapakoneta – early name was *Wapaghkonetta*, a combination of the names of a Native American chief and his squaw
Coshocton – From *Cush-og-wenk* meaning "black bear town" or *Goshoch-gung* meaning "union of waters"
Sandusky – from the Wyandot word *Ot-san-doos-ke*

Out with the old, in with the new

Athens, Boston, Holland, Lexington, London, Paris, Miami, Vienna, Richmond, and Washington. Just put "New" in front of these monikers and you've got some Ohio city names. New London—named for the English city full of tradition—is home of the C.E. Ward Company which has produced such traditional clothing as church vestments and regalia for fraternal organizations since 1891. After the Civil War, New Lebanon resembled the Middle East country. A gang war led to the burning of the town in 1876. New Holland, founded in 1818, added several other country names to its early history. The settlement became known as a center for Poland-China hogs!

How did they get those names?

Town names come from many places. Some honor famous people forgotten over the years. Others are translations from foreign languages or just practical concoctions. The origins of some Ohio place names include:

Akron – from the Greek *akros* meaning "high." Akron was built on the highest elevation along the Ohio and Erie Canal.

Defiance – "I defy the English, the Indians, and all the devils in hell to take it," said General Mad Anthony Wayne when he built Fort Defiance at the confluence of the Auglaize and Maumee rivers.

Bucyrus – B*u* from "beauty" and *cyrus* for the founder of the Persian Empire

Felicity – originally Feelicity—but for obvious reasons one "e" was dropped

Euclid – named by surveyors who honored their profession's patron saint—the great mathematician Euclid, the "father of geometry"

Elyria – founder Herman Ely took the last three letters of his own last name and the last three letters of his wife Maria's first name

Massillon - the town founder's favorite author was Frenchman Jean Baptiste Massillon

Mansfield – named in honor of the surveyor general of the United States, Jared Mansfield, by two surveyors who worked under him

Trotwood – A mailman named the town after Betsey Trotwood, a character from Charles Dickens *David Copperfield*

Van Wert – last name of Isaac Van Wert who captured Major John André—a spy in the Revolutionary War—along with John Spaulding and David Williams

During the 1840s, the U.S. Post Office was trying to get things a little more organized. They wanted town names for each place the mail was dropped. Adamsville submitted its name for approval but the name was already being used. After several more submissions were rejected, local resident Sylvester Wood came up with the solution. He and his family had just returned from a trip to Texas and the Rio Grande. Surely no other town in Ohio would be called Rio Grande, he reasoned. Wood also thought Raccoon Creek was about the same size as the Texas river. Originally settled by a group of Welsh in 1818, the new name—pronounced *Ryo Grand*—was accepted. The town that shares its name with the Texas river boasts another kind of sharing. The University of Rio Grande, a private university established in 1876, shares its 178-acre campus with Rio Grande Community College—the only such arrangement in the nation.

Share and share alike

CITY HALL

President-maker

Millionaire businessman Marcus A. Hanna (right) of Cleveland was so proficient at fund-raising that he was given a seat on the state Republican Committee. From there, he became powerful enough to boost William McKinley into the governor's mansion. In 1896, Hanna's pre-convention persuasion (and $100,000 of his money) gave McKinley the Republican nomination for president on the first ballot. He was repaid by an appointment as national chairman of the Republican Party. He turned down the job of postmaster-general in the McKinley administration because he wanted to be a senator. When Senator John Sherman became McKinley's secretary of state, Hanna got his wish and served out Sherman's term and another term as well. Early in 1901, Hanna was touted as the "logical" choice of the Republican party for president. Supported by eastern business interests, the champion of "stand-pattism," or "keeping things the way they were," looked like the "safe" candidate. But Hanna died suddenly in February 1904.

Thirty-one-year-old Dennis J. Kucinich became the youngest mayor of a major city when he assumed office as Cleveland's mayor in 1977. Known for his big mouth, he called city council members and businessmen "buffoons" and "lunatics." After firing popular police chief Richard Hongisto, the mayor barely survived a recall election by 236 votes. Kucinich's luck ran out on December 15, 1978, when the city couldn't come up with $15.5 million it owed six Cleveland banks. Local bankers didn't like the abrasive mayor and they decided to get even by not extending credit. Not one to back down, Kucinich staged a media event of his own as he withdrew his personal savings of $9,100 from Cleveland Trust. The banks were using "blackmail and intimidation," he said, "I am going to take my clean money out of this dirty bank." That same day Kucinich's brother Perry stole $1,396 from another Cleveland bank and was arrested, putting a strange twist on the day's events.

Young and abrasive

A real hot head

Mayor Ralph Perk presided over Cleveland's city hall during some pretty dark days—1971 to 1977. The city wasn't enjoying much positive publicity and the mayor didn't help. Perk tried to cut a metal ribbon with a blowtorch to open a national metals convention and a column of flame shot up. The descending sparks ignited his hair and the event was "freeze-framed" all over the nightly news. Not only did Cleveland have a river that burst into flames but also a combustible mayor.

Boss Cox A saloonkeeper turned politician, George B. Cox was elected to Cincinnati's city council at age 24. It was the only elected office he ever held. He sold his tavern in 1881 and became a millionaire real estate promoter and the political boss of a corrupt Republican machine. Between 1888 and 1910 "no man had a chance to get on the Republican ticket without the approval of Cox." Loyal to his supporters, he kept a card file detailing the nasty habits of his enemies. In a *New York World* interview dated May 15, 1911, Cox said he liked politics because he was good at it and bosses were just a fact of American life. Young men should stay out of politics because it was too dishonest, he said, and "... whether you [were] successful or not ..." there was "... only abuse ...."

Good government
Dayton was the first major city in the United States to adopt the manager-commissioner form of city government in 1913.

City government reform came to Cincinnati with the 1924 charter that shifted power from the "easily controlled uneducated masses" to the more educated elite. A professional city manager was hired. The 30-member city council elected from small neighborhood districts was replaced by a nine-member council elected from the city at large. Most members on the new city council came from the Charter Party, a group of liberal Republicans. Today, the city is once again debating whether to popularly elect a mayor.

FAMOUS NATIVES

Tecumseh's namesake

Many great men have called Lancaster home. There was Henry Stanbery, who defended President Andrew Johnson during his impeachment trial, and Senators Thomas Ewing and John Sherman. But perhaps the most famous of all was John Sherman's brother William Tecumseh Sherman (left). Born in 1820, Tecumseh was orphaned in 1829. He and his brother were taken in by Thomas Ewing, a friend of the family. It was Mrs. Ewing who added the name "William" when Tecumseh was baptized. Senator Ewing got William an appointment to West Point. Offered a Confederate commission, Sherman turned it down and later became the Union general who "marched through Georgia" and burned Atlanta. His Georgia campaign is regarded as the first battle in which modern warfare—designed to discourage the enemy by destroying supplies—was used. Sherman's famous line, "War ... is hell," was given in a speech at Columbus in 1880.

In 1938, a group of Hollywood publicity types were looking for an American town with a population under 5,000 that could claim the longest list of illustrious citizens. Cadiz won and was dubbed "the proudest small town in America." The 10 names submitted by Cadiz included John A. Bingham, Civil War statesman; Bishop Matthew Simpson, prominent abolitionist; Edwin M. Stanton, Lincoln's secretary of war; and Clark Gable, actor.

The O.J. connection

Canton-native Captain Margaret York of the Los Angeles Police Department (and wife of O.J. Simpson trial judge Lance Ito) recently bought property in Minerva as a vacation getaway. "I've never been anywhere as beautiful as Minerva." she said. "It has good, solid Christian values ...."

CLAIMS TO FAME

Flying the red, white, and blue

You thought Findlay was known for Marathon Oil Company. It is—but it's also been officially recognized as Flag City, USA. John Cook thought that every house in Findlay should fly the American flag on Flag Day, June 14, 1968. He talked to business leaders and enough money was collected to buy 14,000 small flags and a plaque to honor veterans of the armed forces. These flags continued flying until Flag Day 1974. At the urging of several local service clubs, Congressman Tennyson Guyer introduced House Joint Resolution No. 1003 and Findlay was officially declared Flag City, USA in 1975.

Can you imagine a town in the 1990s that doesn't sell alcoholic beverages? Westerville is such a place and claims to be the "Dry Capital of the World." The Anti-Saloon League moved its headquarters from Washington to Westerville in 1918. The town had been dry since 1858 and seemed like the perfect spot for a prohibitionist organization. Considered the "father of Prohibition" and one of the authors of the 18th Amendment to the Constitution, native-Ohioan Ernest Cherrington was head of the organization and editor of its newspaper, *The American Issue*. From the small town of 2,500, Cherrington's organization worked through churches to promote the abolition of saloons and other institutions they felt were breeding places for crime. They mailed so much literature—about 40 tons a month—that Westerville was the first small town in America to have a first-class post office.

In 1875 a businessman tried to open a saloon on Main Street and he was bombed out. He tried again four years later and another explosion occurred. After Prohibition someone else caused a big commotion by trying to sell beer at a local pool hall. The Moose Lodge of Columbus got wind of the dispute and rented a bus to take members to the pool hall in Westerville where 46 men and 2 women said they "drank the best beer" they'd every tasted.

The proudest of the proud

Here she comes again!
During the early years of the Miss America pageant, contestants were allowed to win more than once—a three-time winner could claim the title, Golden Mermaid. Mary Campbell of Columbus won twice—in 1922 and 1923—and was first runner-up in 1924. No one was ever Golden Mermaid.

Other Miss Americas from Ohio
Marilyn Meseke, Marion, 1938
Jacqueline Mayer, Sandusky, 1963
Laurie Lea Schaefer, Columbus, 1972
Susan Perkins, Columbus, 1978
Kaye Lani Rae Rafko, Toledo, 1988

No drinking allowed

VOTE "DRY" FOR US

The big grind   🏠 Berea claims to be the "Grindstone Capital of the World." At one time, 80 percent of the grindstones in the United States were shipped from the area. From Berea's quarries came the sandstone that ground grain into flour and the best building materials in the state for houses, courthouses, and monuments. But don't count Amherst out of the sandstone plaudits. It bills itself as the "Sandstone Capital of the World" and claims the world's largest sandstone quarry.

Sobriety city   🏠 Akron is called the "birthplace of aviation" for good reason, but the town also played a major role in helping alcoholics get their feet back on the ground. Two alcoholics—Dr. Robert H. Smith of Akron and New York stockbroker William G. Wilson—met in May 1935 to discuss their drinking problem and how they could promote sobriety. From that beginning, Alcoholics Anonymous was born. In 1937—with two small AA groups in Akron and one in New York—the two founders met at Dr. Bob's Akron home to begin work on a book that would spell out their self-help program. *Alcoholics Anonymous* came off the press in 1939. Today the organization claims more than one million members in 28,000 groups all over the world.

They wanted an image

Gahanna is a farm community that wanted an image people would remember. Bunnie Geroux, owner of Culpepper's Herb House and an herb expert, thought promoting herbs might do the trick. She designed a garden and planted 100 different kinds of herbs next to the municipal building, organized an Herb Board, and recruited women to travel around the state educating people about herbs. Her efforts were successful in 1973 when Gahanna was designated "Herb Capital of Ohio." In 1974, the first Herb Days were held. To date, the town has been so successful that the state approved a $100,000 grant for the construction of the Ohio Herb Education Center, which will include a 20,000-square-foot building, a high-tech herb library, 5 acres of gardens, and a greenhouse for 30 kinds of herbs.

FOUNDED 1849
Gahanna
WELCOMES YOU

Buy us, please!   🏠 The *Dayton Daily News* is listed as one of the Top Ten newspapers to watch during the 1990s. Some other prestigious names are on the list—the *Boston Globe*, the *Chicago Tribune*, and the *New York Times*. While the employees are grateful for the recognition, circulation is going down. One employee pleaded with the public, "Don't watch us ... Buy us, or we won't be around to watch."

MONUMENTS AND MUSEUMS

See "the real thing"   🏠 A 95-year-old Coca-Cola cooler greets visitors at Butch's Coca-Cola Museum in Marietta. Butch Badgett and his wife started collecting Coca-Cola memorabilia 15 years ago as they visited art sales. Today, they not only have the museum but two garages and six rooms full of memorabilia at Butch's dad's house. For 50 cents a person—or $1 a family—you can see more of the "the real thing" than anywhere else.

Ahead of its time

When the Mormons dedicated their temple on March 27, 1836, in Kirtland, they may not have realized that they had constructed a perfect passive solar building. Positioned to take advantage of the sun, the "enveloped" building—with a wooden structure inside a stone structure—had 27-1/2-inch-thick walls. The building was cool in the summer and warm in the winter. The lighting was also unique. The entryway window provided natural light that shone on a curved surface in the light well and diffused into the temple's main room. This technique was used in Middle Eastern buildings by A.D. 100, but it was unusual in this hemisphere. These accomplishments are incredible since none of the early members of the Mormon Church in Kirtland had any architectural training.

🏠 Dennison is halfway between Columbus and Pittsburgh because a steam engine could only travel about 100 miles before it needed more fuel. The Pittsburgh, Cincinnati and St. Louis Railway built the depot in 1873 and the town of Dennison was born. Almost 3,000 people worked in the railroad yards and shops during the railroad's heyday. Between 1942 and 1946, 1 million World War II soldiers passed through the depot. The Salvation Army sponsored groups of volunteers from eight counties who—with just one hour's notice— provided cookies, fruit, and sandwiches for the soldiers in the depot's canteen while the train refueled. The busiest canteen outside Chicago and New York, young soldiers thought the stop was a "dream"—a place where they got good food and good company for free. They dubbed the town "Dreamsville" and Glen Miller wrote a song of the same name. In 1989, students from Buckeye Joint Vocational School in New Philadelphia who were learning the building trades began restoring the old depot. Today the depot houses the Dennison Railroad Museum.

Like a dream

The Wyandot Popcorn Museum in Marion is home to the largest collection of popcorn poppers and antique peanut roasters in the world, including an 1892 corn popper and Paul Newman's Dunbar Popcorn Wagon. Native Americans first popped corn by shelling it, popping it in a pottery popper, and then sifting the popped corn in a reed basket (above).

THAT CALLS FOR A CELEBRATION

Feels good all under

In 1992 Piqua's Heritage Festival, usually held on Labor Day weekend, was rained out. Some creative citizens decided another kind of celebration was in order. Since Piqua was once the "Underwear Capital of the World," why not celebrate that heritage in early October? Drop-drawer long johns—called union suits—were invented in Piqua and eight factories produced the undergarments in the early 1900s. (Today the factories are gone.) As of 1995, The Great Outdoor Underwear Festival entertains 20,000 to 30,000 underwear enthusiasts each year, appropriately clad in long johns or any similar undergarment. The Sunday parade features entire bands wearing nothing but boxers. Organizers didn't choose to hold the festival in the summer for obvious reasons—one promoter said, "You can't get too 'kinky' in October."

You look just like ...

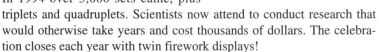 The citizens of Twinsburg wanted to honor the city's founders—identical twins Moses and Aaron Wilcox — during their bicentennial in 1976. In 1827 the brothers gave the town $20 and a piece of land for the new schoolhouse on condition that the town change its name from Millsville to Twinsburg. Today, Twin Days has become a worldwide celebration of multiple births. The inaugural celebration in 1976 drew 36 sets of twins. In 1994 over 3,000 sets came, plus triplets and quadruplets. Scientists now attend to conduct research that would otherwise take years and cost thousands of dollars. The celebration closes each year with twin firework displays!

I'll have a pumpkin burger, please

Mayor George Haswell started the annual Circleville Pumpkin Show way back in 1903 when he arranged a small exhibit of corn and jack-o-lanterns in front of his place on West Main. A more formal organization came together on August 8, 1946—the Circleville Pumpkin Show, Inc.—to operate the ever-growing festival. The whole purpose of the celebration was " … to promote and encourage fellowship among patrons, visitors, and citizens of the community and to promote the general welfare of agricultural, manufacturing and mercantile interests." Today the show, touted as the "Greatest Free Show on Earth," is the sixth-largest festival in the nation and enjoyed by well over 300,000 people during its four-day run.

Just in time for breakfast

 The return of Hinckley's buzzards—technically turkey vultures—has been called Ohio's "social event of the year." Since 1959, the town's annual celebration has attracted thousands of people. Every March 15, the menacing-looking birds begin to come back to roost after a winter in Florida. The first Sunday after the big birds return, the town sponsors Buzzard Day, complete with a pancake breakfast and buzzard memorabilia galore. There are lots of tales about why the buzzards chose Hinckley. One goes back to 1818 when a Medina County farmer went on a hunting spree, killing more than 17 wolves, 21 bears, and 300 deer in one afternoon. Buzzards can see eight times better than humans and apparently saw the flies and carcasses from hundreds of feet in the air. Perhaps they passed the story of that feast from generation to generation! A more likely explanation, however, is that Whipp's Ledges near Hinckley are perfect roosting places for the birds.

ON THE ROAD

Two rivers, one bridge

Zanesville's Y-bridge is "the only bridge in the world which you can cross and still be on the same side of the river"—so says *Ripley's Believe It or Not*. The Muskingum River and the Licking River that empties into it divide the town into three sections. Early residents wanted a good way to reach all parts of the city so they built a single span to the middle of the Muskingum, then an artery to the left and one to the right. Rebuilt five times in the same spot, the latest renovation was completed in 1984. Travelers on the National Road that passed through Zanesville often received funny directions to Columbus. "Just head on down Main Street and when you get to the middle of the bridge, turn left." The city—known as Y-bridge City—claims to have the only Y-bridge in the world. Zanesville's policemen have an embroidered "Y" on their uniform patches.

I can do anything you can do—better!

Along the Bridgeport-Zanesville section of the National Road, S-shaped bridges were built. Some say that workers didn't want to cut down big trees so they just curved the bridges. But another story survives. Supposedly a bridge builder named John McCartney and an engineer got into a boasting contest at a saloon one night. The engineer pushed a piece of paper across the bar with the letter "S" scribbled on it. "McCartney," he questioned, "can you build that bridge?" McCartney replied affirmatively, built one, and others popped up along the road. Besides the Y-bridge, Zanesville also claims a working S-bridge.

Covered bridges and barns

🏠 Some say Ohio used to have 2,000 covered bridges; others say up to 3,500. In any event, Ohio once had more covered bridges than any other state. Today the state is second to Pennsylvania with 136 covered bridges. A 35-mile scenic route along the Little Muskingum River in southern Ohio, not only boasts covered bridges but also old Mail Pouch Tobacco barn paintings. In 1946, a recently discharged Buckeye soldier, Harley Warrick, got a job with the Mail Pouch Tobacco barn painters. It wasn't a bad job at $28 a week and incentive pay of 1-1/2 cents a square foot. During Warrick's first 20 years as a Mail Pouch artist, he worked six days a week and decorated two or three barns each day with the familiar paintings.

Bridge stats
- One of the longest bascule bridges (drawbridges) in the world is Lorain's Erie Avenue Bridge, completed in 1940. Its main span is about 330 feet long.
- Cincinnati's Roebling Suspension Bridge, which spans the Ohio River, was the prototype for another John Roebling creation—the Brooklyn Bridge.
- Silver Bridge, a suspension bridge spanning the Ohio River at Kanauga, was completed in 1928. It was the first bridge painted with aluminum paint and the first to use steel eyebars instead of the usual steel cables—two standard practices today.

The hard and short of it

In 1891, Court Avenue, which wound around Bellefontaine's courthouse, became the nation's first concrete street. The city also boasts the shortest street in the world—McKinley Street stretches a mere 30 feet.

A CITY SCRAPBOOK

Dreams unrealized

A former California miner, Dr. James Lee, discovered gold in Belleville in 1853. Gold rush fever lasted a very short time. Dr. Lee's find was worth only $30 and probably arrived in Belleville from Canada in a glacier during the Ice Age. The town's dreams of riches quickly vanished.

The Wellington rescue

In 1858, John Price, a former slave who lived in Oberlin, was apprehended by a U.S. Marshal and jailed in a Wellington tavern. The slave-catchers had the Fugitive Slave Act on their side. But 50 Oberlin residents went to Wellington, defied the law, and freed Price. Oberlin took great pride in seeing that no runaway slave was ever caught. The U.S. district attorney arrested the "mob," which included 12 African Americans. Refusing to post bond, 20 stayed in jail as a protest. Two were ultimately tried and served some jail time. During the trial, Cleveland's businesses closed and a protest attracted 10,000 people to Public Square. Ohio Governor Salmon P. Chase and Joshua R. Giddings—the first abolitionist elected to Congress in 1838—helped facilitate a compromise that freed the others.

The president's men

John Gray worked as a youth on George Washington's Virginia estate and at age 17 joined the Revolutionary Army. In 1829 he moved to Ohio to become a farmer. His tombstone in McElroy's cemetery reads "John Gray died March 29, 1868, aged 104 years, 2 months, 23 days. The last of Washington's companions. The hoary head is a crown of glory." And the personal valet of Washington, Richard Stanhope, was given his freedom and 400 acres near Heathtown where he was a minister and a well-digger.

Don't get mad—get even

Nothing went right for Jim Slater. During the mid-1800s the Bairdstown farmer lost his wife and his property, and was convicted of setting fire to another farmer's crops. Slater continually proclaimed his innocence. Before his death in a poorhouse, he cursed the small village he thought had done him wrong. And terrible things started happening. Slater's lawyer's family died suddenly and the district attorney ultimately was sentenced to an insane asylum. The man who bought Slater's farm lost his mill in a fire and was harassed by creditors. He moved on to Arkansas where his wife and daughter died. In 1890, Bairdstown burned to the ground.

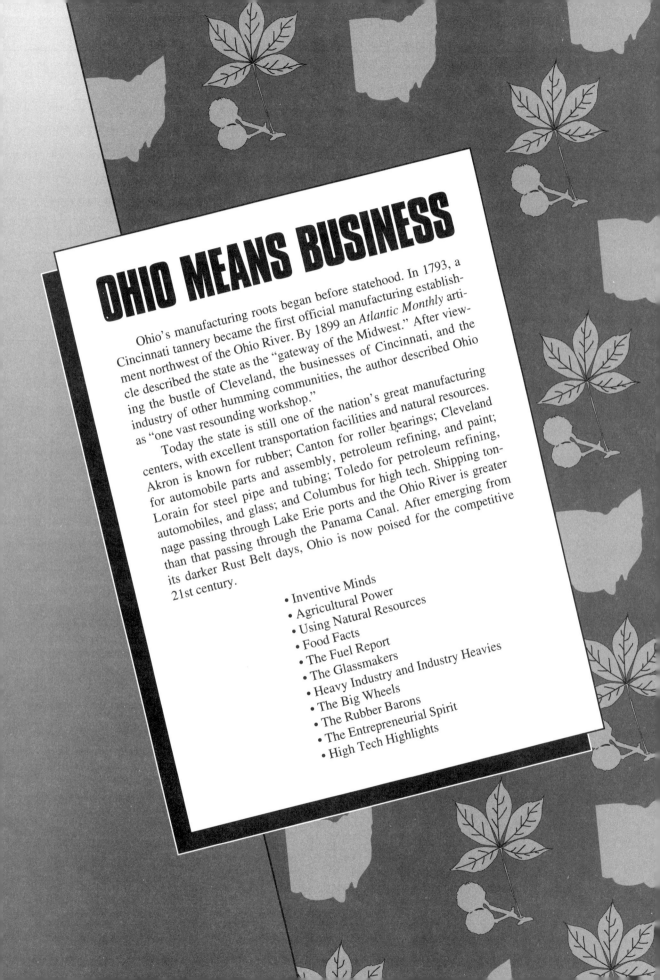

OHIO MEANS BUSINESS

Ohio's manufacturing roots began before statehood. In 1793, a Cincinnati tannery became the first official manufacturing establishment northwest of the Ohio River. By 1899 an *Atlantic Monthly* article described the state as the "gateway of the Midwest." After viewing the bustle of Cleveland, the businesses of Cincinnati, and the industry of other humming communities, the author described Ohio as "one vast resounding workshop."

Today the state is still one of the nation's great manufacturing centers, with excellent transportation facilities and natural resources. Akron is known for rubber; Canton for roller bearings; Cleveland for automobile parts and assembly, petroleum refining, and paint; Lorain for steel pipe and tubing; Toledo for petroleum refining, automobiles, and glass; and Columbus for high tech. Shipping tonnage passing through Lake Erie ports and the Ohio River is greater than that passing through the Panama Canal. After emerging from its darker Rust Belt days, Ohio is now poised for the competitive 21st century.

- Inventive Minds
- Agricultural Power
- Using Natural Resources
- Food Facts
- The Fuel Report
- The Glassmakers
- Heavy Industry and Industry Heavies
- The Big Wheels
- The Rubber Barons
- The Entrepreneurial Spirit
- High Tech Highlights

INVENTIVE MINDS

You don't have to be a parrot

$ Before Bob and Joe Switzer of Cleveland came along in the 1930s, you had to be an exotic parrot or rare fish to display the incandescent Day-Glo colors synthesized by the Switzer brothers. Their experiments with dye and resin produced fluorescent yellow, orange, red, and pink that seemed to glow in the dark. Procter & Gamble first used the Switzers' fluorescent orange and yellow pigments on their Tide detergent boxes in the 1950s. Since that time Day-Glo colors have made products all but jump off the shelf into a consumer's shopping cart. Today the Day-Glo Color Corporation—company motto, "you can't miss them"—sells dry pigment, inks, and paints to the plastics and fabric industries.

Cashing in

$ In 1879, Dayton saloon-keeper James J. Ritty found a way to keep sticky-fingered bartenders honest. He invented a machine that counted the number of business transactions and kept a running total of sales. He and his brother patented the mechanical money drawer on November 4, 1879. In December 1884, John Patterson—who had purchased three of Ritty's cash registers—bought a controlling interest in Ritty's company for $6,500. He renamed the firm National Cash Register, which later became NCR. The National Cash Register Company brought millions of dollars to Dayton both directly and indirectly and was the catalyst that made Dayton the center of the precision-tool industry. NCR was acquired by AT&T in 1991.

1914 model

Paint the town

$ People have been painting their interior house walls since 1500 B.C. but the first commercial, ready-mixed paint didn't appear until the 1880s. In 1870 in Cleveland, Henry Sherwin and his business partner Edward Williams believed that factory-crafted paint would benefit from standardized measurements and ingredients. It took them 10 years to develop pigments that could be ground finely enough to remain suspended in oil. Sherwin-Williams then encouraged Americans to do their own interior and exterior painting by setting up local paint distributors. These dealers taught homeowners how to prepare surfaces, choose colors and brushes—and clean up afterward. Ready-mixed paint created a frenzy that caused owners of fine wooden furniture to ask years later, "Why would anyone ever paint this piece?"

COVER THE EARTH

1905

A self-starter

By 1909 National Cash Register engineer Charles Kettering had made the cash register electric and was head of the inventions department. He once said that "the desire to know is infinitely more important than knowing how." He took that inquisitive spirit and created improvements for the automobile that moved the entire industry along. Kettering founded Delco (Dayton Engineering Laboratories Company) with Edward Deeds for the express purpose of creating electrical improvements for cars. By 1912 the first Kettering electric starter was part of the Cadillac. And by 1914, Henry Ford was offering it as an option on all Model T's. Delco later became a subsidiary of General Motors where Kettering was director of research from 1920 to 1947. By the time he died, Kettering held 140 patents for such things as safety glass and fast-drying car paint. Not all his interests revolved around automobiles. He also helped found the Sloan-Kettering Institute for Cancer Research.

Bell had the right number

Barnesville-native Elisha Gray was involved in a famous legal battle with Alexander Graham Bell—both claimed the invention of the telephone. In 1869, Gray was one of the founders of the company that became Western Electric Company. Bell filed his patent application on February 24, 1876—the day Gray filed a *caveat* or notice that he intended to file a patent for the same invention. It seems that Bell used several devices Gray invented—a liquid transmitter and an electromagnetic metal-diaphragm receiver—in his telephone. But Bell was awarded the patent on March 7, 1876, and a long legal battle followed, with Western Electric finally agreeing to monopolize telegraphy and Bell getting the telephone business. In 1885, Philip Reis entered the fray when he filed a lawsuit in the U.S. District Court in Cincinnati—claiming to be the *real* inventor of the telephone.

Sucking up

In 1907, James Murray Spangler, a luckless Canton janitor, found that his employer's heavy, inefficient carpet cleaner aggravated Spangler's chronic respiratory condition. To make his job easier, Spangler built a cleaner, lightweight carpet sweeper from a soapbox, a roller brush, a small fan motor, a broom handle, and a pillowcase. He patented his new electric suction sweeper on June 2, 1908, and began selling it door to door in the Canton area. One of Spangler's first customers was his cousin, Susan Hoover, wife of a prosperous New Berlin saddlemaker. William Hoover, impressed by the new device, purchased Spangler's rights to the machine, and started manufacturing Model O sweepers in a corner of his saddle shop. When hundreds of homemakers responded to a *Saturday Evening Post* ad offering a 10-day free trial, Hoover became a household word.

For old and new inventors

A new $38 million five-floor steel and glass museum called Inventure Place opened the summer of 1995 in downtown Akron. The museum not only houses the National Inventors Hall of Fame but also hands-on exhibits such as a 20,000 square-foot Inventors Workshop. Inventure Place also franchises "Camp Invention" and "Camp Ingenuity" for children.

A wizard and a tinkerer

With only three months of formal schooling, Milan-native Thomas Alva Edison logged a total of 1,093 patents before his death in 1931—the only American inventor with more than 1,000 patents. His *New York Times* obituary was probably one of the longest in history at 4-1/2 pages. Labeled retarded by a Port Huron, Michigan, teacher, Edison taught himself through reading. His favorite book, *The School of Natural Philosophy*, detailed chemistry experiments that could be done at home. By the time Edison was 10, he had a laboratory in the family basement where he began a life of scientific inquiry.

With money saved from different early inventions, Edison opened his own laboratory at Menlo Park, New Jersey, in March 1876—a 2-1/2-story building with a machine shop. Dubbed the "Wizard of Menlo Park," Edison's genius flourished there with his team of scientists, although his management skills were less than desirable. A ceaseless tinkerer, he would start a project, notice something interesting, and veer off in a different direction. Some say his inability to stick to one thing was probably why he invented so many useful products. He lived according to his famous quote—"Genius is one percent inspiration, ninety-nine percent perspiration," published in *Harpers Monthly* in 1932. He never thought something couldn't be done; the key was finding out how to do it. Usually remembered for the incandescent lamp, the motion-picture projector, and his most original invention, the phonograph, many of his patents were related to sound because Edison was deaf. There were 389 for electric power and light, 195 for the phonograph, 150 for the telegraph, 141 for storage batteries, and 34 for the telephone.

Thanks, but no thanks

Columbus-native Granville T. Woods—holder of 60 patents—was referred to as the "black Edison," an appellation he didn't appreciate. Woods sued the "Wizard of Menlo Park" twice for patent infringement and won both times. He turned down Edison's offer of employment—after the second lawsuit. Before his death in 1910, Woods was dubbed the greatest African-American inventor of his time. One of his more ingenious inventions was the telegraphony—with the flip of a switch you could speak into a telephone or, if you didn't feel like talking, tap out a message in Morse code.

AGRICULTURAL POWER

The big buzz

A.I. Root, a jewelry manufacturer, purchased a swarm of bees in 1865 for $1. Several years later his A.I. Root Company of Medina was making products for beekeepers. Today, it ranks as the largest company of its kind in the world, selling more than 200 different beekeeping products, including live bees.

($) Who better to drain part of the Black Swamp than the Dutch? They had plenty of experience in their homeland reclaiming land. Dutch settlers arrived in the Celeryville region in 1904 to raise onions, celery, lettuce, and radishes in the fertile muck. It took a Reynoldsburg resident—Alexander Livingston—to top off these salad ingredients with tomatoes. An internationally recognized horticulturist, Livingston worked for 20 years to produce the first tomato suitable for canning. He introduced his "Paragon" tomato in 1870—a fruit much different than the wild tomatoes, called Jerusalem or love apples, that he'd first discovered as a 10-year-old boy. Even pigs wouldn't eat that sour watery fruit. Now thanks to Livingston, Ohio cans about 5 million cases of tomatoes each year.

Tossed salad

Top crops and national rank

Tomatoes	2
Mushrooms	4
Soybeans	4
Corn for grain	5
Tobacco	8

($) In 1883, Frederick Baker began building windmills in Napoleon. Frederick Aller and Samuel Heller bought his patent rights in 1885 and the company they started still produces about 400 handmade windmills each year. One of four windmill companies in the nation, the Heller-Aller Company sells windmills to cattle ranchers and farmers who use them to maintain water levels in farm ponds. Other rural customers simply want an inexpensive way to get water.

Made the old-fashioned way

What has broad stripes, bright stars, and flies?

According to the *American Heritage* editors, it is a red, white, and blue Bicentennial manure spreader. In 1976 the New Idea Farm Equipment Company of Coldwater, Ohio, decorated a Model No. 224, 10-ton manure spreader with hand-painted stars and stripes and a banner that read, "Proud to be a part of America's agricultural heritage." The machine was decorated as a tribute to the nation's 200th birthday and to company founder Joseph Oppenheim, who invented the manure spreader.

($) Ohio's southern tobacco lands are simply an extension of Kentucky's tobacco-growing areas. The state's only surviving tobacco market is located in Ripley, where burley tobacco is still the most important cash crop. Every November through February the tobacco auctioneer's cry can be heard throughout the town. Ripley holds a three-day tobacco festival the fourth weekend in August to celebrate the history of the plant with tobacco-worm races, a tobacco show, and plenty of good food.

Just one left

($) Ohio ranks number one nationally in Swiss cheese and milk sherbet production and number three in ice cream production.

Dairy diary

Don't forget the little guy

$ Patrick Conway, a teacher from Chicago, and his brother, a bank loan officer, dreamed of owning a microbrewery. They followed their dream to Cleveland and established Great Lakes Brewing Company which won the Microbrewery of the Year award at the World Beer Championships in September 1994.

Fruit of the vine

The Cincinnati region has been producing wine since the 1820s. The Sandusky area, including the Lake Erie Islands, is the second-largest wine-making region after Cincinnati. The largest vinifera—or old-world grape vine-yard—east of the Rocky Mountains is 25 miles off Ohio's Lake Erie shore on North Bass Island. This 70-acre vineyard produces grapes for four Ohio wineries. The state's largest and oldest winery—Meier's of Silverton near Cincinnati—first planted grapes on the Isle St. George in western Lake Erie in 1845. The small island has a temperate climate with a 200-day growing season. In 1982, the federal government designated the area as a "specific viticultural area" because of its unique grape-growing characteristics. The Lonz Winery, opened during the Civil War (as Golden Eagle Winery) on Middle Bass Island, was the largest wine producer in the nation by 1875. Today, Ohio ranks fourth for number of wineries and sixth in wine production nationally.

It replaced potato peelings

Austrian Charles Fleischmann thought the way Americans made bread was appalling—the yeast for their bread dough was made from fermented potato peelings. Fleischmann went to Austria and returned with yeast samples used in Viennese bread. He and his brother Maximilian took their samples to well-known Cincinnati distiller James Gaff who joined the Fleischmanns in 1868 to produce compressed yeast cakes for Gaff, Fleischmann & Company. In 1929 the Fleischmann Company (Gaff had died) consolidated with several other companies to form Standard Brands. By 1937 their one-pound cakes of baker's yeast were bringing in almost $20 million a year—more than any other product made by Standard Brands.

USING NATURAL RESOURCES

Coal hard facts

$ Ohio ranks 12th of 26 coal-producing states. Belmont, Meigs, Harrison, Tuscarawas, and Vinton counties are the leaders in the state's coal production.

- The first electric locomotives successfully used in a U.S. bituminous coal mine were built by Jeffrey Manufacturing Company of Columbus in 1888 and installed at Ironpoint mine about 1890.
- The world's largest mobile excavating machine or dragline is "Big Muskie," operated by the Central Ohio Coal Company at a Muskingum County site. The machine boasts a 310-foot boom and a bucket that holds 5,933 cubic feet.

Ⓢ Papermaking is one of Ohio's oldest and most important industries—the first paper mill in Ohio was completed in 1806 by John Bever and John Coulter in Columbiana County. Bookseller and printer Peter G. Thomson moved papermaking into a new era, however. His formula for business success was: "First establish good credit, then use it as much as you can …." In 1893 the Hamilton-based businessman put together enough capital to start a company that manufactured paper coated with glue and clay by 1894. Before the development of coated paper, photographs often reproduced as blobs of black ink. By 1935, Thomson's Canton- and Hamilton-based operations were joined to form the Champion Paper and Fibre Company. The company developed a way to coat cardboard with wax—and later plastic—by 1935 and cardboard milk cartons soon appeared on supermarket shelves. Thomson's company purchased a clay mine in Georgia, timberland in North Carolina, and expanded internationally by using his business success formula, but not every transaction was designed to increase productivity. The company sold 80,000 acres of prime spruce forestland to the federal government that became the heart of Great Smoky Mountains National Park.

Borrow as much as you can

Rock hounds

Ohio produces the most lime and has more cement, clay, gravel, gypsum, sand, and sandstone than the other state. These natural resources occur in deposits near the shoreline or in the bedrock beneath Lake Erie. Limestone and dolomite quarries are located near Toledo, Marblehead, and Sandusky. The state ranks number four in the nation in salt production, with the largest operations under Lake Erie. Morton International's mines are located offshore from Painesville, 2,000 feet under water. Some people suggest that the state has enough salt to supply the country for another 150,000 years.

FOOD FACTS

Ⓢ About 1854, Akron grocer Ferdinand Schumacher sold cooked oatmeal—cut in cubes—from big candy jars. He later built German Mills, which became American Cereal Company in 1891 after merging with such companies as the Quaker Oats Mills of Ravenna. The new company adopted "Quaker Oats"—the Ravenna operation's trademark. The Quaker trademark may have been the brainchild of Henry D. Seymour—one of the Quaker Oats owners—who got the idea from an encyclopedia article about the Quakers. But his partner William Heston claimed he'd seen a picture of Quaker leader William Penn who symbolized the quality he wanted in his oatmeal. Whatever his origin, the Quaker Oats man made it big as American Cereal Company put his image on billboards all over the nation—and overseas. An extra large billboard near the White Cliffs of Dover was pulled down after the British Parliament passed an act requiring its removal. Today Quaker Oats' 36 adjacent grain silos in downtown Akron hold hotel rooms instead of oatmeal. The Hilton Inn at Quaker Square (right) is part of a hotel and mall complex created in 1975 by Jay Nusbaum from the original Quaker Oats' buildings.

Sleeping in the silos

If he'd only thought of flavoring

Mt. Vernon dentist William Finley Semple patented chewing gum in 1869, but not as a treat. He was interested in promoting oral hygiene—especially for farmers who could chew the stuff while they worked in their fields and not have to brush their teeth. His patent No. 98,304 reads: "My invention consists in compounding with rubber, in any proportions, other suitable substances … that form the scouring-properties of the same, (to) subserve the purpose of a dentifrice." His "gum" was called "red rubber" because it came from the substance used to mold false teeth.

The top banana

$ Chiquita Brands International—a $2.7-billion company based in Cincinnati—is the top banana in bananas. Traditionally, Europe was Chiquita's biggest market for the yellow fruit until the European Union slashed quotas and raised tariffs in 1993. Chiquita executives enlisted the help of the federal government to protect their European market. Officials think that Chiquita's "banana wars" might be the first test case for the World Trade Organization—a global mediation body created by the General Agreement on Tariffs and Trade (GATT) signed by 124 nations in 1994. But that's no quick process—it takes at least 18 months to mediate any dispute.

Those famous holes

$ In 1913, Cleveland's summer heat melted Clarence Crane's chocolates and put his candy-manufacturing company at risk. To regain his summer sales, Crane made hard mints and punched holes in the middle with a pill-making machine. Since the new confections looked like life preservers, Crane marketed his concoction to candy stores with the slogan, "Crane's Peppermint Life Savers … 5¢ … For that Stormy Breath." New York salesman Edward Noble bought a package of Life Savers and was so impressed he caught a train to Cleveland, intending to convince Crane to advertise Life Savers on New York trolley cars. Instead, Noble bought the rights to the candy for $2,900. His investment yielded big profits and by 1943 the former salesman had amassed enough cash to purchase the American Broadcasting Company.

CRANE'S PEPPERMINT LIFE SAVERS

REGISTERED TRADE MARK APPLIED FOR

5¢

1913

Boy, what a chef!

$ Hector Boiardi worked in European hotel kitchens for many years before he ended up in Cleveland in 1929. He and his brothers started a restaurant that became so popular they sold their spaghetti dinners in jars. In 1936 the brothers began marketing the chef's specialties under the phonetic spelling of the family name—Chef Boy-ar-dee. After Richard Boiardi served Hector's spaghetti to John Hartford, an executive of the A&P grocery-store chain, Chef Boy-ar-dee dinners started appearing on the shelves of A&P stores, and later on the shelves of every grocery store in America.

It's chili

You can't have it "your way," but you can have it 3-way, 4-way, or 5-way—Cincinnati's chili, that is. The city's secret chili recipe came from a Greek immigrant named Nicholas Lambrinides who started Skyline Chili with his three sons. After their father's death, Lambrinides' sons came to the factory every day until October 1994 to mix the secret spices themselves. This chili isn't like the southwestern variety—it's more like a sauce. A 3-way is chili on spaghetti with cheese; a 4-way is chili with beans or onions on spaghetti with cheese; and a 5-way combines all of the previously mentioned ingredients. You can get a taste of Cincinnati chili at any of Skyline's 80 restaurant locations in Ohio, Indiana, Kentucky, and Florida.

Stuffed on Stouffers

Vernon Stouffer planned on making his fortune in transportation, but his bus company and his trucking companies both failed. In 1924 he went to work in his parents' luncheonette in downtown Cleveland. Stouffer realized that serving food at only one location limited their business potential. He founded the Stouffer Corporation in 1929 and opened a chain of restaurants. In 1954 he introduced frozen versions of his most popular entrées and side dishes and marketed them to grocery stores. In 1973 Stouffer Corporation became part of Nestlé, the giant Swiss conglomerate.

1956

💲 Jerome Smucker—seeking a use for his mill when apple cider season was over—came up with an old family recipe for apple butter. He started making the spread for local farmers in 1897, writing his signature on the paper lid of every crock. Soon city folks wanted the product so Smucker expanded his mill and began packing the apple butter in half-gallon and gallon crocks for grocery stores. By 1915, his Orville mill was producing $59,000 worth of apple butter. Today, strawberry preserves is Smucker's signature item.

With a name like ...

💲 Bernard (Barney) H. Kroger began his business career as a door-to-door salesman. In 1883, he pooled his $372 with a friend's $350 to open a grocery store—The Great Western Tea Company—on Pearl Street in Cincinnati. Barney bought out his partner, B.A. Branagan, and by June 1885, Kroger had four grocery stores and a loyal following. He believed in hard work, quality, and honesty. "... I have known it [pink salmon] to be sold ... as first-grade merchandise. That was done in stores that started little, stayed little, and always will be little—little in business ideals and little in business success," he once said. Today, the legacy Barney Kroger built has expanded to more than 1,000 Kroger grocery stores. Still known for quality, the Kroger Company also has a sense of humor. During the recent baseball strike, a Kroger ad in the *Cincinnati Enquirer* caused some welcome chuckles. The copy read: "Holly Farms Whole Fryers, $159, Cottonelle Bath Tissue, $249, Pepsi 6-Pak $379. " The ad further explained that the prices were for baseball players and owners—all other customers would pay $1.19.

Barney's way

Where's the beef?

One of the big-three fast-food chains, Wendy's International began as Wendy's Old Fashioned Hamburgers in Columbus in 1969, the brainchild of high-school dropout R. David Thomas. He had earlier purchased a Kentucky Fried Chicken franchise, where Thomas honed his fast-food and franchising skills. Ready to go on his own, he chose the name "Wendy's"—the nickname of his freckle-faced daughter, Melinda Lou Thomas. (Her siblings couldn't pronounce Melinda Lou so they called her Wendy.) Most folks know Dave Thomas from his TV commercials, but who can forget the 1984 ad campaign that featured Clara Peller asking "Where's the Beef?" Winner of three Clio awards, the ads boosted Wendy's sales 31 percent. Today Wendy's International operates in 33 countries and Thomas has his high-school diploma which he received in March 1993 from Coconut Creek High School in Ft. Lauderdale, Florida—45 years after he dropped out. Adopted as a child, one of Thomas's other interests includes the Dave Thomas Foundation for Adoption. The profits from his two books, *Dave's Way* and *Well Done!*, support this nonprofit organization.

> **Here's some beef**
> A Cleveland doctor, James H. Salisbury, invented the steak that bears his name—Salisbury steak.

He stayed down on the farm

Bob Evans began selling his homemade sausage in 1946 at a 12-stool restaurant near Gallipolis. Demand for the sausage increased so rapidly that Bob Evans Farms Sausage was organized in 1953. Ten years later the business, now headquartered in Columbus, entered the big time as The Bob Evans Farms (BOBE) on the New York Stock Exchange. Today the company operates more than 350 full-service restaurants and sells food products under several brand names. In Rio Grande, you can visit the 1,100-acre Bob Evans Farm, featuring the very first Bob Evans restaurant and his original home—called the Homestead—which is listed on the National Register of Historic Places. The founder retired in 1986 and returned to his Gallia County farm.

THE FUEL REPORT

Almost a "boom town"

When Dr. Charles Oesterlin came to Findlay in the 1830s, he thought the gas seepages around Findlay and Hancock County indicated the presence of a gas field. The doctor found backers in 1884 and started drilling. At 618 feet, there was so much gas that the flame on the surface shot six feet into the air. This first well produced about 250,000 cubic feet of gas per day and set off a drilling spree all over northwest Ohio. On the morning of January 20, 1886, the city was awakened by the roar of a new gas well that ultimately produced 20 million to 50 million feet of gas per day. The gas saturated the city for five days before it was brought under control. Residents weren't allowed to light fires for fear of making Findlay a real "boom" town. When the well was controlled, the flame shot more than 100 feet in the air and could be seen 25 miles away. Findlay offered free gas (gas jets burned around the clock to show off the abundance of gas) to manufacturers who would build factories and 50 new industries moved in. In 1888, Edward Orton, who earlier said there was no gas in Findlay, predicted the gas would run out in ten years. This news delighted the local people because Orton's other predictions had been wrong. However, this time he was right, and by 1891 the gas boom was over.

First producing oil wells

$ Trumbull County had the first major producing oil wells in Ohio, beginning with a well drilled on the farm of William Jeffries in 1860. Oil was 30 to 60 feet below the surface—fairly easy to reach with simple hand drills. The wells yielded about 20 barrels a day and sold for $10 a barrel.

The world's first billionaire

$ By the time John D. Rockefeller was about 20 years old in 1859 he was a successful commission merchant who bought and sold grain and other agricultural products. In 1863, Rockefeller, Samuel Andrews, and Maurice Clark built an oil refinery near Cleveland. Two years later Rockefeller bought out his partners, and in 1867, Henry Flagler—the man who later made Florida the nation's vacation destination—came on board. In 1870, Standard Oil Company was incorporated and by 1880 the huge company controlled almost 95 percent of the nation's oil. In 1882, Standard Oil and associated companies became the Standard Oil Trust. Nine trustees, including Rockefeller, controlled about 40 corporations through a stack of legal papers that hardly anyone could understand. In her *History of the Standard Oil Company*, Ida Tarvell concluded that, "you could argue its [Standard Oil's] existence from its effects, but you could not prove it." When the Ohio Supreme Court ordered the company dissolved in 1892 for violating a state law against monopolies, Rockefeller simply transferred Standard's assets to different companies and continued operating as Standard Oil of New Jersey. In 1911 the U.S. Supreme Court declared the company illegal and in violation of the Sherman Anti-Trust Act—Standard was ordered to divest itself of 33 companies. Today, most of the descendants of Standard Oil don't bear the standard name—Mobil Oil, Amoco, Chevron, and Exxon all originated from companies in the original trust, and Standard Oil of Ohio was purchased in 1987 by British Petroleum Company.

Paradoxically, the world's first billionaire was a devout Baptist who worked full-time giving away money after 1897. Before he died, he handed out more than $80 million for such projects as the founding of the University of Chicago. Pretty good for the son of a traveling quack doctor who had no medical training.

Down but not dead

💲 In 1993, 904 new oil-drilling permits were issued in the state with most sites located in Muskingum, Coshocton, Holmes, Portage, and Stark counties. Although production continues to decrease, the state tallied 8,282,023 barrels of oil. Oil and gas production in the state was worth $276,764,511 in 1993, the lowest since 1979.

Marathon's current trademark (right) has changed significantly since 1946 (below).

Combining oil and steel

Founded in 1887 as The Ohio Oil Company, the business was renamed Marathon Oil Company in 1962 to more accurately reflect its worldwide oil and gas business, which counts more than 4,000 service stations and 9,000-plus miles of oil pipeline today. In 1982, Marathon was purchased by United States Steel—now USX Corporation. Seven years later, Marathon's headquarters were moved to Houston, Texas, although the company maintains a significant presence in Findlay.

1946 · BEST IN THE LONG RUN · MARATHON

1995 · MARATHON

THE GLASSMAKERS

Glass capital of the world

💲 Edward Libbey wanted to be a minister but when a throat infection destroyed his voice, he went to work in his father's glass factory in Massachusetts. In 1888, he left the glass factory he inherited from his father, loaded 50 railroad cars with machinery, and moved to Toledo where he founded Libbey Glass Company. One day an expert glassblower, Michael Owens, showed up looking for a job. He was hired as Libbey's superintendent. Owens first move was to fire everyone and hire a new crew that he trained himself. Edward Ford, son of plate-glass manufacturer John Baptist Ford, came to the city in 1896 and opened a plate-glass plant that became one of the largest in the world.

Owens patented several inventions that modernized the glass industry. His first invention was a machine that opened and closed glass molds mechanically, eliminating the need for "mold boys." Other innovations included an automatic blowing machine (1895) that was first used for tumblers and a machine that made bottles (1903). In 1912, Libbey, on Owen's advice, purchased a patent for unperfected flat-glass machinery and in a few years Owens had adapted it to a practical process. In 1916 Libbey-Owens was formed and by 1930 Ford's plant joined them to form Libbey-Owens-Ford. All of Toledo's present glass companies—Libbey-Owens-Ford, Owens Corning Fiberglas, and Illinois Owens—originated with these three glass pioneers.

On the cutting edge

- More than 200 patterns of glass were produced by companies in Findlay, Ohio, before the natural gas supply ran out in 1908.
- Fostoria became home to glass companies that produced beautiful glass for the table or lighting the home.
- Founded in 1905, Hocking Glass Company in Lancaster merged with the Anchor Corporation to become Anchor-Hocking Glass.

HEAVY INDUSTRY AND INDUSTRY HEAVIES

$ William Procter and James Gamble started a soap and candle-making business in Cincinnati in 1837 with a capital investment of $7,192.94. By 1859, P&G sales had reached $1 million and the Moon and the Stars became the unofficial trademark of the company beginning in the 1850s when dockworkers used the symbols to distinguish boxes of Star Candles. During the Civil War, the company got a big boost from soap and candle orders for the Union Army. In 1933, Procter & Gamble soap brands sponsored one of the first "soap operas," a radio serial called "Ma Perkins." P&G began using television advertising in 1939—which later became its mainstay—by sponsoring a major league baseball game between the Cincinnati Reds and the Brooklyn Dodgers. The company had grown so large by 1955 that it was split into six operating divisions: food, soap, toilet goods, paper products, buckeye cotton oil, and cellulose. As of June 1995, Procter & Gamble employed 96,500 people with operations in 58 countries. P&G markets more than 300 brands in over 140 countries. Some of those products include:

- Crisco –the first all-vegetable shortening—introduced in 1911
- Tide detergent introduced in 1946 and Joy dishwashing liquid launched in 1949
- Crest, the first toothpaste with fluoride, introduced in 1955
- Pampers first test marketed in 1961 unsuccessfully. Improved Pampers product eventually gained a huge share of the disposable diaper market.
- P&G's first product in the snack market— Pringles—introduced in 1968

Not only has P&G been a pioneer in marketing products worldwide, it has also pioneered employment practices that are now standard in many companies.

- P&G employees began getting Saturday afternoon off—with pay—in 1885.
- P&G has the oldest continuous profit-sharing plan in the nation, begun in 1887.
- P&G was one of the first companies to adopt comprehensive sickness, disability, and life insurance programs in 1915.
- A November 1994 *Money Magazine* survey named P&G the number one company in the United States for employee benefits.

What don't they sell?

It floats

The negligence of a Procter & Gamble soap-mixing machine operator in October 1879 gave the world Ivory— the soap that floats. When the machine beat the mixture to a froth so light the cakes floated, the foreman was ready to dump the soap back into the pot for reboiling. Harley Procter, son of the founder, thought the soap would sell and convinced his partners to give him $11,000 to advertise it in 1882. He also thought of the name for the soap while listening to a Psalms reading —"the ivory palaces"—in church. Consumers liked the floating soap that was promoted as 99-44/100 percent pure.

1875 trademark

Procter&Gamble

Beyond the sun

$ David Kurtz founded Cleveland Cap Screw Company in 1901 with $2,500. Today the company—now TRW—generates about $17,000 in revenue every minute. Charles Thompson joined the young firm in 1904 as a welder and by 1926, the company's name was Thompson Products. A merger in 1958 with Ramo Wooldridge Corporation made the company The Thompson-Ramo-Wooldridge Corporation. Executives joked that the corporate name was shortened to TRW in 1965 because "we got tired of writing Thompson Ramo Wooldridge in hotel registers …" Headquartered in Lyndhurst, TRW has played a big role in the U.S. space program. The company built *Pioneer 10* (in California), a spacecraft that had traveled 25 Astronomical Units from the sun (2.3 billion miles) by July 1981. By 1983 *Pioneer 10* was the first man-made object to leave our solar system.

Moonbase America

The Parker Hannifin Corporation of Cleveland produces more than 800 product lines for pneumatic, electric, and hydraulic devices used by other companies to manufacture everything from microchips to automotive parts. When Copley High School teacher Carolyn Staudt needed Parker Hannifin's help, however, the company wasn't too "big" or too busy to contribute to her project called Moonbase America. Staudt was looking for a way to make science interesting for her students and a 6,400 square-foot full-scale simulation of a moonbase was her way of doing that. Parker Hannifin gave the students a Motion Mate robotic arm and the technical assistance they needed to modify it for use in a moon-rock mining experiment. In 1992, after two years of work, Moonbase America was occupied for six days by about 100 students who learned firsthand what it would be like to live and work on the moon.

How do you unload an iron ore ship?

When the *Ontonagon* arrived in Cleveland in 1856 with iron ore, the work of unloading was done by hand. It took up to five days for the longshoremen to unload a single ship. In 1899 Cleveland's George Hulett designed an automatic unloading machine which his employer Webster, Camp & Lane Company of Akron convinced Andrew Carnegie to try at his Conneaut dock. If the machine worked, Carnegie would buy it; if it didn't, the unloader would be removed. Hulett's unloader rested on a rail-track assembly that moved along the dock. A vertical leg with a modified clamshell bucket at the lower end unloaded 275 tons of ore an hour. An operator in the cab above the bucket rode in an arc over the ship. The idea of riding the bucket up, over, and into a ship was frightening, but Hulett finally found a daring operator. The test was successful and Carnegie bought the machine for $40,000. More Hulett unloaders were built, allowing for construction of larger ships and thereby reducing shipping costs.

Hot pigs

You normally think of a pig as a chubby animal with a snout, but to iron-furnace workers of southern Ohio's Hanging Rock region in the 1800s, a pig was an oblong chunk of molded iron. By the end of the Civil War era there were 46 iron furnaces in the state, each with its own name—Empire, Monitor, Latrobe, Young America. Lawrence County claimed to have the first—Union Furnace, built in 1826—and also the most—with 16. Impressed with the quality of Ohio iron, the British purchased large quantities for armaments during the Crimean War which began in 1853. The iron from Jefferson Furnace west of Oak Hill was used to cover the Union ironclad, *Monitor*. During the Civil War, demand for iron was so high and production so fast that the pigs were often loaded while they were still hot. Many wagons, racing to market, caught fire and never reached their destinations. When the Jefferson Furnace stopped producing in December 1916, Ohio's charcoal iron industry was dead.

$ In 1868 the first Bessemer-Kelly converter was introduced at the Cleveland Rolling Mill Company, and Ohio's steel era began.

It started in Cleveland

$ Canadian Cyrus Eaton came to Cleveland to stay with his uncle—the pastor of John D. Rockefeller. The great industrialist took a liking to the bright young man and taught him everything he knew. As a result, Eaton was a millionaire before he was 30 years old. But he wanted something more. Eaton—who disliked the Eastern business establishment—wanted to make the Midwest the steel empire of the nation. In 1927, Republic Iron and Steel—organized in 1899 from 30 small iron companies—was the nucleus around which Eaton began building his company, with headquarters in Youngstown. The Depression slowed things down a bit, but the business continued growing, employing thousands. In 1982, however, a recession and foreign competition hit the steel industry so hard that sales plummeted 38 percent as U.S. mills worked at 50 percent capacity. In order to survive, Republic Steel merged with LTV Corporation in 1983 to form Ohio's largest steel company today—LTV Steel Corporation based in Cleveland.

A Midwest bias

Easy as L-T-V
In 1947, James Ling organized the Ling Electric Company. In 1960, he merged his company with Temco Aircraft and Ling-Temco Electronics was born. And in 1961, Ling-Temco merged with Chance Voight Aircraft, adding the V to present-day LTV.

America's Ruhr Valley

Dubbed the "Ruhr Valley of America," the Mahoning River Valley once boasted 25 miles of steel mills. Steel dominated everyday conversation and made the front-page news in Youngstown. It all started with James and Daniel Heaton in 1802 and their small smelter on Yellow Creek (site of present-day Struthers). In 1826 the first coal mine opened in Mahoning Valley and soon operators of two charcoal-burning furnaces in Youngstown discovered that Mahoning coal could be used in smelting iron ore. Union Iron & Steel was Youngstown's first steel plant in 1892. Most of the nation's seamless steel pipe and tubing came from Youngstown Sheet and Tube before "Black Monday"—September 19, 1977—when the Lykes Corporation, parent company of Youngstown Sheet & Tube, announced the closing of their mills. By 1981, four more mills were gone and 25,000 steelworkers were unemployed. The city became a national symbol of industrial decline.

Youngstown Historical Center of Industry and Labor Museum provides an overview of the impact of the iron and steel industry on Youngstown and other Mahoning Valley communities. The permanent exhibit is entitled "By the Sweat of Their Brow: Forging the Steel Valley."

Some steel stats

In 1994 Ohio's steel shipments reached their highest level since 1979. The state is America's second-leading steel-producing state, employing more than 30,000. Mansfield's Armco, Inc., boasts state-of-the-art electric furnaces, with operations in Coshocton, Dover, and Zanesville. One of the company's newest products is stainless, rust-resisting steel for floors and walls of prefab houses. Massillon-based Republic Engineered Steel is owned by its 5,000 employees. Copperweld Steel of Warren is the nation's leader in the production of thermally-treated bars. And Canton's Timken Company produces specialty steel in 100 facilities located all over the world.

A labor log

- 1825 – The Franklin Typographical Society, the state's first trade union, was organized by Cincinnati's journeyman printers.
- 1852 – Ohio became the first state to limit women's working hours to no more than 10 hours a day—outside the house.
- 1886 – 16,000 Ohio workers participated in 83 strikes. The American Federation of Labor was founded in Columbus that same year.
- 1890 – Cleveland-native John P. Green introduced a bill making Labor Day a state holiday. In 1894, Congress declared Labor Day a national holiday.
- 1942-1943 – More than 1,000 strikes involving 500,000 people were staged in Ohio. At the General Tire and Rubber Company there were 24 wildcat strikes. Workers protested wage controls, inflation, and long hours.
- 1947 – Senator Robert Taft of Ohio sponsored the Taft-Hartley Act, which passed over President Truman's veto. Among other things, the act allowed states to pass "right-to-work" laws.
- 1959 – About 61,000 Ohio steelworkers participated in a national 110-day strike.
- 1965 – Ohioan I.W. Abel became president of the United Steelworkers of America.

On Strike

Truman was out of line

President Truman decided to nationalize the country's steel mills in 1952 when the Steelworkers of America threatened a massive strike. The United States was in the middle of the Korean conflict and the president declared a national emergency. Cincinnati-attorney Charles Sawyer, Truman's secretary of commerce, found himself in control of 68 steel mills and boss of 600,000 steelworkers. Steel company owners went to court, using Youngstown Sheet and Tube for the test case. In 1952, the U.S. Supreme Court declared the federal government's action unconstitutional in *Youngstown Sheet and Tube v. Sawyer*.

THE BIG WHEELS

$ Akron residents were treated to the steam carriage of Achille Philion in 1887. His machine clunked down the streets at about three mph. One man tended the upright brass boiler, which furnished power, and another steered the contraption. In 1898, Carley Motz, an Akron engineer and inventor, built a gasoline car. What was said to be the first motorized patrol wagon in the world—designed by Frank Loomis, engineer for the Akron Fire Department—chugged into service in 1900.

See the U.S.A. the slow way

Alexander Winton—who laid the foundation for Cleveland to become an auto-parts center—came to that city in 1884 to start a bicycle business. By 1895 he had built his first gasoline-powered bicycle, which led to his first gasoline-powered car a year later. It was a funny-looking contraption with a two-cylinder vertical engine, electric ignition, and pneumatic tires. The Winton Motor Car Company of Cleveland was organized in 1897, the year the inventor made an 800-mile test drive from Cleveland to New York in 78 hours and 43 minutes—actual running time—in his automobile.

Did you know?

If you drive a Chevrolet Cavalier or Pontiac Sunfire, it was probably assembled at General Motors' Lordstown operation. Its 5,500 employees turn out more than 450,000 cars a year.

Japan, Ohio-style

In 1982, Honda of America began making Accords in Marysville, a small town northwest of Columbus that had one movie theater and no motel before the carmaker moved in. This was the first auto plant in the country operated by the Japanese. Today, Honda is one of the largest employers in Ohio with a workforce of more than 10,700 associates at four manufacturing plants (two in Union County, one in Logan County, and one in Shelby County). Honda manufactures more than 500,000 cars, 120,000 motorcycles, and 575,000 engines annually in Ohio and more than 100 Ohio companies supply parts to the carmaker. Honda continues to grow in Ohio. By 1998, the company will add at least 400 jobs, invest over $200 million, build an all-new V6 engine, assemble almost 100,000 additional cars a year, and increase engine production to 750,000 units annually.

A show of shows

If you want to see what's new in automobiles, the International Exposition Center in Cleveland hosts one of the largest auto shows in the world every year. Built during WW II as a tank plant, the I-X Center—a 1.7 million square foot builting with outdoor parking for 10,000 vehicles—sits on a 188-acre site next to Hopkins International Airport. One of the world's largest buildings and a leading exposition center since its opening in 1985, the I-X Center also hosts the world's biggest indoor amusement park every year.

You could walk and pass it

His merry Oldsmobile

Geneva-native Ranson Eli Olds produced the first commercially successful American-made car in 1902, the Oldsmobile Runabout. The car with the curved dashboard inspired the song "In My Merry Oldsmobile" and the first enduring car "jingle" was born.

Traveling in style

Ⓢ On January 31, 1995, Andy Mauck unveiled his new minibus at Mauck Special Vehicles in Plain City. He dreamed up the new vehicle in 1979, began sketching it, and in 1989 started putting the product together. When he quit his engineering job with a Dublin-based firetruck maker, Mauck thought group transportation was a great idea, but it was lacking in comfort and style. His MSV 1120—a cross between a bus and a van, measuring 25 feet long—solved those problems, while transporting up to 18 people. The minibus sells for $80,000 to $120,000 and will be marketed to corporations.

Autopawn

Beannie Taylor owns a one-of-a-kind business in Columbus—Autopawn USA. Opened in October 1994, Taylor, who loans cash for vehicles, got the idea from a similar business in Orlando, Florida. Each vehicle accepted must have a clear title before Taylor makes a loan for a percentage of the vehicle's value. One car on his lot was pawned seven times in four months. Autopawn's unique inventory has included a pontoon boat, a Jaguar, and a dump truck. Although Taylor doesn't ask his clients why they need cash, with certain customers it's easy to tell. "Some call a cab from the lot and head directly to a racetrack," Taylor said in a recent newspaper article.

THE RUBBER BARONS

It was a very Goodyear

Ⓢ Connecticut-native Charles Goodyear's passion—to make rubber stronger—drove him into poverty and earned him the nickname the "India rubber maniac." Before Goodyear came along, rubber tended to melt to a sticky consistency when exposed to heat and become brittle and hard in the cold. Goodyear accidentally discovered the secret of vulcanization when he dropped a piece of sulfur-cured rubber on a stove in February 1839. The end result was a material that maintained its shape in severe heat and cold. Goodyear received 60 patents for his rubber-making processes, and his vulcanized rubber was used in 500 different products. He should have been a rich man, but he died $200,000 in debt in 1860 because of mismanagement. Frank and Charles Seiberling memorialized Goodyear in 1898 when they named their new Akron business the Goodyear Tire and Rubber Company. Most people know the company for the Goodyear blimp—which began floating through the air in 1925. Over the years more than 300 airships have been constructed, with many named after America's Cup winners because Goodyear Chairman Paul Litchfield was a sailing enthusiast. The term *blimp* probably originated when Lt. A.D. Cunningham of Great Britain's Royal Navy Air Service playfully tapped the taut fabric skin of an airship and pronounced the resulting sound, "blimp."

Where have all the tires gone?

Of the four major tire companies that used to call Akron home, only Goodyear Tire and Rubber remains. In 1990, Michelin of France bought Uniroyal/Goodrich and moved headquarters to Greenville, South Carolina. Bridgestone—now the Japanese parent of Firestone Tire and Rubber—is headquartered in Nashville, and General Tire, now headquartered in Charlotte, North Carolina, is owned by a German company, Continental AG.

It's good to be rich

Former Civil War surgeon Dr. Benjamin Franklin Goodrich (right) established the first rubber company west of the Allegheny Mountains in 1870 in Akron. An early BFGoodrich Company product was the first rubber fire hose. In 1896, the company produced the first automobile tires (Goodrich was no longer living), and later innovations included the first rubber-wound golf ball, the first tubeless tire, and the first space suits for the *Mercury* astronauts. The BFGoodrich Company no longer produces or sells any of these products. Since the 1980s, the company has focused exclusively on expanding its global presence in the aerospace and special-ty chemicals industries. BFGoodrich Aerospace provides systems, compo-nents, and services to aircraft manufacturers and operators worldwide and BFGoodrich Specialty Chemicals provides plastics, additives, and adhesives to a variety of customers.

Firestone and Ford

$ While working at his uncle's buggy factory in Detroit, Columbiana-native Harvey Firestone probably drove the first rubber-tired vehicle. He later moved to Chicago and opened a tire store, but journeyed on to Akron in 1900 to start Firestone Tire & Rubber. Henry Ford secured the company's fortunes when he ordered 2,000 sets of pneu-matic tires. By 1908, Firestone was provid-ing pneumatic tires for Ford's famous Model T. In an effort to break the grip on rubber prices held by Far East rubber grow-ers, Firestone, believing "Americans should grow their own rubber," started his own plantations in Liberia, West Africa, in 1926. Firestone's boyhood home and farm build-ings—called Firestone Farmstead—can be seen today at Greenfield Village in Dearborn, Michigan.

Make it like Rubbermaid does

$ The company that asks, "Don't you wish everything was made like Rubbermaid?" might have a different motto if it had stayed with its original product—toy balloons. Known as the Wooster Rubber Company in 1920, Horatio Ebert and Errett Grable changed the compa-ny's focus when they saw a rubber dustpan James Caldwell was selling door to door. In 1934 the two men combined Caldwell's product line with Wooster Rubber and marketed the first Wooster Rubber dustpan. During the 1950s the company expanded into plastic products by intro-ducing the dishpan. They also changed the company's name to Rubbermaid and now produce a wide range of products for almost every aspect of life from Little Tikes toys to household storage systems.

THE ENTREPRENEURIAL SPIRIT

Vanishing art

💲 Etch A Sketch was created by Frenchman Arthur Granjean who called it *L'Ecran Magique*, meaning "The Magic Screen." The Ohio Art Company, whose representatives had seen Granjean's invention at the Nuremberg Toy Fair in 1959, bought the rights for the U.S. market and introduced the first one on July 12, 1960. The window on the front of

the Etch A Sketch is filled with powdered aluminum so fine that it sticks to everything. The knobs control nylon strings fastened to a movable metal bar with a stylus attached. In 1986 the company introduced the Etch A Sketch Animator, a computer-operated device that allows an artist to draw a series of pictures that becomes a "flip-book-style" cartoon. Those who want to preserve their drawings can drill holes in the bottom of the frame, very carefully remove the aluminum powder, and spray a fixing agent into the holes—making sure to glue the knobs to prevent any movement. Serious artists often make their work permanent—California artist Jeff Gagliardi Etch A Sketched the Mona Lisa and Michelangelo's creation scene from the Sistine Chapel.

Symbols of swing

💲 Rudolph Wurlitzer opened his musical instrument factory in Cincinnati in 1861. His first big order came from the federal government—drums and trumpets for the Civil War. When sales plummeted during the Great Depression, the company came up with the Wurlitzer Simplex—the first of the well-known jukeboxes popular during the Swing Era.

Financing the feds

Sandusky-native Jay Cooke made money off the federal government by financing the Civil War. In 1862 he was the special agent in charge of selling $500 million in government bonds for the United States Treasury. Three years later, he oversaw another $830-million sale. Cooke lost his fortune in 1873 but he ultimately met all his financial obligations and went on to make another fortune.

Making people smile

💲 Founded in 1850 in Cincinnati, Gibson Greeting, Inc., is the oldest greeting card company in the nation and American Greetings, established in Cleveland in 1906, is the largest publicly-owned greeting card company in the world. But the Amberley Greeting Card Company of Cincinnati, founded in 1966 in the basement of brothers Herb Crown and Ralph Cronstein's home, also sells millions of cards all over the world. In the beginning the two brothers sold their line of cards during the week and packed orders on the weekend. Today, their popular lines include Studio, Slightly Bent, Victoria II, Native Trails, and the ever-popular Our Towners.

💲 Columbus is an insurance center—home to more than 50 life, health, and casualty companies, including Nationwide Insurance. Founded by the Ohio Bureau Farm Bureau Federation with $10,000, Nationwide began with 3 full-time employees and 20 part-time agents who didn't even take commissions. The company was established because rural insurance customers believed they were being charged urban rates. Apparently their hunch was right because Nationwide has grown to include 27 insurance companies along with numerous other subsidiaries that generate $37 billion annually.

They're on your side

💲 The U.S. Shoe Corporation began in 1931 when Stern-Auer Company and United States Shoe Company merged. By 1939 the company's Red Cross brand was the top-selling shoe in the world, but when World War II broke out, the government banned the use of the name for obvious reasons. Red Cross became Gold Cross until 1949 when the FTC restored the Red Cross trademark if the company added a disclaimer— "Not connected with the Red Cross." Today the company owns Casual Corner and Petite Sophisticate apparel stores and Lenscrafters, a two-store company purchased in 1984 that has grown to more than 400 optical centers.

It's more than shoes

💲 When Leslie Wexner, founder of The Limited, Inc., opened his first store at Columbus's Kingsdale Shopping Center on August 10, 1963, total sales at closing time were $473. He launched the new company from his kitchen with $5,000 borrowed from an aunt. Today, the $7.3-billion business is a conglomerate with 12 retail divisions—including Victoria's Secret (catalog and stores), Express, Lane Bryant, and Lerner New York—and more than 4,500 retail stores. Paradoxically, The Limited's phenomenal success was achieved by Wexner's adage "think small"—or cater to the needs of each customer. The optimistic founder, whose personal fortune is estimated at nearly $2 billion, continues to invent and reinvent his growing organization. Known for his generous philanthropic gifts, Wexner is now developing New Albany, a completely new kind of community in the northeast corner of Franklin County.

Expectations are definitely not limited

Other Ohio companies and how they rank in size in the state

No. 5 – Borden Incorporated, Columbus, food products
No. 6 – Federated Department Stores, Cincinnati, department stores
No. 8 – American Electric Power, Columbus, electric utility
No. 11 – Dana Corporation, Toledo, vehicle components
No. 52 – Huffy Corporation, Miamisburg, bicycles
No. 61 – Diebold Inc., Canton, ATM's and security products

Weaving a legacy of quality

When John W. Longaberger was only 15, he began learning the art of making baskets by working part-time at the Dresden Basket Company, owned by his father. In 1936 he and his wife bought a basket shop in Dresden and started the Ohio Ware Basket Company. To support his large family, John worked in a paper mill during the day and made baskets at night. A stickler for quality, he even cut down his own maple trees to ensure that the basket strips were just right. The Longaberger kids sold their father's baskets door to door. In 1973, John's son Dave thought his

father's baskets might sell well in stores since decorative collectibles were all the rage. When demand increased, Longaberger taught several local people to weave baskets and the Longaberger Company was born. Dave Longaberger took over in 1974 after his father's death. Today, each Longaberger craftsman dates and signs the handmade baskets and a national direct sales force markets the baskets and pottery through home parties. Dresden celebrates its Longaberger heritage at Main and Fifth streets where the world's largest basket—48 feet long and 19 feet wide—sits (left).

The nose knows

Thelma Williams—leader of a half-dozen middle-aged female sniffers at Hill Top Research in Miamiville—earns about $40,000 a year by using her nose. Every day she and her crew test the efficiency of deodorants, antiperspirants, foot sprays, and mouthwashes by sniffing the feet, armpits, and open mouths of real people. The company uses about 500 paid test subjects whose natural "rankness rates" must fall between four and eight, on a scale of one to ten (with ten being the most foul-smelling). Test subjects use unscented soap and avoid antiperspirants and deodorants for 10 days before testing. Subjects are sniffed before they use antiperspirant or other products being tested. After using a product, the subjects are again sniffed to see if their odor level has dropped to a two-or-less rating, the level most manufacturers want. Testers of antiperspirants sweat it out in a specially designed "hot room" where the temperature is 100°F. If a client firm needs its product tested with "emotionally engendered sweat," a psychologist comes in to stir up "heated" debate.

Instead of mica

💲 On May 2, 1913, Herbert Faber and Daniel O'Connor opened their formica plant in Cincinnati. Back then the new product was used to insulate materials for the electrical industry—not to cover kitchen counters. Prior to *formica*, meaning "in place of mica," mica was the insulating material of choice. It wasn't until 1939 that the company started making the decorative sheets of formica that we're all used to—a new type of melamine resin and a better manufacturing process made the new product a household word.

Concrete spread

$ In 1995, the inventor of Sakrete, 94-year-old Arthur Arvil, still goes to work every day to oversee the company that has sold over 1 billion bags of the no-fail concrete mix all over the world. Arvil's product is composed of kiln-dried Portland cement, sand, and gravel. All the purchaser has to do is add water (you can even add too much) and it still "spreads like butter." In January 1994, Cincinnati-based Sakrete began marketing a "lightweight" concrete called Conlite that weighs half as much as Sakrete and is 70 percent stronger.

Builder of malls and champions

$ Edward J. DeBartolo, Sr., was the 95th richest man in America (*Forbes* magazine estimated his worth at $850 million) when he died at age 85 in 1994. DeBartolo turned a family real estate business—the Edward J. DeBartolo Corporation—into one of the largest managers of retail and shopping space in the country. Born Anthony Paonessa in Youngstown, Ohio, in 1909, he started working for his stepfather's construction company at a young age and took the DeBartolo surname while he was in high school. At age 13 he wrote construction bids for various projects. By 1937, he was building homes in Youngstown and, after World War II, he saw that the future was in suburbia. He built his first shopping mall in Youngstown in 1948 and went on to develop more than 200 mall properties in 20 states, later moving into industrial parks, hotels, and office towers. His business allowed him to indulge in his first love—sports. Owner of three racetracks—Thistledown in Cleveland, Remington Park in Oklahoma City, and Louisiana Downs in Bossier City, Louisiana—he also owned the Pittsburgh Penguins hockey team when they won their first Stanley Cup. He sold the Penguins in 1992. DeBartolo's son Eddie owns the San Francisco 49ers.

HIGH TECH HIGHLIGHTS

High frequency pioneers

$ If you've ever been caught in a speed trap, you're probably familiar with radar detectors manufactured by Cincinnati Microwave (CNMW). Founded by engineer Jim Jaeger in 1976, CNMW still produces laser and radar detectors, but it has also moved into newer fields. It was the first company in the world to manufacture a cordless phone that guarantees privacy and four times more range—the 900 MHz digital spread-spectrum model. In 1994, a wireless modem—for use in a wireless communication network being developed by the cellular carriers—came off the line. CNMW products are not sold in retail outlets, but are ordered by mail or phone. What makes these products even better is that they're manufactured entirely in the United States.

A major thoroughfare on the information highway

⑤ For a monthly fee, you can ride on the information highway with Upper Arlington-based CompuServe. Established in 1969 as a computer time-share service, CompuServe is one of the largest on-line services in the world, with 2.6 million subscribers as of April 1995. Through the huge data communications network, subscribers can tap into more than 1,700 databases (from newspapers to information about new car models), bulletin boards, and E-mail services.

Beginning in 1995, CompuServe provides access to Internet's World Wide Web, which allows computer users to communicate with computers all over the world. Purchased by H&R Block in May 1980, CompuServe received *PC Magazine*'s Editors Choice Award as the best on-line service for business in 1993, 1994, and 1995.

For those in a hurry

There's an unusually tall tower at Fujitec America's headquarters near Lebanon, but it's a necessary building for the manufacturer of the "Rolls-Royce of elevators." The 108-foot tower is used for research purposes and to test elevators and escalators. Fujitec builds computer-controlled elevators that "remember" the traffic habits of a building and position themselves to be in the right place at the right time. Adapting technology and artificial intelligence makes it all possible. If you're looking for a fast trip—and an interesting sensation—Fujitec also sells the fastest elevator in the world, which speeds up and down at 2,000 feet a minute. For the less adventurous, the company still sells the more familiar hydraulic elevator.

Meteoric rise of Metatec

⑤ CompuServe co-founder Jeffrey M. Wilkins began a new company—Discovery Systems—in 1985. Renamed Metatec Corporation in 1991, the high-tech company, which bills itself as "a one-stop source of CD-ROM expertise," is now a leader in the CD-ROM field. Headquartered in Dublin, Metatec is divided into three divisions: the Publishing Services Group, whose *Nautilus CD* magazine reaches almost 20,000 subscribers; the Software Services Group, which specializes in developing new CD-ROM applications; and the Manufacturing Services Group, which produces CD-ROM discs for customers all over the world. Look for Metatec stock on the NASDAQ National Market System—it's listed as "META."

OHIO ORIGINALS

"Poetry is in so flourishing a state on our side of the river that the limits allotted to this department are preoccupied." A Kentucky poet received that rejection notice from an editor of the *Cincinnati Literary Gazette* in 1824. And the state's creative life hasn't slowed down yet. The Ohioana Library in Columbus keeps track of 40,000 Ohio writers. The prestigious Ohio Book Fair in Wooster spotlights 100 Ohio authors annually. Readers buy 13,000 books at the one-day event.

Besides writers, there are world-class art museums, opera companies, orchestras, painters, and sculptors. From fine art to folk art, Ohio is the place.

- Of News and Newspapers
- The Finer Sounds
- Places for Art
- Cartoon Characters
- Palette and Canvas
- Building Originals
- Moving to Music
- Just for Kids
- Rhythm and Rhymes
- The Fiction Writers
- Sculptors and Carvers
- Rare or Strange

OF NEWS AND NEWSPAPERS

The daily grind begins

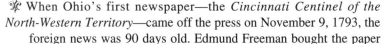

❧ When Ohio's first newspaper—the *Cincinnati Centinel of the North-Western Territory*—came off the press on November 9, 1793, the foreign news was 90 days old. Edmund Freeman bought the paper from William Maxwell, changed its name to *Freeman's Journal* and moved to Chillicothe in 1800. Nathaniel Willis took over from Freeman after his death that same year. Willis began publishing the *Scioto Gazette* on April 25, 1800, making the *Gazette* the state's oldest newspaper with its original name. It's also the oldest continuously published newspaper west of the Alleghenies.

Swaying the nation

❧ As editor of the Findlay *Hancock Jeffersonian*, David Ross Locke published letters in 1861 penned by his abolitionist alter ego, the Reverend Petroleum V. Nasby. The "Nasby Letters" helped unite Northern public opinion against the South. Lincoln once said that "next to a dispatch announcing a Federal victory, he read a Nasby letter with the most pleasure." In 1865 Locke bought an interest in the *Toledo Blade*, which included a weekly edition subtitled "Nasby's Paper" that reached 200,000 people. He moved on to New York where he edited the *Evening Mail*, founded an advertising agency (Bates & Locke), and wrote a play, *The Widow Bedott* (1879). Leaving the big city behind, he returned to Toledo where he wrote his last Nasby letter on December 26, 1887, less than two months before his death. He left behind an estate worth $1 million.

A European hero

❧ There's a birthday celebration every year in Tirnova, the ancient capital of Bulgaria for "the liberator," J.A. MacGahan, born in New Lexington in June 1844. MacGahan's reports for the London *Daily News* detailed Turkish cruelty in Bulgaria during that nation's struggle for independence and turned European sympathy toward the Bulgarian cause. In thankfulness, Bulgarians labeled the journalist, "the liberator." The newspaperman, who spoke nine languages and could shoot and ride like a Cossack, died of typhus in Constantinople in 1878. The Ohio Legislature arranged for a cruiser to bring his body home for burial in New Lexington where a small monument marks his accomplishments.

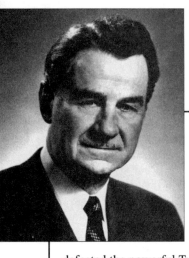

Bringing the world home

Known as a "citizen of the world," Lowell Thomas began life in the small town of Woodington in 1891. At age eight, his family moved to Colorado where he later began his career as a newspaper reporter. He was working on a Chicago newspaper when an assignment took him to Alaska and adventure. During World War I, his reports from the front gripped the nation. It was Thomas who let the world know the story of the man known as Lawrence of Arabia who organized the Arabs and defeated the powerful Turks. Thomas's thirst for adventure led him to "visit more remote areas than any other living man ...." When he became a radio commentator during the 1930s, 20 million fans tuned in each day to hear Thomas's unbiased reports. But writing and speaking weren't his only interests. He once managed a baseball team and loved to take his friends on rattlesnake hunts.

Don't believe everything you read

Toledo-native Janet Cooke was a feature writer for the *Washington Post* when she won a Pulitzer Prize in 1981. Her gripping story, "Jimmy's World," about an eight-year-old heroin addict from the slums of Washington, D.C., caught the nation's attention. But her story began unraveling when Vassar College called the *Post*—Ms. Cooke was not an alumnus as she claimed. Then the Associated Press revealed that Cooke hadn't received a master's degree from the University of Toledo either. After intensive questioning, Cooke admitted the whole story was a fake. She resigned and the *Post* relinquished the Pulitzer—the unfortunate incident marked the first time a "fake" won the prestigious award. Teresa Carpenter, a reporter for the *Village Voice*, received the Pulitzer in Cooke's place.

🎭 Real-life situations mark the writing of America's humorous chronicler of suburban life—Erma Bombeck. Born in Dayton, she knew what she wanted to do since the eighth grade. "I wanted to write light stuff and read every humorist I could get my hands on." After the birth of her first child in 1953, she devoted her time to home and children. Eleven years and three children later, she had lots of personal material related to keeping house and raising children. Bombeck convinced the Kettering-Oakwood *Times* to pay her $3 a week to write a column. Later the *Dayton Journal-Herald* picked it up and before long Bombeck's column was syndicated in more than 800 newspapers. In 1967, her first book, *At Wit's End*, was published. Ten others followed, including best-sellers *The Grass Is Always Greener Over the Septic Tank*; *If Life Is a Bowl of Cherries—What Am I Doing in the Pits?*; and her latest endeavor, *A Marriage Made in Heaven ... or Too Tired for an Affair*. Married for over 45 years to Bill, the Bombeck family adventures are much more slow-paced today. In 1993, she remarked, "Now we drink coffee on our patio in the morning and watch birds, talk to our kids—a teacher, a writer, and a retailer—and bask in their accomplishments."

Family matters

On the air

- CBS TV journalist Edie Magnus—seen on "Eye to Eye"—hails from Cincinnati.
- Host of ABC's "20/20" Hugh Downs was born in Akron on Valentine's Day in 1921.
- TV newsman and journalist Sander Vanocur was born in Cleveland on January 8, 1928.
- TV journalist Marlene Sanders was born in Cleveland on January 2, 1931.

Writing what he thinks
Dayton-native Clarence Page, columnist for the *Chicago Tribune*, won a Pulitzer Prize in 1989 for commentary.

THE FINER SOUNDS

The Queen City's symphony

❦ Cincinnati already had two music schools when the Ladies' Music Club—headed by Mrs. William Howard Taft—organized the Cincinnati Orchestra Association in 1895. This was the first orchestra in the nation founded by females. The fifth-oldest and ninth-largest symphony in the nation today, the orchestra gave its first performance at Pike's Opera House on January 17, 1895. Earning a national reputation for excellence, things turned a bit sour by 1992 when the orchestra accumulated the largest deficit of any orchestra in the country—$8.5 million. Today, the debt-free orchestra performs at two locations—the Cincinnati Riverbend Music Center on the banks of the Ohio and the largest symphony hall in the country, Music Hall with 3,417 seats. Known as the Grand Dame of the Queen City, the building is a National Historical Landmark.

We'll sing, and sing, and sing, and sing

❦ Cincinnati's German population always loved music. Numerous musical organizations were established, and in 1842 the Midwest's first *Sangerfest* took place at the Old Armory Hall. The fun was somewhat dampened when a cholera epidemic broke out. The Dutch singers were blamed "… with their jubilee, drinking, and sour wine, [they] brought the cholera." Thirty years later, a gentleman named Theodore Thomas came to town and began a less deadly tradition—the May Festival.

Begun in 1873, the May Festival is now the oldest continuing choral and orchestral music festival in the nation. Indiana University professor Robert Porco, son of Steubenville steel workers, drives 130 miles round trip each week to conduct the 160-voice all-volunteer chorus. But Cincinnati's Germans aren't the only lovers of song festivals in Ohio. Jackson began its annual *Eisteddfod* (Welsh for "song festival") in 1922. This ancient Welsh custom began with the Druids in what is now Great Britain.

Unique settings for the classics

❦ *Time* magazine touted the Cleveland Symphony Orchestra as "the best band in the land in 1994." Founded in 1918 with Nikolai Sokoloff as conductor, the orchestra has a unique summer home in the Cuyahoga Valley National Recreation Area. Blossom Music Center, a 5,000-seat outdoor amphitheater known for its "perfect acoustics," is located in an 800-acre woodland. Just a little farther southeast, the Youngstown Symphony Orchestra is the only "metropolitan-size" orchestra in the country with its own permanent home. The Edward W. Powers Auditorium was built by the Warner brothers—Sam, Jack, Harry, and Albert—in 1931. The Warners moved on to Hollywood and greater fame, but they left behind the 2,351-seat theater that ultimately became home for Youngstown's classical music makers.

❧ The first home of the Cincinnati Opera was the Cincinnati Zoo. From 1920 to 1972, the opera pavilion hosted the best—Placido Domingo and Beverly Sills—often accompanied by a lion's roar or a donkey's bray. When Beverly Sills made her "zoo debut" in 1965, a newspaper story read "La Traviata starring Beverly *Seals*"! Peacocks took the worst rap for interrupting performances. The ushers spent the first half of every act chasing the screeching birds away from the gate. But the performers and the audience loved the informality. As Sills once said, it was "kind of like going to summer camp." Today, the nation's second-oldest opera company performs in Music Hall.

It was like summer camp

❧ Portsmouth-native Kathleen Battle made her operatic debut in 1972 at the Spoleto (Italy) Festival. After her New York City Opera debut in *Tannhäuser* in 1976, she went on to the Met in 1981 with *The Magic Flute*. She won Grammy Awards in 1987 and 1988. At times her quick temper has overshadowed her extraordinary voice. Workers at the San Francisco opera wore special T-shirts after her performances imprinted with "I survived the Battle."

A winning battle

PLACES FOR ART

A home for museums

Cincinnati's Union Terminal was one of the last train stations built in the nation. Opened in 1933, the art deco building cost $41 million—the most expensive train station ever built. The building boasted the highest reinforced concrete half-dome in the Western Hemisphere—high enough to house a 10-story building inside. The basement of the terminal was about the size of 12 football fields. By 1972 train service had stopped and Cincinnati bought the gigantic building. An ad in *The Wall Street Journal* once advertised the colossus, "World-famous Cincinnati Union Terminal for lease—$1 per year." Around 1985, the Cincinnati Museum of Natural History and the Cincinnati Historical Society were looking for a new home and the terminal was certainly big enough. In November 1990, the structure reopened as Museum Center (right)— now "one of the top 10 new tourist attractions in the United States."

Showdown in Cincinnati

"Obscenity" thrust Cincinnati into the national news in 1990. That's when the Contemporary Arts Center and its director, Dennis Barrie, were accused of staging an obscene display called "The Perfect Moment." The plaintiff charged that Robert Mapplethorpe's pictures showed nude children engaged in sadomasochism. Barrie, who countered that the First Amendment guaranteed freedom of speech, was ultimately acquitted. The Cleveland native moved on to become executive director of the Rock and Roll Hall of Fame and Museum in Cleveland in 1992. Now what could be controversial about rock 'n' roll?

A showcase for contemporary art, the Wexner Center for the Arts opened in November 1989 at The Ohio State University. Designed by Columbus architect Richard Trott and New Yorker Peter Eisenman, the building has been featured in every architectural magazine and recognized as a work of art itself.

For American art

Youngstown claims a national art first—the first museum in the nation built exclusively to house American art. When local industrialist Joseph Butler, Jr., tried to buy a Winslow Homer painting entitled *Snap the Whip* in 1876, he thought the $500 price tag was too high. Today the painting he finally paid $5,000 for in 1919 is priceless. You can see Butler's famous purchase at the Butler Institute of American Art. Opened in 1919, the museums's permanent collection contains 11,000 works—from Frederic Remington to John Singer Sargent. The Donnell Gallery of American Sports Art is the only museum gallery of its kind in the nation. All the sculpture, drawings, prints, and paintings portray sports themes.

CARTOON CHARACTERS

The color strip begins

On February 16, 1896, a boy in a bright yellow shirt—"The Yellow Kid"—appeared on the pages of Joseph Pulitzer's *New York World* and captured the nation's imagination. The character was drawn by Lancaster-native Richard Outcault who is credited as one of the originators of the modern color comic strip. Pulitzer thought giving the kid a yellow shirt would draw more attention to the cartoon and thereby increase circulation. It did—within a year "The Yellow Kid" was pitching everything from chocolate molds to high chairs. But just as quickly as he burst on the scene, his popularity faded. Perhaps it was overkill—there were two "Yellow Kids" at the same time. Outcault left the *World* for Hearst's *Journal* so Pulitzer hired another artist to continue drawing the original strip. The competing newspapers were called "yellow journals." By 1900, Outcault was the highest-paid artist in the nation with his $50,000 salary. In 1902, the cartoonist created Buster Brown and his friend Mary Jane (based on his own son and daughter) and later licensed their use to the Brown Shoe Company of St. Louis.

Born in the same month as Outcault, Madison-native Frederick Opper shares the honor as originator of the comic strip. Opper's most famous strip was "Happy Hooligan," begun in 1899. Early in his career he was a technical illustrator for Thomas Edison.

The funnies   William A. Rogers could claim the title as America's first syndicated cartoonist. Born in Springfield in 1854, he drew cartoons for several Midwest newspapers by the time he was 14. We don't know what Rogers' salary was then but we do know that cartoonist Jerry Siegel of Cleveland—who created and sold the rights to Superman for $130 in 1939—could have made a bundle. Ouch! Hillsboro-native Milt Caniff made a good living from "Terry and the Pirates" and "Steve Canyon." Marjorie Buell introduced "Little Lulu"—the Bart Simpson of a bygone era—in 1935 on the pages of *The Saturday Evening Post*. Little Lulu retired in 1984 and Ms. Buell died in 1993 in Elyria. Other Ohio cartoonists you might recognize on the "funny pages" include:

- Dayton-native Cathy Lee Guisewite created the syndicated "Cathy" comic strip in 1976 and wrote *The Cathy Chronicles* in 1978.
- Kent State graduate Tom Batiuk taught at Elyria's Eastern Heights Junior High until his character "Funky Winkerbean" took off in 1973. You can see his byline on "Crankshaft" today. For those who think drawing comic strips is easy, Batiuk says "not true." He works six days a week in a studio over his garage.
- Mike Peters came to Ohio in 1969 as editorial cartoonist for Dayton's *Daily News*. Garry Trudeau of "Doonesbury" fame and his wife, TV journalist Jane Pauley, will probably never forget their visit to Dayton. Peters met the couple at the Dayton Airport along with the Patterson Coop High School Band. He then took his friends to dinner at a Bob Evans restaurant followed by bowling in Beaver Creek. His explanation—he wanted to "show them the real Ohio."

> **Pulitzer-Prize winners for editorial cartooning**
> 1953 – Edward D. Kuekes
> 1961 – Carey Cassius Orr
> 1981 – Mike Peters
> 1991 – Jim Borgman

- Ziggy was created by young "artist trainee" Tom Wilson while he worked at Cleveland's American Greetings Company in 1966. By 1969, Wilson, who now lives in Lakewood, had syndicated his shapeless character. His son, Tom, Jr., resides in Cincinnati and works with his dad via the fax machine.
- Lakewood cartoonist Art Sansom created Brutus Thornapple—"The Born Loser"—in 1965. The Cleveland native began his career as an illustrator in 1945 and worked on other people's comic strips for 20 years before trying his own. His son Chip came on board in 1977, became part of the byline in 1986, and took over when Art died in 1991.

Mutant art

✺ "What on earth is a Teenage Mutant Ninja Turtle?" That's the question West Salem artist Ryan Brown (right) heard when he participated in the first Ohio Book Fair in 1987. He didn't actually invent the turtles but he was a staff artist at Mirage Studios of Haydenville, Massachusetts, where they were created. He did design 13 characters for the Mutant Turtle toy line and worked on their comic-book adventures. The self-confessed "cartoon geek" and toy inventor's "Wild West C.O.W. Boys of Moo Mesa" is hitting the air waves in Europe after two years on American television. (C.O.W. stands for Code Of the West). His crazy Western characters inhabit comic books, storybooks, and videos with equally crazy titles, such as "Legend of Skull Duggery" and "A Sheepful of Dollars." Brown's imagination is always active—he signed a book series deal in 1995 for his new idea, *Hallowieners*.

PALETTE AND CANVAS

A home-run painter

✺ His mother insisted that he wear white knickerbocker suits until he was eight years old. Of course, "I was faced by a continual need of self-defense …" George Wesley Bellows later wrote. But in the summer of 1892, the 10-year-old lost his "sissy" image by discovering sports. As part of a local baseball team, he learned to play so well that the Cincinnati Reds wanted the young shortstop to play for them. As much as Bellows loved athletics, he loved to paint even more. In New York City, Bellows studied under Cincinnati-native Robert Henri whose adage was, "Anything that strikes you as real is worthy of being painted." The young artist took that to heart as he portrayed the people and events of New York City. His realistic boxing scenes, such as *Stag at Sharkey's* (1909) and *Dempsey and Firpo* (1924), made him famous. But he also painted landscapes, seascapes, and at least 140 portraits. Famous by age 25, no one knows what Bellows could have accomplished if he hadn't ignored the pain in his abdomen. His appendix ruptured on January 2, 1925, and six days later the artist was dead of peritonitis at age 42.

On his honor

Although most people know him as as a founder of the Boy Scouts of America with Ernest Seton and others in 1910, artist and Cincinnati-native Daniel Carter Beard illustrated books, including Mark Twain's *Connecticut Yankee at King Arthur's Court*.

Nature spoke to him

✺ Watercolor artist Charles Burchfield (self-portrait at left) was a shy youngster in Salem where he learned to love nature—in fact, it was his best friend. "I have never learned to talk and have only listened to the trees." Buildings had lifelike qualities too. He wrote that, "The houses have faces. The windows are eyes. Some houses smile at you; others frown." Although he left Ohio to perfect his painting technique in New York, Salem was always a big part of him. During the latter part of his career he tried to recapture the innocence of his youth when he walked "… along a dusty road in the hot sunshine—barefoot, a big straw hat on my head, a pail of wild raspberries in one hand." While eating lunch with his wife on January 10, 1967, he suffered a massive heart attack and died in West Seneca, New York. But his paintings—often called "an extension of the watercolor tradition of the Cleveland School of Art where he studied as a young man"—are a reminder of the sensitive eyes of one of Ohio's best.

The spirit lives on

You might not know the name Archibald M. Willard, but you're probably familiar with the Bedford artist's famous painting, *The Spirit of '76*, which he sketched during a July 4th celebration in Wellington. Originally called *Yankee Doodle*, the painting was first exhibited at Philadelphia's Centennial Exposition in 1876. Today, it hangs at Abbott Hall in Marblehead, Massachusetts. Ohio also claims a connection to another "Revolutionary" painting, *Washington Crossing the Delaware*. Springfield-native Thomas Whittredge posed as Washington while Emmanuel Leutze painted the scene. *Signing the Constitution*, which hangs in the Capitol Building in Washington, D.C., was the work of Morgan County-native Howard Chandler Christy.

The canvas is a screen

Who needs a canvas when you have a computer screen? In 1965, Charles Scuri, an art professor at The Ohio State University, became fascinated when he saw a computer making pictures. He learned computer programming and developed a brand-new art form using the computer. Now head of the Advanced Computing Center for the Arts at the university and founder of Cranston/Scuri Productions, he uses the computer to create images for television and educational purposes. Scuri is "recognized as the first person anywhere with a traditional art background to realize the potential of computer art."

BUILDING ORIGINALS

❧ Native Americans called the beautiful rolling hills of Logan County *Mac-o-chee*. In this beautiful setting, two of Benjamin and Elizabeth

Piatt's sons built "castles" that still stand. Abram, a Civil War general and farmer, moved into Castle Mac-A-Cheek in 1868. But Donn's home, Castle Mac-O-Chee (left), took longer to complete. The original small structure was purchased in 1824, but Donn left Ohio to assume a job as the charge d'affaires at the French Embassy in Paris. During the 1860s he returned to Mac-O-Chee to give his home a simple Swiss chalet look. After he retired in 1879, his remodeling ideas became grander. The addition of a Flemish-inspired limestone front that wrapped around part of the old house made the 36-room home look like a French castle. Governor Tom Corwin remarked that "A man can better live and die here than any place I have ever seen." Donn Piatt died at Mac-O-Chee in 1891.

❧ Frank Seiberling, founder of Goodyear and Seiberling Rubber companies, constructed one of the best examples of Tudor Revival architecture in the country. Built between 1912 and 1915, the house is 300 feet long and cost $2 million to build. It's called *Stan Hywet* (meaning "stone quarry") Hall and Gardens. Located on a 70-acre estate in Akron, the house encompasses 65,000 square feet. Its 65 rooms include 23 fireplaces, 25 bathrooms, 18 bedrooms, 20 sets of French doors, and more than 21,000 panes of glass. It took 24 servants to keep the mansion running and clean.

A man's house is his castle

Home sweet home

Plans to build a castle

Everyone has built sandcastles—and Gallia County-native Jan Adkins has made that endeavor easier and very authentic. Her book *The Art and Industry of Sandcastles* gives detailed instructions about constructing Chinese castles, English castles, Norman castles, and the Tower of London out of sand.

Maya's memorials

❄ Ross Perot hated the design and called it "unheroic." Several congressmen thought it was a "statement of shame and dishonor." But most Vietnam veterans think the Vietnam Memorial, dedicated in 1982, is a fitting symbol for a war that caused so much heartache. When 21-year-old Maya Lin's design was chosen from more than 2,500, the young architect from Athens was studying funerary (burial) architecture at Yale. Lin also designed the Civil Rights Memorial in Montgomery, Alabama, and the Elizabeth Baker Peace Chapel at Juniata College in Pennsylvania, both dedicated in 1989. Before deciding on a design Lin studies every minute detail—history, people, emotions, and psychology. Lin now lives in New York where she is also a sculptor.

MOVING TO MUSIC

Shaking and quaking

❄ An illiterate blacksmith's daughter, Ann Lee, thought she saw Jesus Christ and founded a sect that eventually made its way to Ohio. Called the Shaking Quakers—or Shakers—the group practiced the strictest celibacy and lived simple lives. They met together in the evenings for reading, singing, and dancing. Their strange dance movements—said to be caused by spirits that inhabited their bodies—became set dance patterns by the time the group came to Ohio. They stomped, bounced, hopped, and shuffled to get rid of sin and enter a "state of ecstasy" and thankfulness to God. In 1930, a modern dance pioneer named Doris Humphrey found that Quaker shaking was good material for choreography. Her composition, "The Quakers," has been performed widely over the years. In 1994, it was presented by the University of Akron Repertory Dance Company (left), which only seemed fitting. The Shakers built four settlements near Akron including North Union (now Shaker Heights) where they lived from 1822 to 1889.

Piece quilt for peace

❄ The troubles of the former Yugoslavia seem very distant to most Americans, but a Columbus-based professional dance group is trying to change that. Known as *Zivili*—a Croatian word meaning "To Life!"—the group performs the music and traditional dances of Croatia, Bosnia, Slovenia, Serbia, and Macedonia. In addition to preserving traditional songs and dances, Zivili promotes peace. "In my country, there is winter and there is war, and sometimes you wonder which is worse. Yugoslavia does not exist anymore. But people do and people are willing to make peace," said one dancer. To that end the company constructed a "peace" quilt called *Mir* that was auctioned off in February 1995 and later displayed at the Columbus Art Museum.

✸ Glen Tetley wanted to be a doctor before he saw his first ballet. Born in Cleveland in 1926, the talented dancer and choreographer was awarded the Queen Elizabeth Coronation Award in 1980 by the Royal Academy of Dancing—the first time such an award was given to a non-British resident. Another talented Ohio native, Suzanne Farrell (born Suzanne Ficker), hails from Cincinnati. She joined the New York City Ballet when she was just 16 and became a soloist in 1963. George Balanchine created roles especially for the talented ballerina in *Don Quixote*, *Union Jack*, and *Vienna Waltzes*. This remarkable dancer came back from hip-replacement surgery to dance in 1988, less than a year after her surgery.

On their toes

JUST FOR KIDS

✸ A master of scary children's stories, Robert Lawrence Stine was born and grew up in Columbus. With about 45 million books in print, he's found a winning formula. Now living in New York City, the prolific author turns out two books a month from his Manhattan apartment. His *Goosebumps* and *Fear Street* series demand a disciplined writing schedule. "I'm usually at the computer by 9 A.M. I say to myself that I'm going to write 20 pages. I don't finish until I've done my 20 pages and that's how I get so many books done." The name *Goosebumps* came from a horror movie listing in *TV Guide* and many of his characters' names are straight out of his son's school directory. The post office knows Stine well—he gets about 2,000 letters every week from kids—"I read 40 of your books and I really think they're boring"—and from moms—"My son never read a book in his life and I caught him reading under the covers with a flashlight. Can you write faster?" But there's one person who won't read a Stine book—his 14-year-old son, Matt.

He gives kids goosebumps

African-American first
In 1974, Ohio-native Virginia Hamilton won the Newberry Medal for *M.C. Higgins the Great* to become the first African American so honored. *M.C. Higgins the Great* is the story of a poor African-American boy in the rural South.

✸ You probably wouldn't want the Herdman children in your home, but Barbara Robinson has made them so popular they probably are—on the pages of the author's books. The Portsmouth native wrote *The Best Christmas Pageant Ever* (1972), which was adapted to a play that delights audiences every Christmas. Robinson tries to portray the good in children, even when it's hard to find. Her other books include *My Brother Louis Measures Worms* (1988) and the latest Herdman adventure, *The Best School Year Ever*, published in 1994.

There's good in every kid

RHYTHM AND RHYMES

Poet for his people

Born in Dayton in 1872, Laurence Dunbar was the only African American at Central High School. He self-published his first book of verse, *Oak and Ivy*, written in "Negro dialect" in 1892, while working

as an elevator attendant. Another collection, *Majors and Minors*, was printed in 1895 and a copy sent to William Dean Howells, who praised the poet. *Lyrics of a Lowly Life* was published in 1896 with an introduction by Howells. After 1896, Dunbar lived in New York and Washington, D.C., where he worked at the Library of Congress as a reading-room assistant. In the early 1900s, he became ill with tuberculosis and died in 1906 at age 33. His home was bought by the state of Ohio in 1936 as a historical memorial.

Greeting-card inspiration

Helen Steiner Rice (left) has lifted the spirits of millions with her inspirational verse. Coping with the untimely death of her father in 1918 and her husband Franklin's suicide in 1932 increased her ability to relate to the problems of others and offer comfort and compassion. Born in Lorain in 1900, Rice wrote greeting card verse at Gibson Art Company in Cincinnati from 1932 until her death in 1981. A religious, generous, and caring person, Rice established a charitable foundation prior to her passing. Recently, her biography, *Helen Steiner Rice: Ambassador of Sunshine*, was published by Baker Book House.

A separate house for poetry

Some people don't appreciate poetry. Such was the case with Alice and Phoebe Cary's stepmother—to her, reading or writing poetry was a waste of time. To avoid the whole controversy, Mr. Cary built a separate house for his wife and himself. Then the two girls were free to write all the poems they wished. Born near Mount Healthy, the two sisters published *Poems of Alice and Phoebe Cary* in 1849. They moved to New York City where they held an open house every Sunday evening. P.T. Barnum, George Ripley, and Horace Greeley were among their guests. Alice became the first president of the first women's club in America, the Woman's Club—later known as Sorosis.

The Poet Laureate

Most people know Rita Dove for her Pulitzer Prize-winning poem *Thomas and Beulah*, based on the lives of her grandparents. But Dove started writing very young. At age 10, she made her spelling words into a short book called *Chaos*. While attending Miami University in Oxford, Dove "decided … I would try to be the best writer I could." And she hasn't disappointed. Honors and awards include a Guggenheim Fellowship, Fulbright Scholarship, and, in 1993, Poet Laureate of the United States—the first African American and the youngest poet (she was 40) to be so honored. Now a professor of creative writing at the University of Virginia, she's added playwrighting to her resume. She wrote *The Darker Face of the Earth* in blank verse and staged it at the Oregon Shakespeare Festival in Ashland in 1994. Is Broadway next?

THE FICTION WRITERS

✵ Known as the "hobo author," Jim Tully spent eight years writing his first novel, *Emmett Lawler*. It consisted of one 100,000-word paragraph. Tully had little formal education and a patient friend helped him rewrite the manuscript into a readable book that was published in 1922. A man of varied occupations—tramp, farm laborer, chainmaker, circus roustabout, prizefighter, reporter, and tree surgeon—the St. Marys native is said to have been a "contributor to the development of the 'hard-boiled novel of low life.'"

The never-ending paragraph

He wanted to be a writer

"I called upon my old friend Clarence Darrow, the lawyer … He is deeply interested in letters, and should have devoted himself to literature …." So wrote young journalist Brand Whitlock while he was trying to decide on whether to follow a career in law or letters in 1898. In fact, Darrow, who was a friend of William Dean Howells, published two novels, *Farmington* (1904) and *An Eye for an Eye* (1905) and his autobiography, *The Story of My Life* (1932). But Darrow was no John Grisham and his secret desire to be a famous author was eclipsed by his legal prowess (see p. 164).

✵ The Bill Hawley mystery series, written by Berea's Gene Lazuta (pseudonym Leo Axler), sells best in Arizona and New York—but he's never received much fan mail from the Cleveland area. His third book, *Grave Matters*, was published in February 1995. Former Norwalk police captain, James Martin, created the character, Gil Disbro. Readers in Texas and Florida quickly bought his fourth book, *A Fine and Private Place*, but Cleveland paid little attention. And the creator of the Milan Jacovich series, Less Roberts, who moved to Cleveland Heights in 1990, says his books sell best in New York City, Chicago, and Los Angeles. His fifth book in the series, *Lake Effect* (1994), is being considered for a movie by two Hollywood producers—but Cleveland hasn't taken much notice.

Their books are hits outside Ohio

✵ Steubenville-native Dard Hunter was the first man to produce an entire modern book all by himself. That means he made the type and the paper and wrote the text. The Dard Hunter Paper Museum at MIT bears the name of the man who elevated the science of papermaking into an art form. This was no quick process; it took 30 years for him to make eight of the handmade masterpieces. He passed his knowledge on in his book, *Papermaking by Hand in America* (1950). His son, Dard, Jr., cast the type for the book.

Master bookmaker

Straight from the pen

William Sydney Porter panicked and skipped town after being accused of robbing a bank. When he returned home because of his wife's illness, he was arrested, convicted, and sentenced to five years at the Ohio Penitentiary in Columbus. During that stay, from April 1898 to July 1901, he wrote at least 12 short stories including "Alias Jimmy Valentine." Some people think he took his pen name from a prison guard named Orrin Henry. But a more intriguing possibility might be that O. Henry is an acronym for *Ohio Penitentiary*. Whatever the truth , O. Henry is honored as the "father of the modern American short story."

It beats fixing teeth

❧ Coerced into studying dentistry by his father, Pearl Zane Gray spent four years in an unsuccessful practice in New York City. By 1900, he decided he wanted to write and self-published his first novel, *Betty Zane*, in 1903. He dropped his first name because readers thought he was a woman and changed Gray to Grey. With the publication of *Riders of the Purple Sage* (1912), *Desert Gold* (1913), *The Call of the Canyon* (1924), and *The Thundering Herd* (1925), Zane Grey became the "father of the adult Western." He also earned enough money to move to California. A prolific writer, he published 90 books while he was alive. Twenty books were published after he died and he's still racking up the sales today.

God wrote the words— she got the royalties

❧ During the Civil War, President Lincoln referred to her as "the little lady who made this big war." But all Harriet Beecher Stowe wanted when she began writing her anti-slavery sketches was enough extra money to buy a silk dress for church. She was stuck at home with six children while her husband taught at Bowdoin College in Maine. Harriet got her story material from her memories of living in Cincinnati for 18 years where her father, Lyman Beecher, was head of Lane Theological Seminary. She remembered runaway slaves on the underground railroad and John Rankin's house. The more she wrote, the more convinced she was that she was the abolitionist spokesperson for God. On March 20, 1852, the first copies of *Uncle Tom's Cabin* came off the press. At year's end, 2.5 million copies had been sold in Europe and the United States. Harriet had enough money for clothes and three houses—one in Andover, Maine, an eight-gabled mansion in Connecticut, and a winter place in Florida. She died on July 1, 1896, at age 85 after she wrote her doctor, "I make no mental effort of any sort. My brain is tired out."

Listed with the best

In 1978, *The Bastard*, written by Dayton-native John Jakes, became the first book published originally in paperback to be listed on the *New York Times* best-seller list.

❦ William Dean Howells' big break came while he was working at the *Ohio State Journal* in Columbus. When Abraham Lincoln became the Republican presidential nominee, Howells was enlisted to write the candidate's biography, which he unenthusiastically did. Lincoln won and Howells was rewarded with a job as U.S. consul in Venice where he studied, read, and developed his writing skills. After returning to the United States, he worked as assistant editor at the *Atlantic Monthly* and, later, as editor. In 1881 he resigned from the *Atlantic* to concentrate on writing novels. The result was his most memorable book, *The Rise of Silas Lapham* (1885). The dominant figure in American letters for over 30 years, Howells published 30 novels before his death in 1920.

Bi-coastal rivals

Not everyone appreciated Howells' gifts, however. Fellow Ohioan Ambrose Bierce referred to him as "that lousy cat of our letters." Bierce headed West, worked at Hearst's *Examiner* in San Francisco, and became the "literary dictator of the West." A master of satire and wit, Bierce published the *Cynic's Word Book* (later called *The Devil's Dictionary*) in 1906. Some of his definitions might apply today—

Conservative, n. *A statesman who is enamoured of existing evils, as distinguished from the Liberal, who wishes to replace them with others.*

❦ Somehow, in a fast-paced society, Xenia-native Helen Hooven Santmyer took 60 years to write a masterpiece, ... *And the Ladies of the Club*. She began the book about life in Waynesboro during the 1920s. The Waynesboro Women's Club was the vehicle through which she portrayed the experiences of four generations, from 1868 to 1932. Santmyer hoped to rebut Sinclair Lewis's version of small-town life, portrayed in *Main Street*, with her strong, independent characters. And she did just that when her best-seller was published in 1986, just two years before her death.

It took a long time to finish

A genius or a dolt?

While managing a paint factory in Elyria, Sherwood Anderson simply walked out one day and never came back. He left his wife, moved to Chicago, and spent the rest of his life writing. Some called him the "Dostoevsky of the corn belt" and a great short-story writer. Others thought he had nothing to say—his writing approached "... the inadequate use of a foreign language." Although he is remembered for *Winesburg, Ohio* (1919), only one of his novels ever made money. *Dark Laughter* gave him the means to buy two newspapers—one Democratic and one Republican—and a nice home in Virginia. Always a restless man, he supported left-wing political causes in the 1930s as his interests shifted to what one critic called "the negative approach." A prolific writer, he published a book a year until his death in 1941.

Pulitzer Prize for Letters

1927 – Louis Bromfield, *An Early Autumn*
1972 – James Wright, *Collected Poems*
1987 – Rita Dove, *Thomas and Beulah*
1988 – Toni Morrison, *Beloved*

Pulitzer Prize for History

1918 – James F. Rhodes, *A History of the Civil War*
1938 – Paul H. Buck, *The Road to Reunion, 1865–1900*
1946 – Arthur M. Schlesinger, Jr., *The Age of Jackson*
1954 – Bruce Catton, *A Stillness at Appomattox*

Serious about humor

To cartoonist, humorist, and author James Thurber (left), writing was life. "If I couldn't write, I couldn't breathe," he once told the editor of *The New Yorker*. Best known for his story, "The Secret Life of Walter Mitty," and *The Thurber Carnival* (1945), he disliked being thought of as just a humorist—writing was too serious to him. He worked hard at his craft and only once wrote something quickly. When his wife said the piece sounded like "high-school stuff," he rewrote it six times. He was able to hold as many as 2,000 words in his memory and then dictate his prose to a secretary. But his cartoons—which he took much less seriously—came easily. While working at *The New Yorker* with E.B. White, Thurber often doodled on yellow copy paper, drawing simple, flat characters that White thought were brilliant. The two collaborated in *Is Sex Necessary?* (1929), a humorous self-help book that featured Thurber's cartoons.

After six years with *The New Yorker*—the magazine that rejected 20 of his stories before hiring him—Thurber left to write full-time. *My Life and Hard Times*, *The Thurber Carnival*, *The Beast in Me and Other Animals*, and *The Thurber Album* followed. He received many honorary degrees and awards but declined one from The Ohio State University in 1951 because he believed the trustees' censorship of certain speakers violated free speech. Thurber died in New York in November 1961.

An author and a farmer

When he was 16, Louis Bromfield moved to a farm with his family and toyed with the idea of becoming a farmer. But he opted for Columbia University and journalism. He moved to New York City in 1919 and became part of the original staff of *Time* as a music critic. When he wasn't working at his regular job, he spent his time writing novels. His first four attempts weren't published, but the fifth, *The Green Bay Tree* (1924), became a best-seller. The young author was successful enough to move to Paris where he wrote his Pulitzer Prize-winning novel *Early Autumn* (1926). In 1938 the Bromfields came back to the Mansfield area, bought four farms and named them Malabar—after the coast in India which was the setting for several of Bromfield's books. The author applied farming techniques he learned in France to restore the worn-out land and thousands came to learn his methods. In 1945, two visitors came to get married—Lauren Bacall and Humphrey Bogart. Today Bromfield's farm is Malabar Farm State Park.

SCULPTORS AND CARVERS

Whittled away his time

Elijah Pierce was a Columbus barber who whittled when business was slow. He later turned his barber shop into an art gallery. In 1982, the noted whittler was awarded a National Heritage Fellowship by the National Endowment for the Arts—one of the first 15 folk artists to receive the prestigious award.

❧ During World War II, Dayton sculptress Alice Chatham got a call from the U.S. Air Force. Planes were going higher and faster than ever before and pilots needed a new kind of oxygen mask that would keep them from fainting. Could Chatham design one? The artist created a mask that fit a pilot's head perfectly. Another assignment came in 1947—helmets for test pilots. When Chuck Yeager broke the sound barrier he was wearing a Chatham original. NASA was her next customer—she created a pressurized suit and full-head helmet for the "Project Whoosh" chimps, who were ejected from airplanes at speeds faster than sound. She also devised a harness and mask for the rhesus monkey that became the first animal in space. Among her other inventions for NASA were a space bed, stretch-knit garments for astronauts, and various restraints and tethering devices.

Space gear

What's a sculptor to do?

Called the best-known least-known sculptor in Ohio, Erwin Frey became a teacher at Ohio State in 1925. He received some interesting requests outside the classroom. Could he make casts of corpses' feet for a local manufacturer of burial shoes? A desperate husband once asked Frey to help him get his wife's hands out of a hardened bucket of plaster. While he was trying to make casts of her hands, the plaster hardened too quickly. But his most unusual request came from a wealthy businessman who wanted him to make a full-size nude statue of his mistress. She promised to pose for free. Frey declined. Instead, he agreed to sculpt the less curvaceous president of the university.

"Glass seduced me," said sculptor Christopher Ries who grew up near Columbus. Ries carves blocks of the purest optical crystal like a stone sculptor. Based solely on the cut of the exterior form, he creates an ever-changing, internal fourth-dimension. The work shown above is entitled "Sunflower."

A blue-collar genius

Dover's Ernest Warther was a steel-mill worker by age 14. He began carving to pass the time while tending the family cow. Known today as the world's master carver, Warther never thought of making money from his talent. "… Our roof don't leak, we ain't hungry and we don't owe anybody." He was such a stickler for detail that one of his train models has 10,000 parts. The carver died at age 87 leaving his 64th carving unfinished. Mrs. Warther has her claim to fame also—she collected over 73,000 buttons—no two alike—and arranged them in patterns on the walls and ceilings of the family-run museum in Dover.

RARE OR STRANGE

What a trip!

If you like science fiction, maybe you should pick up a copy of John Uri Lloyd's *Etidorhpa* (Aphrodite spelled backwards), subtitled *The End of the Earth: The Strange History of a Mysterious Being and The Account of a Remarkable Journey*. Lloyd's main character, "I-am-the-man," is kidnapped in Cincinnati and journeys to the hollow center of Earth. He travels through crystal forests, eats magic mushrooms that allow him to fly, and becomes a magician who guards the powers of the universe. Although the book was published in 1895, it was quite popular during the 1960s when a lot of young people were taking their own fantasy trips with the aid of mind-altering substances. Lloyd was a noted pharmacologist. Perhaps Lloyd took a trip—with the help of a laboratory concoction—before he wrote his novel.

Ezee to reed

Cincinnati's Longley brothers—Elias, Cyrenius, Servetus, Septimus, and Alcander—set out to make English easier to read. Through Longley & Brothers they promoted printing, writing, and spelling reforms. Their magazine, *Tip of de Timz*, came off the press in 1848. They organized the American Phonetic Society and published phonetic versions of Goldsmith's *Vicar of Wakefield* and Pope's *Essay on Man*. If the Civil War hadn't disrupted everything, phonetic spelling could have been accepted. Hoo noz? Anyway, the company ceased operations in 1862 and Elias espoused a new cause called phonography (shorthand) and later became a court reporter.

The bard was a fake?

During her writing career Delia Bacon developed the idea that Shakespeare was a hoax and an "ignorant lackey." Francis Bacon actually wrote the bard's work, she said, with the aid of a secret society. Delia went to England to "dig up" evidence—she seriously considered opening Francis Bacon's tomb to retrieve the papers buried with him. But she opted on the side of caution. If there was no evidence in the crypt to support her ideas, she'd look like a fool. Her controversial theory was published in 1857 as *The Philosophy of the Plays of Shakespeare Unfolded*, with a foreword by Nathaniel Hawthorne, who admitted that he had never read the book. Not many others did either, but Delia's question about Shakespeare's authenticity remains today.

Beautiful books

Although Dr. Howard E. Jones of Circleville was a good doctor, he and his family are remembered for *Illustrations of the Nests and Eggs of Birds of Ohio*, a two-volume work published in 1886. Only 100 copies were ever published. Because of the detailed illustrations—first drawn on rock and then colorized—these volumes are often called the "most beauitful books every published in the United States." Five Ohio libraries presently have copies—the University of Cincinnati, Public Library of Cincinnati and Hamilton County, Denison University, Kent State University, and the Ohio State Library.

ON WITH THE SHOW

Show business has deep roots in Ohio. From the days of the showboats along the Ohio River to the new Rock and Roll Hall of Fame in Cleveland, the state is a happening place. Entertainment insiders have tagged Columbus as a new music center, so watch for the New Bomb Turks to make it as big as The Pretenders—formed by Akron-native Chrissie Hynde.

Famous screen stars such as Lillian Gish, Paul Newman, Clark Gable, and Debra Winger were all born in Ohio along with Western greats Annie Oakley and Roy Rogers. And rising stars Luke Perry, Sarah Jessica Parker, and Halle Berry are all Buckeyes. Some of the best movies ever made—*Rain Man* and *The Shawshank Redemption*—were filmed in the state. The list of singers, songwriters, actors, comedians, talk-show hosts, and entertainment centers goes on and on. Let's shine the spotlight on a few.

- Radio, Television, and Movies
- The Music Scene
- On Stage
- Rising Stars
- Western Greats
- Top Billing
- Talk, Talk, Talk
- Theme Parks

RADIO, TELEVISION, AND MOVIES

Some TV shows broadcast or set in Ohio

The king's station

The first radio station in the world to play Elvis Presley music exclusively was Cincinnati's WCVG-AM in 1988.

- "The Dotty Mack Show" broadcast from Cincinnati from 1953 to 1956 on ABC.
- "Mary Hartman, Mary Hartman" featured Louise Lasser as a Fernwood, Ohio, housewife. Developed by Norman Lear, the syndicated show ran from 1976 to 1977.
- "WKRP in Cincinnati" aired from September 18, 1978, until September 20, 1982. Cincinnati has a real radio station with almost the same call letters, WKRC. Native-Ohioans Gordon Jump, Gary Sandy, and Howard Hesseman starred in the series, along with then-newcomer Loni Anderson.
- Popular 1980s sitcom "Family Ties," created by Gary David Goldberg, was set in Columbus. The show starred Michael J. Fox as Alex. The last episode aired in May 1989.

Stupendous success

The oldest of four children, Steven Spielberg was born in Cincinnati in 1947. He moved to Phoenix as a child where he fell in love with movies. In grade school, he borrowed his father's movie camera and made a 3-1/2-minute film starring his friends. By age 17, he'd advanced to full-length movies with a 2-1/2-hour science fiction movie called *Firelight*. He was just 26 when he directed *Jaws* in 1975—a job he almost refused because of lack of experience. Most pundits predicted his next film, *Close Encounters of the Third Kind*, would be a flop but Spielberg scored another hit and an Academy Award nomination for best director. Although the talented director/producer made a string of popular movies including *E.T.: The Extraterrestrial* and *Jurassic Park*, he didn't win an Oscar for best director until 1994—for his Holocaust masterpiece *Schindler's List*. That same year, the master moviemaker, who some sources say earns about $45 million a year, announced the formation of Dream Works SKG, a major movie studio, with partners David Geffen and Jeffrey Katzenberg.

He makes dreams come true

If you think you've written a great movie script, you don't have to find someone in Los Angeles to read it. You can send it to Stepping Stone Entertainment, a Hilliard-based company owned by R.J. Cavallaro. For $75, he'll read your script and if he thinks you might have a hit, he'll try to match you with an interested producer. Cavallaro worked as a location manager and production assistant for such films as *Ordinary People*, *Rain Man*, and *The Natural* before striking out on his own in 1990. A made-for-television movie that aired in November 1994, *Following Her Heart*, was one of Cavallaro's latest successes. The script was written by a North Dakota writer who had never had anything produced previously.

Made in Ohio

The Ohio Film Bureau began working to attract film production to the state in the 1970s. Films shot in the state since then include:

Harry and Walter Go to New York, Columbus, Mansfield
The Deerhunter, Cleveland, Mingo Junction, Youngstown
Harper Valley P.T.A., Lebanon
Brubaker, Junction City
The Instructor, Akron
One Trick Pony, Cleveland
The Second Degree, Cleveland
Those Eyes, Those Lips, Cleveland
The Escape Artist, Cleveland
All the Marbles, Cuyahoga Falls, Niles, Warren, Youngstown
A Christmas Story, Cleveland
Teachers, Columbus
Reckless, Mingo Junction, Steubenville
Mischief, Canal Winchester, Nelsonville
Stranger than Paradise, Cleveland
Gung Ho, Shadyside
Big Business, Youngstown
Eight Men Out, Cincinnati
Fresh Horses, Cincinnati
Light of Day, Cleveland
Plains, Trains, and Automobiles, Cleveland
Tiger Warsaw, Youngstown
Rain Man, Cincinnati
An Unremarkable Life, Youngstown
An Innocent Man, Cincinnati, Mansfield
Major League, Cleveland
Welcome Home, Roxy Carmichael, Clyde, Sandusky

City of Hope, Cincinnati
Tango and Cash, Mansfield, Cincinnati
Diary of a Hitman, Youngstown
Emma and Elvis, Dayton
First You Live, Then You Die, Columbus
Little Man Tate, Oxford, Columbus, Cincinnati
A Rage in Harlem, Cincinnati
Noises Off, Cleveland, Columbus, Mt. Vernon and Pike counties
Paradise, Cleveland
The Public Eye, Cincinnati
Men in Black, Mansfield, Put-in-Bay
Slaughter of the Innocents, Cleveland
Lost in Yonkers, Wilmington, Cincinnati
Chester & Irene, Cleveland
Bottom Land, Dayton
My Summer Story, Cleveland
A Reason to Believe, Oxford
Airborne, Cincinnati
Captain Jack, Granville
Double Dragon, Cleveland
Milk Money, Cleveland, Lebanon
The Shawshank Redemption, Mansfield and surrounding area
Best of the Best Three, Jackson

He knew how to score

When Cleveland-native Henry Mancini saw Cecil B. De Mille's movie *The Crusades*, it was the film score that caught his attention. He decided then and there to become a film score composer instead of a teacher. Over his lifetime, Mancini composed scores for more than 80 movies and won 3 Academy Awards—for *Breakfast at Tiffany's* (1961), *The Days of Wine and Roses* (1962), and *Victor, Victoria* (1982). His Academy-Award winning song, "Moon River" from *Breakfast at Tiffany's,* was so popular it was recorded more than 1,000 times. Although that song was a hit, more people probably recognize Mancini's *Pink Panther* theme today. But the talented composer didn't confine his magic to the big screen. He wrote the TV theme songs for such shows as "Remington Steele," "Newhart," and "The Thorn Birds." He also wrote a textbook entitled *Sounds and Scores—A Practical Guide to Professional Orchestration*. Mancini's brilliant career ended on June 14, 1994, when he died of cancer in Beverly Hills, California.

From book to big screen

- Cleveland-native Ernest Tidyman wrote the novel and screenplay, *Shaft*. He also won a best screenplay Oscar for the movie *The French Connection* (1971).
- Cleveland-native Jack Warner Schaefer wrote Western novels including *Shane* in 1949, which was translated into 35 languages. It was adapted into a film in 1953.
- Cincinnati-native Thomas Louis Berger wrote *Little Big Man* (1964) which later became the Dustin Hoffman film of the same name in 1970.
- Harvard-educated Earl Biggers Derr, born in Warren in 1884, created motion-picture detective Charlie Chan. Chan first appeared in Derr's book, *The House Without a Key* (1925). Biggers published six Charlie Chan novels, all serialized in the *Saturday Evening Post*.
- Springfield-native William Riley Burnett wrote for eight years before selling his novel *Little Caesar* in 1929. James Cagney starred in the movie of the same title. Burnett also wrote the movie script for *Asphalt Jungle* (1949).
- Author of the book *Lollipop* (1962) and the script for the popular film *Easy Rider* (1969), Terry Southern hails from Alvarado.

THE MUSIC SCENE

You can't pretend forever

As a pre-teen in Akron, Chrissie Hynde often dreamed of leaving home—she wasn't interested in school or dating, but she loved listening to bands. After studying art at Kent State, Hynde headed for the London music scene in 1973. Unable to put a rock band together, she returned to Cleveland where she sang with Jack Rabbit. Returning to London just as punk rock was born, Hyde organized The Pretenders whose first single, "Stop Your Sobbing," hit the British Top Thirty. Their debut album *The Pretenders* shot to number one in England and went on to establish the group in the United States. She married Jim Kerr of Simple Minds, became the mother of two children, and told *The New York Times Magazine* in 1986, "I'm 35 and I can't keep pretending I have my head in a garbage can." Hynde is credited as one of the first women to organize a successful all-male rock band.

Not on today's Top Ten
- Cleveland-native Ernest R. Ball, a vaudeville pianist, wrote "When Irish Eyes Are Smiling," "Little Bit of Heaven," and "Will You Love Me in December as You Do in May?"
- The Mills brothers of Piqua were popular from the 1930s until the 1970s. Their hits included "Glow Worm" and "Lazy River."
- Findlay's Tell Taylor wrote "Down by the Old Mill Stream" in 1901 after returning to fish on a stream near the city's present golf course. He remembered the old mill that used to be on the stream and a favorite song was born.
- Westerville-native Benjamin Hanby wrote more than 80 folk songs and hymns but most people know him for his Christmas song, "Up on the Housetop."

Notables—rock, pop, and blues

- Singer Tracy Chapman (right) grew up in Cleveland. While attending Tufts University, the singer was playing in coffee-houses, when a fellow student brought her to the attention of Elektra Records. Chapman is best known for her 1988 hit "Fast Car."
- MIT graduate and Toledo-native Tom Scholz formed Boston in 1976 while he was a designer with Polaroid. His first album, *More Than A Feeling*, sold 6 million copies.
- The Isley brothers of Cincinnati—Rudolph, Ronald, O'Kelly and Vernon—left church music behind to form a group in 1955. They recorded "Shout" in 1959, an R & B hit, followed by "Twist and Shout," which later became a megahit for the Beatles.
- Tommy James of Dayton formed first his singing group, Tommy James and the Shondells when he was 12 years old in Niles, Michigan, in 1960. When that group disbanded, James formed a new Shondells and recorded "Hanky Panky" for Roulette Records—the number-one hit of 1966. Other hits include "Mony Mony" and "I Think We're Alone Now."
- Cleveland-native Benjamin Orzechowski (Orr) performed with Rick Ocasek for 10 years before the two musicians formed The Cars in 1974. Orr debuted as a solo artist in 1987 with *Stay the Night*.
- Five Akron musicians—Bob Casale, Jerry Casale, Bob Mothersbaugh, Mark Mothersbaugh, and Alan Myers—formed the band Devo, known for the hit single "Whip It" in 1980.
- Former artist and dancer Marty Balin—born Martyn Jerel Buckwald in Cincinnati—founded Jefferson Airplane in 1965. He left the group for a solo career but rejoined the band, renamed Jefferson Starship, in 1975. Four years later he went on his own again. In 1989, the original band came together once more with Balin in the lead.
- Robert "Kool" Bell, born in Youngstown on October 8, 1950, formed Kool and the Gang with students from his Jersey City, New Jersey, high school in 1964. He is best known for his number-one hit single, "Celebration."
- Most people associate singer Anita Baker with Detroit, Michigan, but she was born in Toledo in 1958. Although Baker is very successful, she has a way to go to top fellow-Toledan Teresa Brewer who chalked up 38 pop-chart hits by the late 1950s including "Let Me Go, Lover."
- The O'Jays were originally called the Mascots when they formed at McKinley High School in Canton with Eddie Levert, Bobby Massey, and Bill Isles in 1958. Million-selling singles included "Love Train" in 1973, "I Love Music" in 1976, and "Used Ta Be My Girl" in 1978.

Probably best known for his 1988 Grammy-winning duet, "Somewhere Out There," with Linda Ronstadt, James Ingram moved from Akron with his band Revelation Funk in 1973 and toured with Ray Charles for two years. Quincy Jones heard Ingram and featured him on his album *The Dude*, although the album was credited to Jones. In 1982, Ingram won a Best R & B Vocal Performance Grammy for "One Hundred Ways" from *The Dude* to become the first singer to win a Grammy without releasing an album under his own name. In 1985 he won another Grammy with Michael McDonald for "Yah Mo Be There." It wasn't until 1990 that Ingram had his first solo hit, "I Don't Have a Heart," although he had seven previous Top 40 hits.

Going solo took a long time

The 150,000-square-foot Rock and Roll Hall of Fame, designed by I.M. Pei, is located in Cleveland's North Coast Harbor, a development that will include such attractions as the Great Lakes Museum of Science, Environment, and Technology, and the Cleveland Aquarium.

This place rocks

In June 1994, ground was finally broken for the Rock and Roll Hall of Fame—nicknamed "The Building"—at Cleveland's North Coast Harbor after years of squabbling with New York City. Although New York is huge in the rock 'n' roll scene, it was Cleveland DJ Allen Freed, and record store-owner Leo Mintz who first used the term "rock 'n' roll" in the early 1950s to promote concerts featuring the new sound. And Cleveland DJ and lawyer Bill Randle is credited with discovering the King himself, Elvis Presley. Scheduled to open Labor Day 1995, the museum's concept was developed back in 1983 by Ahmet Ertegun of Atlantic Records and Jann Wenner of *Rolling Stone* magazine. "We're not going to show you Bruce Springsteen's guitar or his autograph and leave it at that. We're going to try to make some sense out of it all, to show how things are connected," they said. The new museum features the Rock and Roll Hall of Fame and a permanent collection with such items as Buddy Holly's high-school diploma and Grace Slick's dress from Woodstock. Other exhibits take visitors to "Little Richard's House of Style," which features rock 'n' roll fashion, and the "Roots of Rock," which explores the origin of the music.

Main stop on the blues circuit

In 1957 Frank and Sarah Hines built Hines Farm Blues Club on the outskirts of Toledo in the African-American enclave called Spencer-Sharples near Swanton. Their club became a national rhythm-and-blues center, featuring such greats as John Lee Hooker, B.B. King, Bobby "Blue" Bland, Little Esther Phillips, and Jimmy Ricks. When the outdoor pavilion opened in 1961, Count Basie and his entire orchestra headlined the event for 1,500 guests. But Hines Farm wasn't only music. There were horse races, exhibition baseball games, motorcycle races, hayrides, roller skating, comedy acts, and impersonators—almost anything that was entertainment. By 1976, the blues center most people know little about today was gone, but its brilliance had made it a main stop on the blues circuit for years.

She sounds heavenly

One of the country's most popular Christian singers, Kelli Reisen, hails from Glendale. Her debut album, *Dream of a Lifetime*, yielded four Top 20 Christian singles. It all started when Kelli began singing in church at age three. By age nine she felt singing Christian music was her calling and she never looked back. As a high-school student, the devout Christian, nicknamed God Squad, was singing in commercials and on the radio. Her latest album *Someday* was released in February 1995, one year after she met her music idol, Donny Osmond, on her 30th birthday!

The "I'm a Honky Tonk Man"—Dwight Yoakam—was raised in Columbus where he wrote his first song at age 10. By 18 he was playing guitar on the Ohio Valley roadhouse circuit before moving on to audition at Opryland in 1977. Called "too country," Yoakam didn't make it in Nashville. Of all places, he was discovered by Reprise Records on the Los Angeles "post-punk" club circuit. In March 1986, his first album *Guitars, Cadillacs, Etc.* came out without "… any string sections, choral arrangements … no Nash' trash schlock bull that they played up for the last 20 years," Yoakam said in an interview with *Maclean's*. Five other albums followed with *This Time* (1993) going double-platinum and earning Yoakam a Grammy for the single "Ain't That Lonely Yet."

The honky-tonk man

Country notes

- Imagine how country singer Bobby Bare—born in Ironton in 1935—felt when he realized he had sold the rights to the 1958 hit "All American Boy" for $50! He went on to become a star with such hits as "Detroit City" (1963) and "500 Miles Away from Home" (1963).
- Remember the 1978 country hit, "Take This Job and Shove It"? It was recorded by Greenfield-native Johnny Paycheck.

ON STAGE

Broadway in Cleveland

Cleveland's Playhouse Square Foundation has guided the largest theater-restoration project in North America at Playhouse Square Center. Now one of the country's largest performing-arts centers, there are four restored interconnected theaters—the Ohio (first one restored—opened in 1982), State, Palace, and Allen—with more than 7,000 seats. The center is now home to pop, rock, comedy, and Broadway performances as well as the Cleveland Opera, Great Lakes Theater Festival, Ohio Ballet, Cleveland Ballet, and Dance Cleveland. But in 1972, the area looked much different. The four theaters built as art deco movie houses in the 1920s were scheduled for demolition in a dilapidated downtown Cleveland. A simple act by employees of the Cleveland Board of Education spawned the area's revival—they decided to hold a meeting in one of the forgotten theaters, and interest in the area was ignited. Cuyahoga County bought the Loew's building that housed the Ohio and State theaters and leased them back to Playhouse Square Foundation, the non-profit group guiding the area's redevelopment. Playhouse Square Foundation is credited with spawning Cleveland's dramatic urban renewal.

An artist's conception of Playhouse Square as it may appear in the year 2000 is shown below. The $20-million renovation will feature sidewalk cafes, brick-paved patios, and colorful marquees and neon signs reminiscent of Broadway.

Black face begins

Mount Vernon-native Daniel Decatur Emmett organized the first minstrel show troupe in Ohio, the Virginia Minstrels, in 1842. Minstrels were white performers who blackened their faces and performed on stage singing African-American ballads. In 1859, while a member of Bryant's Minstrels, Decatur penned "I Wish I Was in Dixie" one afternoon in New York. The song was played in New Orleans in 1861 and was soon adopted by the Confederacy. It is said that President Lincoln loved the song. Emmett also wrote "Turkey in the Straw."

Closing a gap

Shanny Mow of Cleveland, deaf since meningitis struck him at age five, has devoted his professional life to bridging the gap between the silent and hearing worlds. As artistic director for Fairmount Theater for the Deaf in Cleveland, he has written 12 plays. *Counterfeit*, the story of two deaf Civil War soldiers, opened at the Fairmount in January 1995. Both deaf and hearing actors performed on stage at the same time.

Pulitzer Prize for drama
- Findlay-native Russell Crouse (with Howard Lindsay) for *State of the Union*, 1946
- Columbus-native Ketti Frings for *Look Homeward Angel*, 1958
- Steubenville-native Tad Mosel for *All the Way Home*, 1961
- Cleveland-native Charles Gordone for *No Place to Be Somebody*, 1970

Winning words
- Robert E. Lee and Jerome Lawrence wrote *Inherit the Wind*, now a classic performed in more than 30 languages. But they also predicted the appointment of the first female Supreme Court Justice with their play, *First Monday in October*, which opened on Broadway October 3, 1978. Other credits include *Mame* and *Jabberwock*, which was written as the opening production for OSU's Thurber Theater.
- When Ketti Frings won the Pulitzer in 1958 for *Look Homeward Angel* she had previously written two unsuccessful books and an unsuccessful play. In fact, her credits were so obscure she had trouble remembering them.

RISING STARS

Same sitcom—same home state

Two Ohio natives starred with Delta Burke on the short-lived 1995 CBS sitcom, "Woman of the House," produced by Linda Bloodworth-Thomason and her husband, Harry. Most people recognized Lakewood-native Terri Garr, whose visits to "Late Night with David Letterman" are legendary, but Patty Heaton, daughter of Cleveland *Plain Dealer* sports columnist Chuck Heaton, wasn't as well known. A graduate of OSU in 1990, Heaton got her big break in a Pabst Blue Ribbon commercial which led to roles on the New York stage before she formed her own theater group called Stage Three. When her company produced *The Johnstown Vindicator* she finally came to the attention of the right people. Heaton moved with her actor/director husband to Los Angeles and got a part in "thirtysomething" in 1989, with later parts in NBC's "Someone Like Me" and ABC's "Room for Two." When the role in "Woman of the House" came up, Heaton made it clear that she couldn't play the part if her character supported abortion—Heaton grew up with strong religious beliefs and has stuck with pro-life stance.

And Justice for Berry

Beautiful Halle Berry wanted to be an actress since she was a child in Cleveland. Popular in high school, she was prom queen, cheerleader, and class president. When she was 17, one of her former boyfriends entered her in the Miss Teen Ohio beauty pageant and she won. In 1985, she was crowned Miss Ohio and later selected as first runner-up to Miss USA. Berry decided to study broadcast journalism at Cuyahoga Community College in 1986, but left to audition for Aaron Spelling's TV show "Charlie's Angels '88." The noted producer encouraged her to continue with acting. Her big breaks came with a role on the TV series "Living Dolls" and a USO tour with Bob Hope. She was later seen as Debbie Porter in "Knots Landing" and went on to film roles in *Jungle Fever*, *Boomerang*, *The Last Boy Scout*, and the TV miniseries "Queen."

But her life became much happier after she found her husband—Atlanta Braves outfielder David Justice—while watching MTV's "Rock 'n' Jock" in 1992. Justice is a Cincinnati native and, after watching him on the show, Berry couldn't get the baseball player out of her head. She called one of his old friends to get his phone number and flew down to Atlanta to meet him. Little did Berry know that Justice, 1990 National League Rookie of the Year, was also a fan of hers. Justice later said he "knew when I saw her I was going to marry her." The two tied the knot at 1:30 A.M. on New Year's Day 1993.

David Justice and his wife Halle Berry holding her 4-year-old co-star in *Losing Isaiah*, Marc John Jeffries.

Hunk from the Heartland

When Coy Luther Perry III graduated from Fredericktown High School in 1984 his life was nothing like the character Dylan McKay from "Beverly Hills 90210," the TV role that boosted him to stardom in 1990. Perry told *Rolling Stone* magazine that his "… high school experience was so hugely different …. We had classes on giving birth to cows and driving tractors." An average student, he was voted the "biggest flirt" in his senior year and had a reputation as a mischievous daydreamer. After high school Perry moved to New York where he landed a role as Ned Bates in "Loving" and appeared in Levi's 501 ads. Often called the modern-day James Dean, the popular actor isn't married—his favorite pet is a Vietnamese pot-belly pig named after his favorite rock star, Jerry Lee.

Friends are forever

A story of the enduring friendship among seven Lorain women made the front page of *The Wall Street Journal* in July 1994. In 1943 the 17-year-old girls—Eleanor Halasz, Gerrie Dudash, Bernie Maxwell, Fran Rottman, Lorry Sandrew, Irene Paskvan, and Fanny Kovacs—dubbed themselves the "Dreamers" and took a solemn oath to remain friends forever. Since that night, the women have met at least once a month for dinner and have supported each other through deaths, divorces, and other hardships. This story of true friendship is now in development as a Hallmark Entertainment miniseries.

Engaged to Elvis

The fourth of eight children, Sarah Jessica Parker (left) was born in 1965 in Nelsonville. A dancer with the Cincinnati Ballet and American Ballet Theater, she made her first professional appearance in the TV special *The Little Match Girl* at age eight. Most people don't recall her film debut in 1979 in *Rich Kids*. She is better known for her roles in *Footloose*, *Honeymoon in Vegas*, and *Ed Wood*.

WESTERN GREATS

Home on the range

You might know him as Leonard Slye, Dick Weston—or Roy Rogers. They're all names for Hollywood's top Western star between 1943 and 1954. Born near Portsmouth in 1912, Slye was part Choctaw Indian. He became a local square-dance caller before heading to California where he changed his name to Dick Weston while he sang with the Sons of the Pioneers. As Roy Rogers, beginning in 1951, he starred in 88 films and hundreds of TV shows with his wife Dale Evans.

The good guy's from Cambridge

William Boyd Lawrence got into the movies as an extra in 1919 where Cecil B. De Mille discovered the Cambridge native. De Mille cast him in *The Volga Boatman* in 1926. Eight years later producer Harry Sherman bought the rights to some Clarence Mulford books about a western Robin Hood named Hopalong Cassidy who rode a white horse named Topper. Boyd wasn't cast as the good guy in the beginning. He played the bad guy in two movies before landing the part of Hopalong. Boyd is credited with the "longest sustained characterization in film history"—a total of 66 Hopalong movies from 1935 to 1948. Although Boyd moved to Oklahoma as a seven-year-old, the town of Cambridge celebrates its famous native son's success each July with a three-day Hopalong Cassidy Festival.

First woman to make her living with a gun

Phoebe "Annie Oakley" Moses was born in Darke County in 1860. Her father died when she was four, and the family of seven children fell into poverty. She developed her marksmanship out of necessity—the family needed money to pay the mortgage. Even though she was a Quaker, guns were allowed for survival and she used her natural skill to kill game and, later, sell animal pelts to the wealthy people of Dayton and Cincinnati. She won a marksmanship contest against her future husband Frank Butler, who was also an expert shot, when she was only 15. In 1885, while performing with the Sells Brothers Circus in New Orleans, Annie Oakley—now married to her manager Frank Butler—signed a contract with Buffalo Bill's Wild West Show where she performed for 17 years. She traveled the world, known for such stunts as shooting a cigarette from Kaiser Wilhelm II's teeth. On one record day, she successfully hit 4,772 of 5,000 dimes and glass balls thrown in the air. An injury sustained in a 1901 train wreck ended her legendary career and she died in Greenville in 1926. The town now celebrates Annie Oakley Day each July and invites visitors to see her memorabilia at the Garst Museum. But her story has been told numerous times on the big screen and on stage. Barbara Stanwyck played Annie in the 1935 movie *Annie Oakley*; and Rogers and Hammerstein wrote the Broadway musical *Annie Get Your Gun* (1940) which starred Ethel Merman, and later became a movie starring Betty Hutton.

TOP BILLING

Matinee idol

How did a shy backstage handyman for touring theater companies with big ears, bad teeth, and foul breath become America's sex symbol? He married or loved the right women and befriended the right people. Cadiz-native William Clark Gable married his drama coach, Josephine Dillon, in the mid 1920s. She helped her younger husband get a role in *The Merry Widow* (1925) and paid to have his teeth capped. (He later acquired false teeth.) Gable befriended actor Lionel Barrymore who got Gable a screen test at MGM which eventually landed him a small part in *Painted Desert* (1931). An affair with Joan Crawford led to parts in two other 1931 films—*Fools Dance* and *Possessed*. Three years later, Gable became a box-office success and won an Academy Award as best actor for *It Happened One Night*. But the 1939 megahit *Gone With the Wind* made him the undisputed "king of Hollywood" and with his marriage to Carole Lombard he finally discovered true love. Gable appeared in 71 films before his death from a heart attack in November 1960 shortly after his last film *The Misfits* was completed. Doctors warned Gable that if he did his own stunts in the movie, his heart wouldn't hold up. His only child was born after his death to his fifth wife, Kay Spreckles.

"Thanks for the Memory"

Born Leslie Townes Hope near London in 1903, Bob Hope's family emigrated to Cleveland in 1907. At age 10, the young performer won a Charlie Chaplin contest and went on to a successful vaudeville career. From 1941 to 1951 Bob Hope was among the top money-making film stars. He sang his theme song, "Thanks for the Memory" in the film, *The Big Broadcast*, released in 1938. Probably the most honored entertainer in the nation, Hope has received the country's most coveted civilian honors for his work entertaining American troops wherever they are stationed in the world. Among these awards is the Medal of Freedom (1969); Congressional Gold Medal (1963); Distinguished Public Service Medal (1973); and Distinguished Service Gold Medal (1971). The Academy of Motion Picture Sciences also recognized Hope's humanitarian service with special Oscars in 1940, 1944, 1952, 1959, and 1965.

No friend of President Nixon

Born in Cleveland in 1925, Paul Newman starred in his first play as a 10-year-old. By 1948 he was on Broadway and starred in *Picnic* from 1953 to 1954. When he was cast as a Roman slave in his first movie, he phoned his agent anxiously wanting back on Broadway and out of films. But Hollywood was eventually kind to the actor. He's been nominated nine times for an Academy Award—eight times for Best Actor and once for Best Picture. He was given an honorary Oscar in 1985 and won one for Best Actor the following year for *The Color of Money*. What most people might not know is that Newman is color blind and his name also appeared on President Richard Nixon's enemies list, submitted to the Watergate Committee in June 1973.

In a world of his own

 Funnyman Jonathan Winters might have been a commercial artist if he hadn't lost his watch. He entered a talent contest in 1949—the first prize was a watch—and won. Son of a Dayton investment banker, Winters probably picked up some of his crazy antics from his grandfather who often walked down the street flapping his arms and asking, "How's the airplane, Orville?" Winters—who is idolized by comedian Robin Williams—claims he can make more than 5,000 sounds.

She loves plastic

Phyllis Diller's favorite memory is "standing in a barn when I was six and singing opera to sheep." The Lima native entered Bluffton College intent on becoming a music teacher, but married Sherwood Diller instead and moved to San Francisco. The mother of five children, Diller focused on what she really wanted—a comedy career—after reading the book, *The Magic of Believing*. She auditioned at San Francisco's Purple Onion at age 37 and became a regular with her outlandish clothes, wigs, and self-deprecation. "I was ugly. I had a badly broken nose … and the wrong hairdo. That gave me a head start on being funny." Diller went on to become a top comedian, author, and proponent of plastic surgery—she had a facelift and her nose fixed in 1971.

She has a pet cause

Doris Day (born Doris Kappelhoff) appeared as a man in one movie, *Calamity Jane* (1953). The former big-band singer and dancer made her film debut in 1948 in *Romance on the High Seas*. Today, the actress who appeared in such hits as *April in Paris*, *Pillow Talk,* and *The Pajama Game* lives on a ranch in Carmel Valley, California. She established the Doris Day Pet Foundation in Beverly Hills which promotes proper animal care. Her CBN TV show, "Doris Day's Best Friends" featured her animal friends and ran from 1985 to 1986.

TALK, TALK, TALK

Honesty is the best policy

Jerry Springer—Cincinnati's answer to Oprah—was born in England and grew up in New York City. But he adopted the Queen City after graduating from Northwestern Law School in 1969. Springer won a seat on the city council in 1971, only to have his political career threatened when it was revealed that he had employed the services of a prostitute. Springer's admission of guilt at a 1974 news conference was accepted by the public, and in 1977, he became mayor of Cincinnati by garnering more votes than any other city council candidate. In 1981, he resigned as mayor and began working for Cincinnati's WLWT-TV as a newscaster. His presence quickly boosted the ratings to number one. In 1991, "The Jerry Springer Show" debuted at the same Cincinnati station where it stayed until 1992 when the show moved to Chicago. As of February 1995, Springer's show was rated second to "The Oprah Winfrey Show" in the "Female Viewers" category.

Did you know? Canton-native Jack Paar, talk-show star of the "Tonight Show" from 1957 to 1962, was once a stutterer.

On air advice

Dr. Sylvia Rimm, a clinical professor of pediatrics and psychiatry at Case Western Reserve University School of Medicine, appears once a month on NBC's "Today Show" to dispense child-rearing tips. She also hosts a national call-in radio show that is aired in 35 states. An authority on underachieving gifted children, her 11th book, *Why Bright Kids Get Poor Grades,* was published in April 1995.

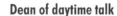

Dean of daytime talk

Phil Donahue was born in Cleveland in 1935 and always had a desire to "prove something." He honed his broadcasting skills at the University of Notre Dame, moved on to his own radio talk show, and then became host of "The Phil Donahue Show" on Dayton's WLWD-TV in 1967. His first guest was Madalyn Murray O'Hare, a controversial atheist. The show was syndicated in 1970 and successful enough to move to Chicago in 1977, where the name was shortened to "Donahue." The format was expanded to 60 minutes and involved the audience—a technique Donahue pioneered. In 1985, Donahue moved to New York City where one of his first audiences pretended to faint during a taping. Always looking for the competitive edge, Donahue broadcast his show for a week from the Soviet Union in 1987 (he was the first Western journalist to visit Chernobyl) and dressed in a skirt for a 1988 program. Still going strong, the "dean of daytime talk shows" celebrated 25 years on the air in 1993. He and Russian journalist Vladimir Pozner also host a call-in talk show on CNBC, "Pozner-Donahue," devoted to current-events topics. Winner of 19 Daytime Emmy Awards, Donahue was inducted into the Academy of Television Arts & Sciences Hall of Fame on November 20, 1993. Donahue once remarked that in "... my next life I want to be Ted Koppel."

A new kind of talk show

⭐ Cleveland-native Arsenio Hall was the first African American to host a successful late-night talk show. As a teenager, the would-be star interviewed imaginary celebrities in his bedroom. Leaving behind an advertising career, Hall became a stand-up comic in 1979 and was discovered by fellow Ohioan, singer Nancy Wilson, at a Chicago nightclub. His big break came when Joan Rivers needed a guest host for her talk show on the Fox network. Audiences loved Hall, but by the time they invited him back he was busy making the movie *Coming to America*. (Hall actually made his movie debut in the little-known film *Amazon Women on the Moon* in 1987.) "The Arsenio Hall Show" finally debuted on Fox on January 3, 1989. The show attracted a young audience—with its rap and soul music acts—in a time slot dominated by "The Tonight Show." Hall was chosen as the first "TV Person of the Year" by *TV Guide* in 1990. But when David Letterman moved to CBS, Hall's talk show was doomed—his last show aired May 27, 1994.

THEME PARKS

Home of "The Beast"

⭐ Kings Island, outside Cincinnati, boasts 600 acres of family fun. Billed as the country's most "popular seasonal theme park," Kings Island has everything from wild animals to wild rides. Its six roller coasters have set some records. The Beast, built in 1979, is dubbed the longest wooden roller coaster in the world at 7,400 feet. And the King Cobra was the nation's first vertical, looping roller coaster when it opened in 1984.

Amazing amusement

In a recent survey, Sandusky—where Cedar Point Amusement Park is located—was ranked as the third most popular vacation destination in the nation. It all began in 1870 when a Sandusky cabinetmaker opened a bathhouse, a beer garden, and a dance floor on the peninsula that juts out into Lake Erie. By the late 1870s, there were 16 bathhouses, and bathing suits could be rented for 10 cents a day. The first "ride"—a water trapeze—carried bathers out over Lake Erie. In 1897, George Boeckling bought the park and renamed it the Cedar Point Pleasure Resort Company of Indiana. Under his leadership, the park became a destination resort. In 1905, the Hotel Breakers—listed as a National Historic Landmark in 1987—opened and welcomed such guests as Presidents Taft, Wilson, Harding, Coolidge, Roosevelt, and Eisenhower. In 1906, the first midway appeared. Today the park that boasts 11 roller coasters—more than any other theme park in the world—is often billed as the best amusement park on Earth.

• The first roller coaster, the Switchback Railway, premiered in 1892. It was 25 feet tall and went 10 mph.
• The park's oldest roller coaster still in use—the all-wooden Blue Streak—opened in 1964.
• The world's tallest roller coaster, the Magnum XL-200, towers 205 feet and speeds along at 72 mph—a virtual scream machine.
• The park's newest roller coaster, the Raptor (above) came on line in 1994.

THE OHIO ATHLETE

Almost no other state can top the sports record of Ohio, home to Olympic athletes, the nation's best coaches, and some of the best athletic teams in history. The state is the birthplace of professional baseball at Cincinnati and professional football at Canton, where the Football Hall of Fame details the history of America's second-favorite sport.

Massillon teenagers look back to such greats as John Heisman; Cleveland's young hear tales of Paul Brown; and Middletown's youth remember hoop star Jerry Lucas. Let's enter the playing fields, the racetracks, the arenas, and the lonely roads of the famous and not-so-famous athletes of Ohio.

- At Bat
- Gridiron Glory
- Hoop Dreams
- The Front Office
- The Coaches' Corner
- College Sports
- In the Ring
- The Olympians
- From the Sports Page
- High-School Tales

AT BAT

Pay for play

◀ The Cincinnati Red Stockings started playing baseball in 1866 as an amateur team. Originally called the Cincinnati Baseball Club, they adopted cricket uniforms in 1867—shirt, cap, long trousers, and red socks. Two years later Cincinnati lawyer A.B. Champion—the Red Stockings president—decided to pay his players and the sports world was shocked. "Baseball should not be prostituted by salary payments," opponents argued. But Champion moved right ahead and the Reds became the first professional baseball team in the nation. Ticket prices doubled, up from 25 cents to 50 cents. Reds captain George Wright received $1,400, and salaries for the rest of the team ranged from $600 to $1,000. The Reds weathered the storm quite well—the team didn't suffer a defeat until June 14, 1870, ending the longest winning streak in baseball history at 92 victories, 1 tie, and 1 loss to the Brooklyn Atlantics, 8-7. Reds owners disbanded the team after 1870 because they couldn't afford the high salaries. Compare that Reds' payroll to 1995's. Some current Reds' salaries include $5.7 million to shortstop Barry Larkin and $3.58 million to pitcher Jose Rijo.

Can't stop "Charlie Hustle"

◀ There was nothing fake about Pete Rose's enthusiasm for baseball. Nicknamed "Charlie Hustle" by Whitey Ford, Rose once said he'd "walk through hell in a gasoline suit to keep playing baseball." In 1963, the Cincinnati boy signed by the Reds was named Rookie of the Year. Part of the "Big Red Machine" of the 1970s—which included Johnny Bench, Joe Morgan, and Tony Perez—Rose batted .300 for nine years straight, from 1965 to 1973. He came back to Cincinnati in 1984 as player-manager, ready to break Ty Cobb's hitting record. On September 11, 1985, fans cheered for seven minutes when Rose hit number 4,192 at Riverfront Stadium. He later claimed Ty Cobb and his deceased father, Harry, were sitting in the stands.

But Charlie Hustle's Major League days came to an end in August 1989, when Baseball Commissioner Giamatti banished the star from baseball for life for conduct related to gambling. Pete Rose finished his career with 3,215 singles, 4,256 hits, and 14,053 times at-bat in 3,562 games. After serving five months in federal prison for income tax evasion, Rose settled in Boca Raton, Florida, where he now owns the Rose Ballpark Cafe and has a nationally syndicated sports talk show, "The Pete Rose Show." His baseball legend lives on—sometimes in unique ways. At the Holyoke (Massachusetts) Community College art gallery, an exhibit in 1994 entitled *The Rose Garden* was composed of 4,256 identical images of Rose on 70 square feet of wall space.

Those skinny legs

The Forest Citys began Cleveland's association with professional baseball on June 2, 1869, in a game against the rival Cincinnati Reds. In 1889 the team was renamed the Spiders because the players were tall and thin. When the team became one of the first four charter members of the American League, Cleveland's moniker became the Blues—the color of their uniforms. The players didn't like that name and changed it to Bronchos in 1902. Early player/manager Napoleon Lajoie was honored when the team became the Naps in 1903. Fans finally settled on Indians in 1915 in honor of the first Native-American player in the majors—Louis F. Sockalexis (right)—a Maine Penobscot who swung a bat for the Spiders from 1897 to 1899.

World champions

◀ The Cincinnati Reds have won nine National League pennants (1919, 1939, 1940, 1961, 1970, 1972, 1975, 1976, 1990) and five World Series titles (1919, 1940, 1975, 1976, 1990). Some say the series win of 1919 was tainted since eight White Sox—labeled the Black Sox—players "fixed" the series and were banned from baseball for life.

The Cleveland Indians won a world title on October 10, 1920, by crushing Brooklyn 5 games to 2. Indian second baseman Bill Wambsganss completed the only unassisted triple play in series history in game five. And Elmer Smith hit the series' first grand slam during the same game. The Indians' win was dampened somewhat by the death of popular player Ray Chapman on August 16, 1920, before the series started. Chapman is the only player to die as a result of an injury during a major league game— an errant pitch "beaned" him on the head. The tribe won the World Series again on October 11, 1948, beating the Boston Braves 4 games to 2.

Who's that girl?

In 1908, the *Cleveland Press*, anxious for a winning major league team, printed the headline "If The Nap Pitchers Can't Win Regularly, Why Not Sign Alta Weiss?" The female pitcher from Ragersville had "all the motions of a regular league pitcher," but she went on to become a doctor.

Faster than a speeding bullet

He quit playing baseball in 1911, but three of his pitching records are still on the books—7,377 innings pitched and 751 games completed with 511 wins. The legend of Cy Young began while he was pitching for Canton in the Tri-State League. He "so battered the wooden fence of the grandstand [with his pitches] that the Canton owner, surveying the damage, remarked it looked as if a cyclone had come through." The Cleveland Spiders bought his contract for $300 in 1890 and his major-league career began—a career that took him to St. Louis and Boston before he retired with Cleveland in 1911. Today, the best pitcher in baseball each year receives the Cy Young Award. But how many pitchers today can come close to Young's accomplishments, which included 20-game winning seasons 16 times and 30-game winning seasons 15 times?

Baseball Hall of Fame
(Birthplace and year inducted)

Walter Alston, Darrtown, 1983
Roger Bresnahan, Toledo, 1945
Edward J. Delahanty, Cleveland, 1945
William "Buck" Ewing, Massillon, 1939
Roland "Rollie" Fingers, Steubenville, 1992
Elmer Flick, Bedford, 1963
Jesse J. "Pop" Haines, Clayton, 1970
Miller Huggins, Cincinnati, 1964
Byron "Ban" Johnson, Norwalk, 1937
Kenesaw Landis, Millville, 1944
Richard "Rube" Marquard, Cleveland, 1971
W. Branch Rickey, Stockdale, 1967
George Sisler, Manchester, 1939
Denton True "Cy" Young, Gilmore, 1937

A brilliant past

• When Bill Veeck bought the Cleveland Indians on June 21, 1946, the tribe entered its Golden Age. He brought in two African-American greats—Lary Doby in 1947 (the first African American to play in the American League), and the great Satchel Paige in 1948, who boosted the tribe to the World Series that year. Paige was a legend with pitches named the "barber," "two-hump blooper," and the "Long Tom." When Veeck bought the St. Louis Browns, Paige moved with him in 1951.

• Owner Frank Lane—nicknamed Trader Lane—made an astronomical 60 trades between December 2, 1957, and December 15, 1959.

• The tribe hired Frank Robinson as player/manager on October 4, 1974—the first African-American manager in the majors. Fans voted Robinson's home run on opening day April 8, 1975, the "most memorable event in club history."

Whose field is this anyway?

◄ "Are we in our ballpark or on the road? I can't believe this." So said Cleveland Indian Carlos Baerga on opening day April 4, 1994, at Cleveland's new $169-million county-owned ballpark, Jacobs Field. President Clinton threw out the first ball of the season at 1:05 P.M. The optimism the new park engendered boosted the Indians to first place before the players' strike hit in August 1994. The Indians hadn't been in first place since 1954. The driving force behind the new ballpark was current Indians owner Akron-native Richard E. Jacobs who bought the club in 1986. Cleveland Stadium remains the home of the Cleveland Browns pro-football team.

Most famous AAA team

If you were a fan of the TV show "M*A*S*H," you've heard of the Toledo Mud Hens. Toledo-native and actor Jamie Farr, who played Corporal Max Klinger, made the Hens a household word. But Farr isn't the only celebrity to wear a Mud Hen cap. Before Jackie Robinson broke the major-league color barrier, catcher Moses Fleetwood (Fleet) Walker played for the American Association Toledo team in 1884—the first African American to play in the majors. Olympic hero Jim Thorpe joined the team in 1921 and Casey Stengel stayed with Toledo for six seasons, guiding them to a 1927 Junior World Series title over Buffalo. Modern major-leaguers Phil Niekro, Rick Cerone, Kirby Puckett, and Cy Young Award winners Willie Hernandez (1984) and Frank Viola (1988) also wore Mud Hen uniforms. TV sports announcer Bob Costas—who bragged on national TV that he was a Hen in the 1970s—was invited to be a guest first-base coach. The curious team name originated before 1900 when wild ducks lived in the wetlands next to the ballpark.

• Dayton-native Roger Clemens pitched his first major-league game as a Boston Red Sox against the Cleveland Indians in Cleveland on May 15, 1984. Two years later he won his first Cy Young Award and repeated the following year—the fourth pitcher to win consecutive pitching awards.

• Cincinnati-native Karl Rhodes, a former West High baseball star, is now a Chicago Cub. He goes in the record book for hitting home runs his first three times at bat as a major-leaguer in 1994.

In the record books

GRIDIRON GLORY

◀ On September 17, 1920, representatives of 10 football teams met in a car showroom in Canton to organize the first professional football league—the American Professional Football Association. The franchise fee was $100 and Jim Thorpe—who played for the Canton Bulldogs then—presided over the new organization. Besides the Bulldogs, Ohio teams included the Dayton Triangles, Cleveland Tigers, and Akron Pros. After the new league collapsed, Joseph Carr of Columbus organized the National Football League in 1922, with some franchises going for as little as $50. There were 21 different teams that first year and it wasn't uncommon for a game to attract fewer than 100 fans.

There were no dawgs in the pound then

Great things come in small packages

When Paul Brown quarterbacked the Massillon Tigers he weighed a mere 135 pounds. He later coached his hometown high school to eight state football championships during his nine-year tenure. In 1942, he led the Ohio State Buckeyes to a national championship. When the All-American Football Conference was organized in 1945, Mickey McBride paid a $10,000 franchise fee and tagged Brown as his head coach. Fans voted for the "Browns" moniker—according to the Pro Football Hall of Fame—to honor their already-legendary coach and he responded by leading the Browns to four consecutive league titles. The Browns became part of the NFL in 1949. Through the 1940s and 1950s, Cleveland dominated professional football with seven divisional titles and three NFL championships (1950, 1954, 1955). Coach Brown—who stayed with the Browns 27 years—probably contributed more to the game than any other coach. He was the first coach to make the job a year-round position, the first to call plays from the sidelines by rotating players in and out, and the first to teach the game of football in an educational setting. Brown also implemented face guards on football helmets, devised the draw play, and developed exact pass routes.

In 1967, a consortium headed by Brown received a pro-football franchise in Cincinnati and chose the name Bengals because an earlier Cincinnati pro-football team had used the same name. Coach Brown retired in 1975, leaving behind an awesome 34-year professional coaching record of 299 wins, 89 losses, and 15 ties.

Hooray for Oorang!

All-around athlete and Olympic champion Jim Thorpe began his football career in Ohio. He joined a group of Native-American athletes who lived "native" style at the Oorang Dog Kennels in Larue and traveled from city to city playing football with the Oorang Indians.

Breaking the color line

◀ In 1946, the color line was broken in professional football by four players. Coach Paul Brown signed two of them—Bill Willis of Columbus and Marian Motley of Canton (born in Georgia but moved to Canton). When the Browns traveled to Miami for a game, Willis and Motley stayed behind because Florida law prohibited integrated sporting events.

Top dawg

The bleacher section at Cleveland Stadium is called the "Dawg Pound." At least 150 plainclothes police aided by surveillance cameras keep the dawgs in the pound from getting too "rabid" during Browns games. The biggest dawg of all—John "Big Dawg" Thompson—is a salesman during the week. But when the Browns are in town, Thompson dons a dog mask, a football jersey marked No. 98, and yells in the stands come rain or shine. "A walking Brown's encyclopedia," Thompson has appeared on "Entertainment Tonight" and in pages of *The Sporting News*.

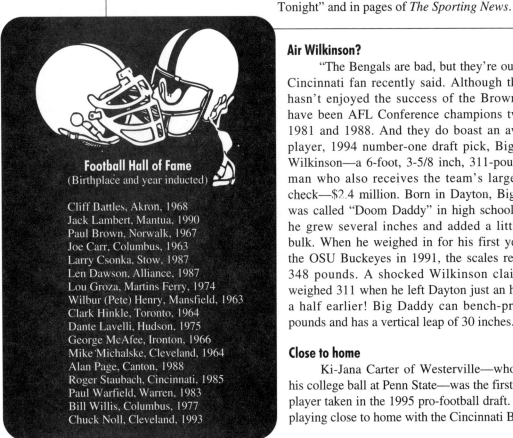

Football Hall of Fame
(Birthplace and year inducted)

Cliff Battles, Akron, 1968
Jack Lambert, Mantua, 1990
Paul Brown, Norwalk, 1967
Joe Carr, Columbus, 1963
Larry Csonka, Stow, 1987
Len Dawson, Alliance, 1987
Lou Groza, Martins Ferry, 1974
Wilbur (Pete) Henry, Mansfield, 1963
Clark Hinkle, Toronto, 1964
Dante Lavelli, Hudson, 1975
George McAfee, Ironton, 1966
Mike Michalske, Cleveland, 1964
Alan Page, Canton, 1988
Roger Staubach, Cincinnati, 1985
Paul Warfield, Warren, 1983
Bill Willis, Columbus, 1977
Chuck Noll, Cleveland, 1993

Air Wilkinson?

"The Bengals are bad, but they're ours," one Cincinnati fan recently said. Although the team hasn't enjoyed the success of the Browns, they have been AFL Conference champions twice, in 1981 and 1988. And they do boast an awesome player, 1994 number-one draft pick, Big Daddy Wilkinson—a 6-foot, 3-5/8 inch, 311-pound lineman who also receives the team's largest paycheck—$2.4 million. Born in Dayton, Big Daddy was called "Doom Daddy" in high school, before he grew several inches and added a little more bulk. When he weighed in for his first year with the OSU Buckeyes in 1991, the scales registered 348 pounds. A shocked Wilkinson claimed he weighed 311 when he left Dayton just an hour and a half earlier! Big Daddy can bench-press 500 pounds and has a vertical leap of 30 inches.

Close to home

Ki-Jana Carter of Westerville—who played his college ball at Penn State—was the first football player taken in the 1995 pro-football draft. He'll be playing close to home with the Cincinnati Bengals.

The pigskin shrine

Located on George Halas Drive in Canton, the Professional Football Hall of Fame (right), opened in 1963, boasts 83,000 square feet of exhibit space in five interconnected buildings. The "hallowed shrine" of professional football traces the game's history from 1892 to the present. A 350-seat movie theater highlights unforgettable games, plays, and players. Busts of each Hall of Famer are displayed in two separate galleries. The 200,000 pigskin fans who visit every year learn why the hall is located in Canton. It was here that the American Professional Football Association was organized in 1920. And the Canton Bulldogs, two-time NFL champions in 1922 and 1923, listed the first big-name football player on their roster—Jim Thorpe. Every year before the induction of new Hall of Famers, the AFC-NFC Hall of Fame pre-season game is played. The last Ohio team to win the contest was the Cincinnati Bengals in 1989 over the Los Angeles Rams, 14-7.

◀ For a man who didn't start his pro-football career until age 27, Roger Staubach's football stats are more than impressive. Nicknamed Roger the Dodger, Staubach led the NFL in passing in 1971, 1973, and 1978. More amazing, he led the Dallas Cowboys to 23 fourth-quarter wins, with 14 of those victories coming in overtime or in the last two minutes. Although his mother wanted him to concentrate on piano lessons, Staubach opted for football and was offered 25 college scholarships after graduating from Purcell High School in Ironton. His first choice was Notre Dame but the Irish wanted Staubach to play basketball and he preferred the gridiron. Retired after the 1979 football season, Staubach now heads his own Dallas real estate firm.

Roger the dodger

HOOP DREAMS

Never say die

Cleveland was granted an NBA franchise in 1970. Jerry Tomko—who suggested the Cavalier name and won the *Plain Dealer* contest—wrote that "the Cavaliers represent a group of daring, fearless men, whose life's pact was 'never surrender, no matter what the odds.'" Throughout the franchise history, the moniker has reflected the Cavaliers' fighting spirit. In 1976 and 1992 the team made it to the Eastern Conference finals.

A million-dollar miss

Sixteen-year-old Mike Holmgren of Strongville had one chance to make $1 million at the NBA All-Star game on February 11, 1995. All he had to do was hit one 3-point shot and the money was his. Chosen at random, Holmgren missed!

Basketball Hall of Fame
(Birthplace and year inducted)

Harold Anderson, Akron, 1984
John Bunn, Wellston, 1964
Henry Carlson, Murray City, 1959
John Havlicek, Lansing, 1983
Edward Hickox, Cleveland, 1959
Neil Johnston, Chillicothe, 1990
Bob Knight, Orrville, 1991
Jerry Lucas, Massillon, 1979
Fred Taylor, Zanesville, 1985

I want one of these

Current Cavaliers owners—George and Gordon Gund—came on board in 1983. The beginning of the 1994-1995 season saw the Cavs move into Gund Arena (below) next to Jacobs Field in the Gateway complex. Noted for its excellent design, a reporter wrote that "you go inside Gund Arena and you think, right away, 'I want one of these.'" Some of the arena's vital statistics include:

- Cost – $148 million
- Height from center court – 133 feet. It would take more than 53 million basketballs to fill Gund Arena.
- Seating capacity – 20,500, fourth largest in the NBA, with 60 percent of the seats in the lower tier
- Bay window – 108- by 48-foot bay window, composed of 189 glass panes, is used as a billboard to advertise activities
- Bathroom facilities were built to accommodate tall basketball players. Shower ceilings rise 8-feet and the sinks are 4-feet high.

No special desire   ◄ Probably the best basketball player in Buckeye history, Jerry Lucas once said he "never had any special desire to be a basketball player." During his high-school years at Middletown High, his team was defeated a mere seven times. Lucas was wooed by over 150 colleges, but chose to play for OSU where he shot 63.7 percent in his freshman year. The Buckeyes—with Lucas and John Havlicek—won the national collegiate title in 1960. Drafted by the Cincinnati Royals in 1962, Lucas later played on the New York Knicks 1973 championship team.

THE FRONT OFFICE

You couldn't move the Mountain

His father fought in the Battle of Kennesaw Mountain, Georgia, and named his son accordingly (without one "n")—Kenesaw Mountain Landis. Born in Millville in 1866, the younger Landis became a flashy lawyer and judge who once tried to summon Germany's Kaiser Wilhelm to the witness stand to explain his sinking of the *Lusitania*. It's no surprise that baseball owners tagged the strong-willed Landis as baseball's first commissioner after the 1919 World Series scandal. Landis demanded and received complete autonomy—none of his decisions could be overruled. One of his first acts as commissioner was to ban for life the eight White Sox players who conspired to fix the 1919 World Series. When Landis died in 1944, he was still commissioner and his strict rules of conduct had rescued America's pastime.

Vacations are important

Some say the flamboyant owner of the New York Yankees, Cleveland-native George Steinbrenner III (right), has mellowed over the years, but pitcher Jim Abott might think otherwise. Born without a right hand, Abott spends a lot of his time off the field raising funds for the Little League Challengers, the Little League division that works with handicapped children. Steinbrenner told the pitcher he should curtail his charitable activities—they might interfere with his concentration on the mound. On the other hand, Steinbrenner also remarked that he was "in no position to judge [Yankee designated hitter] Danny Tartabull" whose teammates criticized him for putting off necessary shoulder surgery so he could enjoy a long European vacation.

The only woman in a man's club

Born in Cincinnati in 1928, Marge Unnewehr grew up in a strict, wealthy German family. Some say she learned her father's management style—"autocratic paternalism"—quite well. When her husband Charlie Schott died in 1968, Marge inherited Schottco and began her business career. The first woman in the nation to receive a GM dealership in a major city, Schott quickly learned how to turn a profit. She became a limited partner of the Cincinnati Reds in 1981, general partner in 1984, and owner (the only female in the majors), president, and general manager in 1985—and the team's free-spending management style was out. "Daddy always taught us it wasn't right to waste money," Schott said. "When I see someone cheat for two bucks it makes me want to throw up." Supposedly she even charged Lou Pinella for three bats he donated to a charity raffle.

Her legendary mouth got her suspended from baseball for a year in 1993, when she allegedly called two Reds players her "million-dollar niggers." On May 18, 1994, the blunt owner was at it again, declaring, "I was raised to believe that men wearing earrings are fruity." The Los Angeles Dodgers later entered the playing field at Riverfront Stadium with earrings dangling from their "fruity" lobes.

THE COACHES' CORNER

◄ Football coach John Heisman was born in Cleveland in 1869. Many of his innovations have made the game what it is today—the forward pass, voice signals, the snap from center, T and I formations, and quarters. As a college player at Penn, he earned one of the first football letters awarded in the country. In his book, *The Principles of Football*, he wrote that "a coach has no time to say 'please' or 'mister'... he must be occasionally severe, arbitrary, and something of a czar." His techniques produced success—he was undefeated as Oberlin's head coach in 1892. He moved on to coach at Texas and Pennsylvania. The Heisman Trophy—first awarded in 1935 by Manhattan's Downtown Athletic Club (where Heisman was a director) to the best collegiate player in the nation—was named after the pioneering coach.

A coach can't be courteous

A football legend

Wayne Woodrow "Woody" Hayes spent his whole career coaching football in Ohio, first at Denison, then Miami, and finally OSU—where the loyalty of the Buckeye fans was so changeable before his

arrival that the school was dubbed "the graveyard of college football coaches." Hayes changed that tradition and stayed 28 glory-filled years, from 1951 to 1978. He won 13 Big Ten titles, 5 national titles, played in 8 Rose Bowls—4 of them consecutive (1972-1975)—and won 4, and coached 58 All-American players, including 3 Heisman Trophy winners. During 1968 to 1976, the Buckeyes lost only 13 games. Hayes once said that "Football is the best single program taught at Ohio State. The education you may forget. You don't forget the football." Hayes was so intense about his profession, however, that his temper flared during the 1978 Gator Bowl when he hit a Clemson University player, an action that cost him his job. To Buckeye fans, the coach continued to be a legend. When Hayes died in 1987, the flags all over Columbus flew at half-mast.

Some dreams might be too big

Perennial nice guy Gerry Faust coached football at Cincinnati's Moeller High School for 21 years before moving to the big time as coach of the legendary Notre Dame Fighting Irish. Faust's dream job ended in 1985 when his 30-26-1 record was far below Irish expectations. (East Liverpool-native Louis Leo Holtz—whose first job was selling cemetery plots—replaced Faust.) Moving on to the University of Akron, coach Faust's Zips almost zipped the 1994 season before pulling out a win over fellow-cellar-dweller Ohio University. John Heisman didn't have much luck as the Zips' coach either—he resigned under pressure in 1894. Always an optimist, Faust tried to put a positive spin on the season when he reminded the press that the Zips fulfilled their preseason expectations—they were picked to finish ninth in the league and they did. Faust—still positive about his years at Notre Dame—dreams of getting a phone call from Notre Dame inviting him back. Faust is available—he no longer coaches Akron football.

The brightest star from Orrville

The biggest star to come out of Orrville, Bobby Knight warmed the OSU bench during the days of the great Jerry Lucas. At OSU, Knight—nicknamed Dragon because he'd jokingly told teammates he belonged to a motorcycle gang, the Dragons—started in just two games. But he loved basketball and just wanted to coach. At age 24 he landed his first head-coaching job at West Point for $99 a month. When he won the

NCAA title in 1976 as coach of Indiana University, Knight was the first coach who had also played on a national championship team (OSU in 1960). For the sport's fan who has everything, the perfect gift might be the limited-edition Bobby Knight doll. The $545 porcelain-and-cloth collector's item comes complete with a red IU sweater and Converse tennis shoes—but it doesn't shout or throw things.

◄ Sid Gillman—inventor of the professional passing game, teacher of Vince Lombardi, and former coach of the San Diego Chargers—is just one of the football coaches whose pigskin roots are planted deep at Miami University of Ohio. Known as the "Cradle of Coaches," the school boasts eight national "Coaches of the Year"—Coach Earl H. (Red) Blaik of Army, 1946; Coach Woody Hayes of Ohio State, 1957; Coach Paul Dietzel of Louisiana State, 1958; Coach Ara Parseghian of Notre Dame, 1964; Coach John Pont of Indiana, 1967; Coach Jim Root of New Hampshire, 1967; Coach Bo Schembechler of Michigan, 1969; and Coach Bill Narduzzi of Youngstown State, 1979. Professional sports organizations have hired famous Miami graduates including "Weeb" Eubank, coach of the New York Jets, and Paul Brown, coach of the Cincinnati Bengals and Cleveland Browns.

Cradle of coaches

COLLEGE SPORTS

Is there any other sport?

An Ohio State University doctoral student surveyed 1,000 Columbus residents and discovered that almost 9 out of every 10 had attended a Buckeye football game. The university team is so dominant every fall that many people believe that's why central Ohio doesn't have a professional team—there wouldn't be enough interest. Buckeye fans—whose mascot, the buckeye tree's leaves and nuts, was drawn by cartoonist Milt Caniff and adopted in 1950—expect winners every year and they are rarely disappointed. The team boasts 26 Big Ten championships, 6 Rose Bowl victories, 5 Heisman Trophy winners, and 138 All-Americans, as well as being the first Big Ten School to play in every major Bowl—Rose, Fiesta, Sugar, Cotton, and Orange.

When Ohio Stadium (right) was completed in 1922—the biggest horseshoe-shaped, double-deck sports stadium in the nation and the first—at a cost of $1.3 million, early doubters thought its original 66,210 seats would never be filled. Now on the National Register of Historic Places, the stadium's current 89,841 seats are sometimes filled beyond capacity—the largest crowd on record was 95,375 in 1991 when OSU played Iowa.

Heisman Trophy winners

The only Big Ten quarterback ever to win a Heisman was also the first quarterback to win the coveted trophy—OSU's Les Horvath. Archie Griffin, the Buckeye's legendary running back, is the only two-time winner in Heisman history. And Desmond Howard was the biggest winner ever, beating the runner-up by 1,574 points.

Frank Sinkwich, Youngstown, 1942	Roger Staubach, Cincinnati, 1963
Les Horvath, Parma, 1944	Archie Griffin, Columbus, 1974
Vic Janowicz, Elyria, 1950	Archie Griffin, Columbus, 1975
Howard Cassady, Columbus, 1955	Desmond Howard, Cleveland, 1991

His plays ran out

◀ Art Schlicter, OSU quarterback from 1978 to 1981, had everything going for him. Named the Big Ten's Most Valuable Player in 1981, he appeared in four post-season bowl games. A pro-career seemed assured, but Schlicter had one problem—he was a compulsive gambler who was barred from the NFL in 1987. He moved to Las Vegas in the spring of 1994 to work as a talk-show host by convincing radio KVEG that his gambling habit was under control. But his luck ran out in January 1995, when the former football star was convicted of bank fraud to the tune of $175,000. Schlicter had involved his talk-show listeners in schemes to cash stolen checks—he even stole 25 checks from his employer. Sentenced to two years in the federal penitentiary in Terre Haute, Indiana, prosecutors estimated that the smooth-talking Schlicter really stole almost $500,000.

The pride of Youngstown

The Youngstown State Penguins coached by Jim Tressel (left) claim the most wins of any Division I-A or I-AA football team during the 1990s. Grabbing national titles in 1991, 1993, and 1994, the team boasts a 61-9-2 record since 1990 and fills the hometown stands with 17,000 cheering fans. Youngstown's mayor sees the Penguins as a vital morale booster and a source of community pride. "…Losing the [steel] mills took a tremendous psychological toll. We're starting to regain confidence and YSU football has been a big part." The town that lost almost 25,000 steelworker jobs in the 1970s is also rich with football talent. Tressel recruits heavily from what he calls the "State of Youngstown"—the area within 100 miles of the university. You might remember one famous YSU alumni—quarterback Ron Jaworski who was originally drafted by the Los Angeles Rams.

Tressel joins another YSU football coach in the record books. Coach Dwight "Dike" Beede is credited with providing referees with the first penalty flags—sewn by his wife—for a Penguin game against Oklahoma City in 1941. The Big Ten commissioner saw a ref using one of the flags in Columbus later and adopted the cloth triangles for the entire conference. By 1948, the NFL was using Beede's invention.

Did you know?
The NCAA Basketball Tournament was first suggested by Ohio State basketball coach Harold Olsen in 1939.

How much is a season ticket worth?

The University of Cincinnati basketball team began playing Bradley on December 21, 1981, beating them seven continuous overtimes later—75-73—on December 22. The Bearcats don't know anything but exciting basketball. Winner of two national collegiate titles, Cincinnati beat OSU in 1961 and 1962 (the only time two schools from the same state played each other in the finals) just after Oscar Robertson starred for Cincinnati. Most recently, Coach Bob Huggins took the team to the Final Four in 1992 and the quarter-finals in 1993. A Bearcat basketball fan who purchased a season ticket for the 1994-1995 season was also required to buy a $70 season football ticket. And, in 1995-1996, that same basketball fan will be required to join the Booster Club—to keep his basketball ticket—at a cost of $550.

A one-man scoring machine

As a freshman at Rio Grande College, Wellsville-native Bevo Francis once scored 116 points in a basketball game but the NCAA didn't count the feat because Rio Grande played a junior-college team. In 1954, the great shooter averaged 46.5 points a game (a Division II record) and dropped 113 points during a single game (also a Division II record). The basketball ace quit college hoops after two seasons, amassing an unbelievable 3,272 points.

IN THE RING

Hair's Don!

You know him by his hair, which rises toward the heavens. Touting himself as the greatest boxing promoter of all time, Don King says his silver frizz is "a burning bush basted in righteous juices …." Whatever his secret for success, King seeks divine guidance before every business transaction. He began his boxing management and promotion career in 1974, by inviting Muhammad Ali to participate in a benefit for Cleveland's Forest City Hospital. Ali said yes and King saved the hospital and went on to sign George Foreman and Ali to fight in his first big extravaganza, "The Rumble in the Jungle." Each boxer was guaranteed $5 million.

Born in Cleveland's ghetto in 1931, King ultimately grabbed the title as "top racketeer" in Cleveland. A fistfight between King and one of his numbers runners—which ended in the accidental death of the runner—got King convicted of manslaughter in 1967. Paroled on September 30, 1971, Governor Rhodes gave him a full pardon in 1983. King wasted no time making money after his incarceration—he was a millionaire boxing promoter several years later and hasn't turned back. "All I'm doing is working in the tradition of America. I am a pioneer, a trailblazer." Today King holds the record for promoting the most championship fights in a single year—47 in 1994.

◀ Youngstown's Boom Boom Mancini won the WBA lightweight title on May 8, 1982, in a first-round knockout—capturing the title his father Lenny had sought. An unexpected tragedy occurred during his title defense in November 1982 against Deuk-Koo Kim of South Korea. During the 14th round, Kim fell unconscious and died four days later. A shaken Boom Boom later lost his title to Livingstone Bramble because, as he said, "I lost my heart." Boom Boom's desire was reignited for a fight against Hector "Macho" Camacho in 1988—the $1.2-million purse had something to do with it. After the fight, both boxers thought they'd won, but Camacho was awarded the win. Today, Mancini no longer boxes. He's married, has two children, and lives in Santa Monica, California, where he's pursuing an acting career. You may have seen him in such movies as *Iron Eagle 3* and *Dirty Dozen 4*. He keeps his hand in boxing as a promoter and matchmaker.

Boom! Boom!

Boxing bits

- Columbus-native Buster Douglas defeated Mike Tyson on February 10, 1990 (Tyson's only defeat), to win the heavyweight title and lost it on October 25, 1990, to Evander Holyfield.
- When Mike Tyson was released from prison in March 1995, he settled in at his home in Southington, outside Youngstown.

THE OLYMPIANS

A real clubman

◀ Cleveland's Edward A. Henig had a very long athletic career. Indian club swinging isn't a major attraction today but back in 1904 when Henig first won the AAU title it was quite popular. Henig tied for the title in 1911 and won again in 1933, 1936, 1937, 1939, 1940, 1942, 1945, 1946, 1947, 1950 and 1951. He also won the gold medal in his specialty in the 1904 Olympics.

Stella or Steven Walsh?

Cleveland-resident Stella Walsh emigrated from Poland and wasn't a U.S. citizen when the 1932 Olympics began. She competed for her native country, winning a gold medal in the 100-meter dash—the first female to break the 12-second mark. Over the course of her career she set more than 1,000 records including five consecutive pentathlon titles from 1950 to 1954. But a most amazing discovery occurred when Walsh was accidentally killed during a robbery attempt in Cleveland. The coroner announced that Stella Walsh was really a man.

Hard work pays off

Although Jesse Owens wasn't born in Ohio, he moved to Cleveland as a youngster and honed his athletic prowess there. True to his mother's adage—"What you puts in is exactly what you gets out"—Owens worked hard. Called the "Ebony Antelope," Jesse earned a place in the record books on May 25, 1935, when he broke five world records and tied another in a track meet between Owens' OSU team and Michigan in Ann Arbor. This feat was accomplished in 70 minutes in spite of Owens' back injury. And who can forget his four Olympic gold medals won at Berlin in 1936 in the 100-meter dash, the 200-meter-dash, the long jump, and men's relay, while the Führer himself looked on? Jolted back to the reality of prejudice upon his return to the United States, the country's greatest athlete received only two job offers—one was a $28-dollar-a-week job as a playground teacher. Suspended from the AAU because he wouldn't attend a track meet, he resorted to racing horses to support himself. Owens worked through those hard times to become a respected lecturer and public relations consultant.

- At the 1924 Paris Olympics, broad jumper Dehart Hubbard of Cincinnati was the first African American to ever win a gold medal. His winning jump measured 24 feet, 5-1/8 inches.
- Figure-skating gold medalist Peggy Fleming first tried ice-skating at age nine while living with her family in Cleveland.

The grand old man

Edwin Moses is a gifted student and hurdler. He earned a degree in physics and two Olympic gold medals in 1976 and 1984 in the 400-meter hurdles. In 1988, at age 33, he amazingly won an Olympic bronze. How did this incredible athlete keep on going? Part of his training routine included ballet, yoga, and martial arts. Moses' wife is an accomplished artist who preserved part of her husband's well-developed physique. A plaster cast of his athletic derriere hangs in the couple's bedroom.

Did you know?

FROM THE SPORTS PAGE

◀ Held in September, the Little Brown Jug—a race for the world's best three-year-old pacers—began in Delaware in 1946. Known as the "Jug," the race wasn't named after homemade brew, but commemorates a champion pacer of the 1800s named Little Brown Jug. Preliminary races during Jug Week include the Jugette for three-year-old fillies and the Senior Jug for four-year-olds and up. The Jug, along with the Cane Futurity at Yonkers Raceway and the Messenger Stake at The Meadows comprise the "Triple Crown" for pacers. While the Little Brown Jug might be the most prestigious race in the state, the Ohio Derby is the oldest, first run at Queen City Downs in Cincinnati in 1876. Today, the race for three-year-olds is held every year at Thistledown near Cleveland.

It's not home brew

Speed demons

- In 1899, Wauseon-native Barney Oldfield drove Henry Ford's Ford-Cooper "999" at an exhibition in Dayton. In 1902, the future car mogul hired Oldfield as chief mechanic of his racing team. Three years later Oldfield began his professional career by winning the Manufacturer's Challenge Cup at Grosse Pointe, Michigan, on October 25, 1902—after one week's practice. Oldfield popularized the automobile through his racing accomplishments. He was the first man to travel "a mile a minute" in 1903 at Indianapolis and he set a speed record in 1910 at 131.724 miles per hour. What made Oldfield try such daring feats? He was fearless, but he also believed "… in the product and I always spell it with a capital M—for Money."
- Medina-native Bobby Rahal won the Indianapolis 500 in 1986. The second woman to qualify for the Indianapolis 500, Lynn St. James—only child of Willoughby-businessman Alfred Cornwall—was named Rookie of the Year at Indy in 1992 and competed in 1993 and 1994. Born Evelyn Cornwall, she became a professional race driver and changed her name after a 1978 race in Atlanta. The St. James was borrowed from actress Susan St. James.

He could do everything

◀ Jockey Willie Shoemaker called rival Eddie Arcaro the "greatest rider I ever saw. He could do everything." The Cincinnati native was the first jockey to win the Kentucky Derby five times—in 1938, 1941, 1945, 1948 and 1952. He won the Preakness six times—in 1941, 1942, 1945, 1948, 1952, 1955. A millionaire when he retired, Arcaro was one of the first three jockeys inducted into the Jockey Hall of Fame.

The Chinese connection

Born in Youngstown in 1929, Arnold Palmer was the first golfer to earn $1 million in prize money. He won the Masters four times (1958, 1960, 1962, 1964), the U.S. Open in 1960, and the British Open in 1961 and 1962. Palmer's company, Arnold Palmer Enterprises, designed the first golf course in the People's Republic of China. The Chung Shan Hot Springs Golf Club in Zhongshan opened in October 1981.

The best of the best

◀ Columbus-native Jack Nicklaus fell in love with golf at age 10. "By the time Jack was 12," his father said, "I couldn't handle him any more. I remember one day I hit as good a drive as I could …. I told Jack, 'If you outhit that one, I'll buy you a Cadillac convertible.'" Jack's drive landed about 30 yards beyond his dad's and he received a Mercury convertible—instead of a Cadillac—when he graduated from high school. In 1959, Nicklaus was the youngest man in 50 years to win the U.S. Amateur Championship, and in 1986, he was the oldest ever to win the Masters. A man of supreme confidence, Nicklaus has won the Masters six times (1963, 1965, 1966, 1972, 1975, 1986); the PGA five times (1963, 1971, 1973, 1975, 1980); the U.S. Open four times (1962, 1967, 1972, 1980); and the British Open three times (1966, 1970, 1978). "When you go head-to-head against Nicklaus," J.C. Snead once remarked, "he knows he's going to beat you, you know he's going to beat you, and he knows you know he's going to beat you." In 1976, Nicklaus inaugurated the Memorial Tournament (he won in 1977 and 1984) at Muirfield Village Golf Club, the course he built for his hometown. Elected to the Golf Hall of Fame in 1978, he has also designed more than 125 golf courses worldwide. His friends and associates broke ground in May 1995 for the Jack Nicklaus Museum at Muirfield Village Golf Course.

◀ Twenty-eight-year-old journalist Steven Newman realized a boy-hood dream when he left Bethel on April 1, 1983, to walk around the world. Four years, 22,500 miles, and four pairs of hiking boots later, the Ripley journalist had completed a trek across Europe, Africa, south-ern Asia, the center of Australia, and North America with his backpack. Walking came naturally to Newman—as a boy, his family was so poor he didn't even have a bike, but the adventure books he read gave him the idea that walking around the world would be the best way to explore places most people don't see, and meet regular people. Shortly after Newman arrived home, a Japanese businessman, disappointed that the young man hadn't walked across Japan, offered to pay his expenses if he would do so. Newman accepted and walked another 2,000 miles.

You gotta have a dream

Ready ... aim ... fire

Competitive shooting was a popular sport in the 1880s. The targets were live pigeons released from cages or glass balls filled with colored powder. But passenger pigeons became extinct (not a surprise) and broken glass was dangerous. A young Buckeye inventor, George Ligowsky (left), patented a new kind of target—the clay pigeon—on September 7, 1880. His idea came from watching young boys skip shells across water. By the 1890s, clay-pigeon shooting was a favorite pastime. In 1887, Cleveland's Paul North developed a better clay pigeon—the Blue Rock—and an automatic throwing machine to advance the sport. Today the American Trapshooting Association Hall of Fame and Museum in Vandalia celebrates the sport of competitive target shooting. The first fifteen Hall of Fame inductees in 1969 included three Buckeyes—Rolla Heikes of Dayton, George Ligowsky, and sharpshooter Annie Oakley. Heikes was the first Grand American Handicap (the major trapshooting tournament) winner in 1900, the first year clay targets were used in the competition.

Cashing in on fame

In the 1960s, television began broadcasting sports events and Mark McCormack, a young Cleveland lawyer, saw an opportunity to use sports heroes and athletic events to market the world's products. He signed Arnold Palmer in 1960 as his first International Management Group (IMG) client, shortly after Palmer won his second U.S. Open title. Not only has McCormack made athletes wealthy—from South African Gary Player to tennis great Chris Evert—he created a completely new sports entertainment field, including made-for-TV sporting events such as the popular "Battle of the Network Stars." His merchandise-licensing activities and corporate sponsorship of the biggest athletic contests on the globe, such as Wimbledon, has made IMG a worldwide giant with 64 offices in 15 countries.

A sports collage

- Akron attorney Eddie Elias founded the Professional Bowlers Association of America (PBA) in 1958. The first PBA tour consisted of three stops—Dayton, Ohio; Paramus, New Jersey; and Albany, New York. Players competed for $49,500 in prize money. When ABC began televising PBA tournaments in 1962, prize money skyrocketed into the millions.
- Greg Snouffer of Delaware is the World Indoor Boomerang Champion.
- Dick Dammel, a Mt. Lookout doctor, finished the Little Miami Triathlon—a 6-mile canoe race, a 10-kilometer run, and a 19-mile bike ride—twice in the same day—once with each of his sons.
- Golfer Louise Kepley of Cincinnati was 52 when she won her fourth women's state amateur golf championship in 1994. She beat her 29-year-old niece, Janie Dumler, by one stroke.

HIGH-SCHOOL TALES

The Waterloo Wonders

The Waterloo Wonders, state basketball champs in 1934 and 1935, could have inspired the Harlem Globetrotters. Five white boys from the tiny town of 150—Orlyn Roberts, Wyman Roberts, Beryl Drummond, Curtis McMahon, and Stewart Wiseman—entertained crowds from all over the state with their winning skills and crowd-pleasing tricks. Ironton writer Stan Morris first dubbed the team the Waterloo Wonders. Some of their on-court antics included rebounding an opposing team's missed shot and giving them one more try; sending several players off the floor to eat popcorn while their remaining teammates continued playing; and bouncing the basketball into the hoop for a score. Sometimes fans got into the game as the Wonders tossed the ball into the crowd and told the enthusiastic recipient to shoot. In a 1935 game against Chesapeake, the Wonders fabulous five were so far ahead at halftime that they left the subs to finish off the win and hurried on to Jackson for the second game of the night. The Wonders beat two teams in one evening—Jackson 45-24 and Chesapeake 47-5. When interviewed by a reporter about their training program, the Wonders coach passed around a pack of cigarettes and everyone lit up! Kentucky coach Adolph Rupp tried to recruit the whole team, but only one player—Stewart Wiseman—went to college. The other four worked at the Frigidaire plant in Dayton and played in the city's industrial league.

Meaningful mascots

The Glenville Tarblooders are in the High School Hall of Fame for their mascot name—they're the only Tarblooders in the nation. The earliest reference administrators can find to the unique name goes back to a 1920s cheer—"Wack, Thud, Tar and blood." But other than that, no one really knows where the nickname originated. On the other hand, the Shenandoah Zeps know the historical significance of their mascot. A zeppelin crashed in Noble County on September 3, 1925.

Shenandoah ZEPS

BUCKEYE BANDITS, BRIBES, AND BURDENS

While Ohio has made many positive contributions to American society, it also has its dark side. Swindler Cassie Chadwick bilked banks for millions of dollars at the turn of the century. In the 1920s, Ohio had the largest Ku Klux Klan membership in the nation. And in the 1930s, the state was the playground of notorious bank robbers John Dillinger and Pretty Boy Floyd. It is also the home state of murderer Charles Manson.

Terrible disasters have struck, too. The Collingwood Elementary School fire in Cleveland in 1908 killed 175 people, one of the worst school fires in United States' history. Over 320 prisoners at the Ohio State Penitentiary in Columbus were roasted to death in their cells during a fire in 1930. Let's take a walk on the wilder side of Ohio.

- Crime Shapes History
- Ku Klux Klan Kollides
- Politics and Corruption
- Felonies and Fakes
- Murderous Madmen
- Deadly Disasters

CRIME SHAPES HISTORY

Hang 'em

☞ The first recorded execution in Ohio was the hanging of John O'Mic in 1812. O'Mic was a Native American convicted of murdering two trappers. Hanging was the method of choice for executions in the 19th century and usually drew large crowds of spectators. In 1885, the gallows at the Ohio Penitentiary consolidated county executions. From 1885 to 1897, 28 people were hung.

Explosive burial

☞ In 1885, Johnsville resident and murderer Valentine Wagner became the first person hanged in the Ohio Penitentiary. Local residents forbade his burial in the village cemetery, so his grave was dug just outside the village limits. To prevent vandalism, 12 torpedoes were embedded in the tomb.

Capital crimes in Ohio
Assassination
Contract murder
Murder during escape
Murder while in a correctional facility
Murder after conviction for a prior purposeful killing or prior attempted murder
Murder of a peace officer
Murder arising from rape, kidnapping, arson, robbery, or burglary
Murder of a witness to prevent testimony in a criminal proceeding or in retaliation

Mob scene

George Andrew Horn and William Henry Gribben were hanged on May 16, 1884, near the Ashland County Courthouse. They were convicted of murdering a fellow townsman. Only a few persons were invited to the hanging, but a crowd of 12,000 showed up. Undeterred by 300 National Guardsmen, they tore down a high board fence and ran to the scaffold. After the execution the crowd continued to gape, reluctant to end the show. The behavior of the spectators provoked stormy opposition and the legislature passed a bill ensuring privacy of execution.

Justice served

In 1897, prisoner Charles Justice may have been clever enough to assemble Ohio's first electric chair, but he wasn't wise enough to stay out of it. Justice served his time for burglary charges, then killed a Greene County farmer and ended up on Death Row. He was executed in 1911 and became the 38th person to die in Ohio's electric chair. But, 17-year-old Willie Haas, the "child murderer of Hamilton County," holds the distinction of being the first murderer executed in Ohio's electric chair. Haas was convicted of killing the wife of a man who had befriended him. He was 16 at the time of the crime to which he confessed. He was executed in 1897, the year the state began using electrocution. His execution drew a large crowd, many of the spectators "pushing and shoving for a better view." The last convicted murderer to be executed by electrocution was Donald Reibolt on April 21, 1963. Reibolt murdered a Columbus grocer.

The state pen

The first two buildings of the Ohio Penitentiary in Columbus were erected in 1813 and 1818 respectively. By 1826 they housed more than 142 inmates. The inmates were employed in various occupations, including wagon making, blacksmithing, coopering, shoemaking, and cloth manufacturing. These products and services were in turn exchanged for goods needed by the prison. Discipline was relatively lax and escapes numerous.

In 1832 a new expanded prison facility was authorized with housing and work space for 500 convicts. With the opening of the new building a different system of labor was introduced. Instead of manufacturing articles, the convicts' labor was contracted out. Recognizing the need for a separate facility to incarcerate females, a women's department was constructed in 1837. Only the "most degraded women" were sent there.

The harshness of the contract system, however, created opposition and by 1850 the system was partially abandoned. The only reading materials allowed were the Bible and a prayer book. Those who didn't follow the rules were taken to a special flogging room where prisoners were beaten with large whips. The Ohio Penitentiary (above) closed in 1984.

Crimetown U.S.A.

Between 1951 and 1962, a crime spree broke out in Youngstown—87 bombings, attempted bombings, and murders. Only two cases were officially solved. The situation was so bad that a letter addressed to Murdertown, Ohio, was actually delivered to a Youngstown address. Police and politicians were in cahoots and the public didn't seem to care. The rackets in Youngstown were profitable and rival gangs were fighting for control. A numbers game called "the bug" was the biggest moneymaker. The blue-collar workers of Slovak, Italian, and Greek descent usually wagered only a quarter, but thousands of quarters added up to about $3 million a year—enough to kill for. Richer gamblers liked *barbut*, a gambling game adopted by Greek immigrants. Youngstown was also a bookmaking center for football, basketball, baseball, and horse races, bringing in $15 million annually. When Mayor Harry Savasten said he was going to clean up the town, he made some interesting appointments. An attorney for the underworld, Russell G. Mock, became his law director, and his choice for chief of police disbanded the vice squad after announcing a war on crime. Finally, Attorney General Robert Kennedy beefed up the FBI presence by adding 20 additional agents in the search for the city's elusive connection to organized crime. Youngstown earned the moniker, "Crimetown," but many residents didn't think that was fair. "We're no worse than other cities. Look at Chicago."

A man called Sue

Mark Pollock, a male inmate at the Warren Correctional Institution, sued the state in 1994. He wanted to be called "Susan Marie" and wear makeup, grow long hair, and dress in women's clothing. Prison officials denied his request whereupon Pollock—or Susan Marie—claimed "these circumstances violated his freedom from cruel and unusual punishment." Susan also wanted $200,000 in damages.

They tied the knot and left the joint

The first prison wedding in Ohio joined Nancy Scott and Thomas Miles on their release date—February 1, 1875. About 1,100 inmates watched the convicted burglars tie the knot at the Ohio Penitentiary. They left immediately after the ceremony.

Crime and punishment

The story of John Demjanjuk's trial before Israel's Supreme Court is like a chapter from one of Dostoevsky's novels. In 1988, Demjanjuk, a retired auto assembly-line worker from outside Cleveland, was sentenced to death for his part in Nazi war crimes. The court believed he was "Ivan the Terrible," the sadistic Ukrainian gas-chamber guard of the Treblinka death camp. After a decade of hearings in the United States, Demjanjuk was stripped of his U.S. citizenship. He was about to be deported to the Soviet Union when Israel intervened and asked that he be extradited to stand trial. The trial, which lasted 18 months, was Israel's first Nazi war-crime hearing since Eichmann's, and only the second in Israel's history. Five witnesses, all death-camp survivors, identified Demjanjuk as "Ivan the Terrible." The judges agreed with the witnesses and Demjanjuk was sentenced to death. Then, in 1992, new evidence emerged. Documents from Soviet KGB files were discovered that suggested that Demjanjuk was not "Ivan the Terrible," and that "Ivan the Terrible" was a native Ukrainian whose fate remains unknown. In light of the new evidence the Israeli Court refused to retry Demjanjuk and on September 22, 1993, he was released and returned to the United States.

Deadly drama

Prisoners at the Southern Ohio Correctional Facility in Lucasville laid siege to the prison for 11 days beginning on April 11, 1993. Four hundred and fifty prisoners barricaded themselves in a cell block, taking guards as hostages. To prove that their demands were serious, the prisoners murdered guard Robert Vallandingham and seven inmates believed to be cooperating with authorities. The deadly drama finally ended on April 21, 1993, when authorities agreed to grant some of the prisoners' demands.

KU KLUX KLAN KOLLIDES

Racism reborn

In the 1920s the reborn Ku Klux Klan embraced the Midwest with its appeal to patriotism and return to fundamental values. Ohio boasted the largest Ku Klux Klan membership—400,000—of any state in the Union. Klan organizers throughout Ohio played upon the fears of the Protestant majority, many of whom were disturbed by rapid social changes affecting the United States after World War I. In Ohio, the Klan organized itself against the Democratic Party, an organization the Klan thought was corrupt and anti-Prohibitionist. The Klan promoted the candidacy of Republican Warren G. Harding. Likewise, in cities around Ohio, crusaders thought the Klan would clean up entrenched corruption. Not surprisingly, the Klan won several municipal elections in 1923, placing "Klan mayors" in Niles, Warren, Girard, Struthers, and Youngstown.

The Wizard comes to Dayton

During the summer of 1923, thousands flocked to Dayton for a Klan Konklave, or convention, featuring the Imperial Wizard Hiram W. Evans. Special trains were chartered by the Klan on the Pennsylvania, Big Four, and B&O railroads to carry delegates to the convention. Reportedly, over 7,000 new members joined the Klan during the event. Speakers denounced journalists, bossism, bootlegging, and anything illegal. The theme of the rally was 100 percent American and nothing less.

Just before the national elections of 1924, the KKK planned a convention for Niles. Events began turning sour when an anti-Klan group organized a counterprotest. Conveniently, local politicians made themselves absent the weekend of the scheduled event. Klansmen arriving in town ran into trouble immediately as anti-Klan groups smashed Klan automobiles and beat or shot passengers. The sheriff called on the National Guard for assistance. Several of the Klansmen had to switch uniforms and reappear as guardsmen. The violence was stopped, but the Klan's reputation suffered. Further violence, factionalism, and misappropriation of funds eroded the Klan's hold in Ohio. By 1925 the Klan had lost most of its power.

A konclave kollapses

Catholic parochial school systems were among the favorite targets of Klan propaganda. Klan sympathizers in the Ohio Legislature introduced bills that outlawed Catholic schools and made it illegal for Catholics to teach in public schools. Neither bill passed, but more successful was the Klan-supported bill introduced in 1925 by Carroll County's Representative Ross Buchanan. The legislation required that each student read 10 verses from the Bible daily. The bill passed both houses, but was vetoed by Governor Vic Donahey because it violated the separation of church and state. Ironically, this was one of the very principles that the Klan accused the Catholic church of violating.

Targets of Klan propaganda

Kan't klean

A request by the Ku Klux Klan to pick up litter on a two-mile section of highway in Union County was turned down by the Ohio Department of Transportation in 1995. The department chairman thought an Adopt-a-Highway sign with the Klan's name on it "would be an extreme distraction to certain segments of the population." Vandals and picketers might hamper the Klan's cleaning activities. Klan spokeswoman Angela Septer of West Mansfield was shocked. She said the Klan just wanted to do something nice for Central Ohio.

POLITICS AND CORRUPTION

Money under the table

Joseph B. Foraker was born in Rainboro in 1846 and served as governor from 1886 to 1890. When the Hearst papers revealed that Governor Foraker had accepted $29,500 from Standard Oil Company's vice president John D. Archbold, Foraker insisted that the money was for legal services rendered in Ohio. Foraker, however, used the funds to lobby against legislation harmful to Standard Oil's interests.

In 1914, Foraker attempted to win the Republican nomination for senator. Warren G. Harding defeated him. Foraker retired from public life and spent his remaining years writing his memoirs.

Robbing the taxpayer

A trusting man, President Harding took part of his "Ohio gang" to Washington and they took every opportunity to line their own pockets. Harry Daugherty, President Harding's mentor and attorney general, put a price on federal jobs and judgeships. Charles Forbes, head of the Veterans Bureau, siphoned off vast sums of money from the Veterans Administration. In 1920, Secretary of the Interior Albert Hall pointed out that commercial drilling was draining the naval oil reserve field at Teapot Dome, Wyoming. He sold that field and another at Elk Hills, California, to private enterprise. In reality, Hall sold the fields at bargain prices to his friends—oilmen Edward Doheny and Harry Sinclair. Doheny and Sinclair made a fortune on the deal. In exchange for his "friendship," Hall received $100,000 in used notes delivered in a little black bag. Hall gave Harding the distinction of being the first president to have a cabinet member go to jail for a crime. Forbes was convicted of fraud, Daugherty was tried for selling pardons, and Jess Smith, who had a job at the Justice Department, killed himself.

Acquitted of mob connections

In the early 1980s, the FBI was still looking for organized crime in Mahoning County—this time in the sheriff's office. Jim Traficant, elected as sheriff in 1980, was accused of taking $163,000 from local racketeers during his election campaign to ignore illegal gambling activities. Because he didn't report the alleged bribes as income, he was indicted for tax evasion. The FBI supposedly had a confession—which Traficant said was a forgery—in which the sheriff admitted taking money as part of his plan to investigate organized crime. In an attempt to prove his innocence in 1982, Traficant said he would plead "no contest" and go straight to jail if FBI agents would take lie detector tests. (Traficant couldn't because of high blood pressure). Loud accusations from Traficant and the FBI filled the Youngstown air. Democratic Party Chairman Hanni tried to commit the sheriff to a hospital for mental tests in October 1982. But Traficant outlasted everyone, as he usually does. He wasn't convicted of any crime and went on to win a seat in Congress in 1984—a feat he's repeated six times as of 1994.

☞ On May 4, 1970, four students were slain and nine others wounded at Kent State University when a contingent of Ohio National Guardsmen opened fire on an anti-war demonstration. The shooting that rocked the nation lasted 13 seconds. Four days earlier, President Richard Nixon announced his decision to invade Cambodia. Angered by Nixon's decision, college students across the nation staged anti-war rallies. Fearing that the demonstrations in Kent might get out of hand, Mayor LeRoy Satrom asked the governor's office to send the National Guard to the university. Ohio Governor James A. Rhodes granted Satrom's request and on May 2, the Guard was ordered to police the campus.

Thirteen seconds of shooting

Although several investigations followed, none could determine why the guardsmen had fired. Neither could they explain the event's disturbing inconsistencies. In 1974, a federal court acquitted the eight guardsmen accused of the shooting. A second civil trial was held in Cleveland six months later. In 1979, a settlement was reached, and the nine wounded students were awarded damages. The parents of the four slain students each received $15,000 to compensate their losses. In May 1990, a long-awaited memorial (right) was dedicated at Kent State as a remembrance of the tragedy.

☞ In 1989 Republican Representative Donald E. Lukens was charged with having sex with a 16-year-old girl. In 1990, new allegations—that he fondled an elevator operator in the Capitol Building in Washington, D.C.—surfaced. When the House decided to investigate, Lukens resigned "for the good of the Congress." After leaving Washington, he served 30 days in Franklin County Jail for the 1989 offense. He still receives his government pension.

The one good thing he did was resign

FELONIES AND FAKES

A consultant in burglary

George Leonidas Leslie was considered by some to be the greatest bank burglar of his time. A wealthy brewer's son, Leslie graduated in architecture from the University of Cincinnati. A brilliant career was predicted for him, but after his parents died in 1865 Leslie left the Midwest and turned to crime in New York. He masterminded the Ocean National Bank and Manhattan Savings Institution robberies, hauling in $786,879 and $2,747,700, respectively. Gangs all over the country hired Leslie as a consultant but he despised most of them because they lacked his cunning and self-control. Frequently, Leslie would break into a bank undetected. If there was less money than expected, he would leave and return later for a bigger haul.

How to steal $350 million

Youngstown entrepreneur Mickey Monus opened his first Phar Mor discount drugstore in 1982. By 1992, the $3-billion chain—hailed as the next Wal Mart—boasted 300 stores in 33 states and 25,000 employees. But in August 1992, the bubble burst when company officials found out Monus and his chief financial officer Patrick Finn had falsified company books to make the business look profitable—the company's value had been overstated by $350 million. In the meantime, millions had been siphoned off over the past three years for personal use and other business ventures. Monus was discovered when he and Finn diverted $10 million of Phar Mor's money into the World Basketball League (WBA)—the league founded by Monus for shorter professional players. When the league suffered financial problems, Monus patched things up with Phar Mor money.

In August 1992, Phar Mor laid off employees, closed stores, and nervous suppliers waited as the company filed for bankruptcy protection. The 34th largest bankruptcy in the nation's history, Phar Mor reported 25,000 creditors. "By the time this case is over, there will be appearances by 1,000 or more lawyers…," said the judge. Finn turned state's evidence and was convicted and sent to prison. Monus—the man who had been Youngstown's savior—was tried on 126 counts of fraud and embezzlement in a trial that began May 31, 1994, in Cleveland. By June 23, 1994, the jury was deadlocked 11 to 1 on all counts. The FBI investigated the possibility of jury tampering and a new trial has been scheduled for 1995.

Physically challenged

Robber Bruce Williams gave new meaning to the term "physically challenged." Shot and paralyzed during an attempted robbery on May 3, 1977, Williams didn't let his handicap stop his criminal pursuits. Within a year, he was charged with five additional crimes, including robbery, theft, and kidnapping. When Cleveland police arrested the wheelchair-bound Williams, he complained about the law-enforcement system's inhumane treatment of handicapped people.

Fox in the henhouse

 From 1882 to 1885 Woodworth was terrorized by burglaries, arson, and murder committed at the hands of the Morgantown gang. The gang's leader was Asariah Paulin, more commonly known as the "Old Fox." Paulin, along with his seven sons and other relatives preyed on the countryside. Finally captured in Pennsylvania, he was returned to Youngstown for trial and, with other members of the gang, sentenced to a long term in the Ohio Penitentiary.

Lady firebug

Halloween night in Cincinnati in 1993 was cold, damp, and miserable. It was the kind of night that makes people want to curl up in front of a roaring fire with a good book. Twenty-nine-year old Debbie Cayze wanted a fire, too, but not in a fireplace. A wife and mother of three children, Debbie was a pathological firestarter. While taking her children trick-or-treating, Debbie took a break from the festivities to set an apartment building on fire. While attempting to start the blaze, things went wrong. The gasoline exploded, trapping and killing her. Police had been watching Cayze since 1990 and suspected her of starting hundreds of unexplained fires in Cincinnati and northern Kentucky. Sadly, her last fire wasn't a mystery—she left herself as a clue.

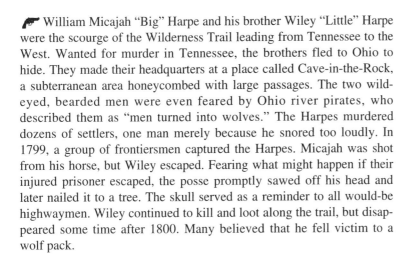 Swindler Cassie Chadwick posed as Andrew Carnegie's daughter. Chadwick was well versed in the swindler's art when she met future husband Dr. Leroy Chadwick in a low-class Cleveland whorehouse. She convinced him that she was there to teach etiquette. Unknown to Leroy, who married Cassie, née Elizabeth Bagley, his bride had spent three years in prison for blackmail and fraud.

Once established as Mrs. Leroy Chadwick, Cassie traveled to New York, where she "accidentally" bumped into a prominent Ohio lawyer named Dillon. After a friendly chat, she asked him to accompany her to her father's home. They pulled up in front of Andrew Carnegie's home and Cassie went inside to visit her "father." She returned with a $2-million promissory note in hand. She made Dillon swear to secrecy, then explained that she was Carnegie's illegitimate daughter. The note, she told him, was guilt money, but it was nothing compared to the $400 million she would inherit when Carnegie died.

Dillon returned to Cleveland and told everyone about the secret Chadwick fortune. Banks began loaning Cassie money indiscriminately at outrageous interest rates—over $1 million a year. They assumed they would be reimbursed when Cassie came into her father's millions.

The scheme began to unravel when a Boston bank became nervous and decided to call in a loan of $190,000. Chadwick couldn't pay and widespread panic ensued. The Citizens National Bank of Oberlin, which had loaned her $800,000, suffered a run on its deposits and went bankrupt overnight. As for Carnegie, he issued a statement, attesting that he did not know Mrs. Chadwick of Cleveland, and furthermore, that he had not signed a note in over 30 years. As for the trip to the mansion, Chadwick had conned her way into the house under the pretense of checking the references of a maid she was considering employing. The promissory note was a fake. Cassie was arrested in 1904 and sentenced to 10 years in prison. She died there three years later.

Cleveland's headache

 William Micajah "Big" Harpe and his brother Wiley "Little" Harpe were the scourge of the Wilderness Trail leading from Tennessee to the West. Wanted for murder in Tennessee, the brothers fled to Ohio to hide. They made their headquarters at a place called Cave-in-the-Rock, a subterranean area honeycombed with large passages. The two wild-eyed, bearded men were even feared by Ohio river pirates, who described them as "men turned into wolves." The Harpes murdered dozens of settlers, one man merely because he snored too loudly. In 1799, a group of frontiersmen captured the Harpes. Micajah was shot from his horse, but Wiley escaped. Fearing what might happen if their injured prisoner escaped, the posse promptly sawed off his head and later nailed it to a tree. The skull served as a reminder to all would-be highwaymen. Wiley continued to kill and loot along the trail, but disappeared some time after 1800. Many believed that he fell victim to a wolf pack.

Men turned to wolves

Public enemy

In the 1930s, bankrobber John Herbert Dillinger (right) was famous for his daring exploits. Within the space of 12 months, Dillinger robbed more banks and stole more money than Jesse James did over 16 years. Dillinger is remembered in Ohio for the 1933 robbery of the Citizens National Bank in Bluffton, his subsequent capture, and his escape from the Lima jail. After the bank robbery, Dayton police detectives received a tip and Dillinger was arrested at his girlfriend's apartment and sent to the Lima. Five of Dillinger's gang helped him escape on October 12, 1933. One gang member, Harry Pierpoint, shot and killed a sheriff. Dillinger continued his bank-robbing spree until 1934, when the FBI set a trap for him in Chicago. Instead, the FBI was duped into participating in an underworld scheme to help Dillinger escape permanently. On July 22, 1934, they shot and killed James Lawrence, a Dillinger look-alike, outside the Biograph Theater in Chicago. Dillinger had escaped—and to this day no conclusive evidence exists that he was ever apprehended.

He really was innocent

Accused of a rape he didn't commit, Brian Piszczek sat in prison for 1,731 days before being exonerated. The Cleveland handyman was found guilty when his victim pointed at him in a courtroom. He wasn't eligible for parole until 2001. In January 1993, Piszczek read a story in *USA Today* about Barry Scheck (of the O.J. Simpson legal team) and the Innocence Project at the Cardozo School of Law in New York. Scheck was an expert on DNA testing. Piszczek contacted Scheck, his mother borrowed the $5,000 for laboratory tests, and on July 6, 1994, DNA tests proved that Piszczek couldn't have been the rapist. He was released from prison—the first person in Cayahoga County proved innocent as a result of DNA testing.

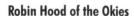

Robin Hood of the Okies

A folk hero in Oklahoma, Charles Arthur "Pretty Boy" Floyd began his bank-robbing career in northern Ohio alongside two other robbers—Tom Bradley and Jack Atkins. The trio knocked over several small banks near Akron, then ran into problems after robbing the bank in Sylvania on March 11, 1930. While trying to escape, they killed a policeman and ran their getaway car into a telephone pole. Arrested and tried, Bradley received the electric chair, Atkins was sentenced to life in prison, and Floyd got 15 years in the Ohio Penitentiary. On the way to prison, Floyd escaped and headed for Toledo. Once there, he teamed up with Bill Miller and the two robbed a series of banks in Michigan. Over the next four years, Floyd carried out a robbing and killing spree. He robbed so many banks in Oklahoma that the insurance rates doubled in one year. In October 1934, Floyd's bank-robbing career ended in Ohio where it began. Trying to escape a dragnet, Floyd ran across an Ohio field and was gunned down by FBI agents. He died on October 22, 1934, near East Liverpool.

MURDEROUS MADMEN

Hippie cultist

Notorious murderer Charles Manson was born in Cincinnati in 1934 to unwed Kathleen Maddox. He spent most of his life in reform schools or prisons. Following his release from the Federal Penitentiary on McNeil Island, Washington, in 1967, he organized a commune-like group of hippies at Spahn Ranch near Los Angeles. Manson was the self-appointed anti-Christ leader of the group—his followers often called him "Death" or the "Devil." On August 8 and 9, 1969, Manson and his cultists broke into the home of film director Roman Polanski and killed actress Sharon Tate, millionaire coffee heiress Abigail Folger, Voityck Frokowsy, Jay Sebring, and Steven Parent. The five victims were shot and stabbed to death. Two days later they repeated their pattern, killing Leno and Rosemary LaBianca. Authorities quickly arrested Manson along with his cult followers Susan Atkins, Patricia Krenwinkel, and Leslie Van Houten. All four were found guilty and sentenced to death in 1971. With the U.S. Supreme Court's decision to abolish the death penalty, they will remain in prison for life.

Cannibal monster

Although referred to as Milwaukee's "Cannibal Monster," Jeffrey Dahmer's first murder took place in Bath Township, Ohio, on June 28, 1978. Dahmer had recently graduated from high school. His victim, Stephen Hicks, was hitchhiking home after attending a concert at Chippewa Park when Dahmer picked him up and invited him in for a few beers. When Hicks said he had to leave, Dahmer, who was alone in the house at the time, snapped. He hit Hicks over the head with a barbell and strangled him, hiding the body under the house's crawlspace. He later pulverized the remains and spread them over his backyard. Following failure at college and a dishonorable discharge from the army, Dahmer moved to Milwaukee to live with his grandmother. There his savageries worsened. By the time he was arrested in July 1991, he had murdered 17 people. Dahmer was beaten to death in prison on November 28, 1994, at Portage, Wisconsin.

Guilty or not?

In 1954, neurosurgeon Dr. Samuel Sheppard of Cleveland was found guilty of murdering his wife Marilyn. The night of the slaying, the couple gave a dinner party. Sheppard fell asleep on the couch before the party was over. During the middle of the night—according to Sheppard—he was awakened by his wife's screams and ran upstairs. He was immediately knocked unconscious by an unknown assailant. When he came to, he found his wife's battered body. Hearing the intruder downstairs he gave chase and was again knocked unconscious. Investigators discovered that Sheppard was having an affair and a mark on his wife's pillow suggested one of Sheppard's surgical instruments. Despite his insistence that he was innocent, Sheppard was found guilty of second-degree murder and sentenced to life imprisonment. While in prison he became the first human to be inoculated with live cancer cells. In 1964, attorney F. Lee Bailey won an appeal for Sheppard, claiming that the trial was flawed by a "carnival atmosphere, and prejudicial publicity." In 1966 a retrial found Sheppard not guilty. He died in Columbus on April 6, 1970.

Foul fanatic

When the Lundgren family moved to Kirtland in 1984 their neighbors welcomed them. Four years later, they felt differently. Jeffrey Lundgren (on right below) was a member and lay minister of the Reorganized Church of Jesus Christ of Latter-day Saints. Over time his religious views began to disturb church officials. Jeffrey began telling fellow members that only he could interpret holy scriptures. In 1987, he and his wife Alice were fired as tour guides at the Kirtland Temple for stealing. In January 1988, he and two dozen followers left the congregation and moved to a farm. As the group's leader, Lundgren ruled with a dictatorial hand. Men received weapons training, disobedient children were beaten, and women were told they could gain their salvation only through sexual rituals. Lundgren promised the group that he would lead them to God, but he also preached that a blood sacrifice must occur before they could go to the promised land.

Dennis and Cheryl Avery and their three daughters joined Lundgren in Kirtland in 1987. The Averys' daughters were withdrawn from school with no request to forward their transcripts. During one night, neighbors were awakened by the sound of a chain saw coming from the Lundgrens' barn. Two days later, Lundgren and his followers had vanished. On January 4, 1989, police found the bodies of the Avery family buried in the barn. After a nationwide manhunt located Lundgren, he was returned to Cuyahoga County where he was tried, convicted, and sentenced to die in the electric chair.

Attorney for the damned

Known as the "Great Defender," Kinsman-native Clarence Darrow represented Tennessee teacher John Scopes who was tried for teaching evolution. Although Darrow lost the famous "monkey trial" in 1925, he won in the court of public opinion. Often associated with unpopular causes, he was a major force in forming the conscience of his time. An opponent of capital punishment, he was extremely successful in defending accused murderers because he perfected the art of jury selection. "Get the right men in the box and the rest is window dressing," he once said. Germans and Swedes made terrible jurists—Germans were too law-and-order oriented and Swedes too stubborn. The best jurists, Darrow discovered, were Irish and Jews because they were very emotional and easily "moved to sympathy." He must have been right. Forty-nine accused murderers he defended were acquitted. Only one of Darrow's clients was ever executed—and that was his first. In 1924, Darrow took on one of his most famous cases when he defended Nathan Leopold and Richard Loeb, sons of prominent Chicago businessmen. Leopold and Loeb killed a 14- year-old boy just because they wanted to commit the "perfect murder." Darrow took up their defense to express his opinions about capital punishment. The judge sentenced the boys to life imprisonment.

DEADLY DISASTERS

Bridge collapses

In Ashtabula on December 29, 1876, the west-bound Pacific Express was running behind schedule due to heavy snowfall. On the outskirts of the city the 11-car, 2-engine train slowly edged onto the bridge crossing the Ashtabula River. Just as the first engine reached the opposite shore, the bridge collapsed. The remaining engine and all 11 cars fell into the ravine and burst into flames. Rescuers were hampered by the heavy snowfall. Eighty-four passengers died and 160 were injured.

Designed for disaster

The fire at Cleveland's Collingwood Elementary School on March 8, 1908, was the most devastating school fire in Ohio's history. Built in 1902, the 2-1/2-story wooden structure was an accident waiting to happen. It had narrow interior corridors and only one fire escape. Approximately 300 children attended classes in the building, with the youngest students taught in the attic rooms. On March 8, a fire started in the basement and quickly spread to the first floor. During fire drills the children had been taught to use this main exit as their escape route but fire and smoke blocked that route. Confusion ensued as scores of children were trampled by their classmates or collapsed from smoke inhalation. The Collingwood Volunteer Fire Company was unable to check the blaze and their ladders didn't even reach the upper floors. Of the 325 people in the school, only 80 escaped without injury. The dead numbered 175. Some of the parents blamed the fire on the school's janitor, Fred Herter, sighting a faulty furnace. One bereaved parent tried to kill him. Herter lost three of his own children in the blaze and was seriously injured rescuing others.

Poisonous fumes

On May 15, 1929, Cleveland's Crile Clinic was a busy facility, treating over 300 patients. On the morning of May 15, an explosion in a basement storage locker set fire to a supply of X-ray films. The burning films released poisonous gas that spread though the ventilation system, killing patients in their beds. The fire was so intense that the windows burst and the poisonous fumes escaped outside. Firefighters and rescuers were overcome by the noxious gases as well. A total of 125 people died as a result of the gas, including some rescuers who succumbed later.

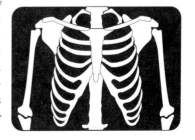

Fiery fortress

The Ohio Penitentiary in downtown Columbus was one of the largest and most overcrowded prisons in the United States when a fire broke out on April 21, 1930. Originally designed to hold 1,500 men, the prison held 4,300. New construction had been started to ease the overcrowding, and that's where the flames erupted. The fire spread quickly from the construction scaffolding to the upper interior tiers of the building. Confused guards refused to open the cell doors. The warden, who was more worried about a possible jailbreak than he was about the fire, called the National Guard and not the Fire Department. By the time the guards decided to open the prisoners' cells the heat had warped the locks and their keys wouldn't work. In the end, 320 prisoners died in the fire, roasted in their cells. Only one prisoner escaped. In the confusion, he changed into civilian clothes and walked away. Warden Preston Thomas was criticized for his response, but no action was ever taken.

Greatest mining tragedy

The Millfield Mine disaster was the greatest tragedy in Ohio mining history. On November 5, 1930, a terrific blast and wall of flame in mine number 6 of the Sunday Creek Coal Company caused 82 miners to suffocate from carbon monoxide gas. Among the victims were the president of the company and eight officials inspecting the mine. The explosion occurred at noon, but it was nighttime before the men were reached. During the night, ambulance sirens constantly shrieked down the valley and the mine whistle wailed unceasingly. Nearly every miner's home in Millfield kept vigil that night for a missing family member.

Burned in Lake Erie

The paddle wheeler *G. P. Griffith* burned in Lake Erie offshore from Mentor on June 17, 1850. Two hundred and eighty six lives were lost.

High winds brought disaster

On September 3, 1925, the American-built dirigible *Shenandoah* (below), under the command of Naval Lt. Commander Zachary Lansdowne flew into an intense electrical storm over Marietta. One strong gust overturned the ship, snapped the interior girders, and ripped open the underside of the gas bag. Six crew members fell to their death. Then the control gondola broke loose, killing Lansdowne and seven other officers. The ship then split into three pieces. The nose section floated over Ohio for more than an hour. The midsection collapsed into a meadow. The tail section with the remaining 18 crew members floated gently down into a forested area near Sharon. Farmers rescued the men from the trees.

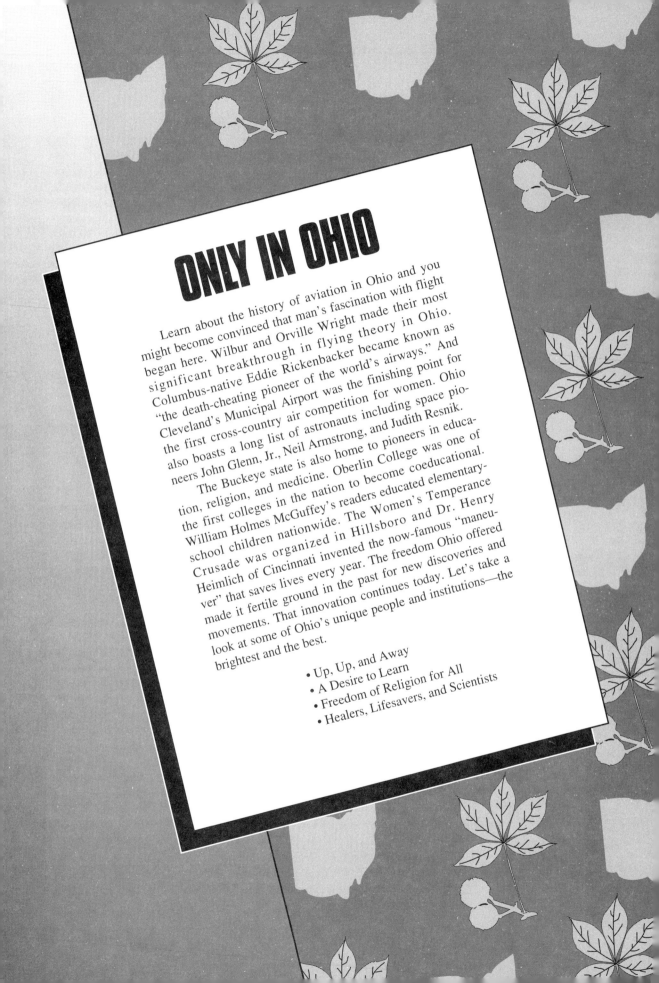

ONLY IN OHIO

Learn about the history of aviation in Ohio and you might become convinced that man's fascination with flight began here. Wilbur and Orville Wright made their most significant breakthrough in flying theory in Ohio. Columbus-native Eddie Rickenbacker became known as "the death-cheating pioneer of the world's airways." And Cleveland's Municipal Airport was the finishing point for the first cross-country air competition for women. Ohio also boasts a long list of astronauts including space pioneers John Glenn, Jr., Neil Armstrong, and Judith Resnik.

The Buckeye state is also home to pioneers in education, religion, and medicine. Oberlin College was one of the first colleges in the nation to become coeducational. William Holmes McGuffey's readers educated elementary-school children nationwide. The Women's Temperance Crusade was organized in Hillsboro and Dr. Henry Heimlich of Cincinnati invented the now-famous "maneuver" that saves lives every year. The freedom Ohio offered made it fertile ground in the past for new discoveries and movements. That innovation continues today. Let's take a look at some of Ohio's unique people and institutions—the brightest and the best.

- Up, Up, and Away
- A Desire to Learn
- Freedom of Religion for All
- Healers, Lifesavers, and Scientists

UP, UP, AND AWAY

First flyers ❖ Famous for their first flight at Kitty Hawk, North Carolina, on December 17, 1903, aviators Wilbur and Orville Wright made Dayton their home base. At the Wright Cycle Company, founded in 1892 in Dayton's West End, the brothers sold, repaired, and manufactured bicycles and earned enough money to pursue their real interest—aviation.

Fascinated by flight, the Wrights first tested their theories with large kites. They soon found that they needed a stronger, more constant wind than Dayton could provide. They learned that the Outer Banks of North Carolina offered strong winds and a place for soft landings. Beginning in 1900, the brothers began making annual trips to Kitty Hawk. In November and December 1901, back in Dayton, Wilbur and Orville made their most significant breakthroughs in flying theory.

Orville Wright

Convinced that their lift and drag tables were not correct, they began a series of experiments that resulted in more accurate tables. They also worked out the problems of stability and control that had made flying impossible until then.

On December 17, 1903, the brothers made four flights at Kitty Hawk. The longest was 59 seconds and went over 850 feet. In 1909 the federal government purchased a Wright Flyer and the first *Air Force 1* went into service. The Wrights also negotiated sales with France, England, Spain, Italy, and Germany, and Wilbur established the world's first flight school at Pau, France. In November 1910 the brothers incorporated the Wright Company. Although the company was very successful, Wilbur and Orville were drawn into lawsuits to protect their patent rights. Still fighting for protection of their patent, Wilbur died of typhoid fever in 1912. Many attributed his early death to the stress of prolonged litigation. Orville continued to run the business, inventing the automatic stabilizer and the hydroplane. In 1915, however, he sold the business to a group of financiers. A millionaire, he was free to study and continue research activities. Neither brother ever married.

Wilbur Wright

On display ❖ You can see the Wrights' first "practical" airplane at Dayton's Carillon Historic Park. If you want to know more about the history of aviation, travel to Wright-Patterson Air Force Base, northwest of Dayton, and visit the world's largest and oldest aviation museum, the United States Air Force Museum. More than 200 planes and missiles and over 1,000 artifacts trace the history of flight.

The death-defying ace

Columbus-born Edward Vernon Rickenbacker, dubbed America's "Ace of Aces," was the most decorated pilot of World War I and one of America's most colorful heroes. Rickenbacker once said, "All my life, engines have spoken to me." War-hero, statesman, self-made man, business tycoon, pioneer in automobiles and aviation, Captain Eddie was one of the luckiest men in the world. He cheated death 135 times, and died at the ripe old age of 82.

During World War I, Rickenbacker earned the rank of captain and his distinction as "Ace of Aces," tallying 26 air victories against the Germans. After the war, Rickenbacker designed and manufactured the first passenger car with four-wheel brakes—the Rickenbacker. But his venture ended in bankruptcy in 1927. After the failure of his company, Rickenbacker purchased the Indianapolis Speedway and later became head of Eastern Air Lines in 1929. On February 26, 1941, Eastern Flight 21 crashed in a wooded area south of Atlanta, with Rickenbacker on board. Upon reaching the hospital, Rickenbacker was mistaken for dead. As a priest administered the last rites, he saw signs of life and asked Rickenbacker if he was Catholic. "Hell, no! I'm a Protestant like everyone else around here," Rickenbacker replied.

In September 1942 during World War II, Secretary of War Henry Stimson asked Rickenbacker if he would go overseas to look into the condition of American airmen. While traveling from Honolulu to Port Moresby, Rickenbacker's military transport crashed into the Pacific Ocean. He and seven other crew members spent 23 days adrift on a raft and were presumed dead, but they were found alive. In his later years Rickenbacker no longer viewed his many escapes from death as luck, but as divine intervention because he had missions to perform. On July 23, 1973, his earthly mission ended in Zurich, Switzerland.

Women's competition

❖ A major opening event of the National Air Races of 1929—the Women's Air Derby—was the first cross-country competition for women. The race began in California on Sunday, August 18, and ended at the Cleveland Municipal Airport on Monday, August 26. If there were any doubts about the capabilities of women pilots, the Women's Air Derby disproved them all. The race—which covered over 2,800 miles—attracted most of the leading international female aviators of the 1930s. Navigation was primitive. Each pilot carried magnetic compasses, Rand McNally road maps, and found their way by dead reckoning. Of the 20 fliers who started the race, 15 finished in Cleveland. Louise Thaden, who at age 23 held the women's international speed, endurance, and altitude records, finished first. Gladys O'Donnell came in second and Amelia Earhart third. Marvel Crosson, a commercial flier from Alaska, was the only fatality.

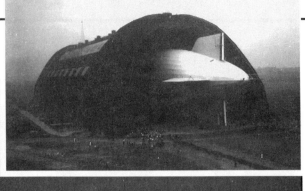

Is it bigger than the Denver airport?

Built in 1929, the Goodyear-Zeppelin Airship Factory and Dock (right) in Akron is the world's largest building without interior support. With nearly 8-1/2 acres under its roof, the airdock is so large that some say "clouds form and rain falls under its cavernous roof." Because airships are extremely vulnerable to wind gusts and crosscurrents, the airdock was oriented and shaped to minimize these problems. Unlike conventional airplane hangars, the building is curved on all sides. Its most unusual features are its "orange peel" doors and rolling arches. The doors open flush with the sides of the building and the three center arches are fixed in position, while the remaining support arches are on rollers to permit the building to expand and contract.

After the zeppelin factory folded, sky cars for Chicago's Century of Progress and a prototype rail zeppelin were built here. During World War II, the airdock became a defense plant and in the 1950s Goodyear built blimps for the Navy. In the 1960s Goodyear Aircraft became Goodyear Aerospace and the airdock became part of the Space Age. In 1986, Goodyear hosted the United Way campaign kick-off in the airdock, the first time in over 50 years that the building had been open to the public. In 1987, Loral Corporation bought Goodyear Aerospace and renamed it Loral Defense Systems-Akron. Once part of a grand plan to make Akron an international "port of call for the world's business," the airdock is now a monument to the history of airships.

Ohio space pioneers

❖ John Herschel Glenn, Jr., became the first American to orbit Earth when his Mercury capsule *Friendship 7* circled the globe three times on February 20, 1962. Born in Cambridge on July 18, 1921, Glenn was a Marine fighter pilot during World War II and became a test pilot during the Korean conflict. In 1957 he made the first supersonic transcontinental flight. Selected for the space program in 1956, he was the oldest astronaut chosen at the time. Retiring from the space program in 1964, he was elected to the United States Senate for the first time in 1974, an office he still holds. He ran unsuccessfully for the Democratic presidential nomination in 1984.

Wapakoneta-native Neil A. Armstrong (left), a licensed pilot by age 16, was a test pilot for supersonic fighters and the X-15 rocket plane after WWII. Armstrong was chosen as part of the second group of astronauts in 1962. As commander of *Gemini 8* on March 16, 1966, he and David R. Scott docked with an unmanned rocket—the first manual docking in space. On July 16, 1969, at 10:56 P.M. EST, he became the first person to walk on the moon during the *Apollo 11* mission. He left the space program in 1971 and taught engineering until 1979 at the University of Cincinnati. Today he is employed by CTA, Inc., in Charlottesville, Virginia. If you want to relive Armstrong's moon walk, visit the Neil Armstrong Air & Space Museum in Wapakoneta where the historic event is portrayed in detail.

***Challenger* fatality**

❖ Born in Akron in 1949, scientist and electrical engineer Judith Resnik joined the space program in 1978—the first Jewish woman and the second American woman in space. On January 28, 1986, Resnik was killed in the *Challenger* explosion on her second space mission.

The sky's the limit

On June 5, 1921, Cincinnati-born aviatrix Laura Bromwell was killed when she lost control and crashed in a single-seat plane near Garden City, Long Island. Some think her seat strap may have been too loose and she lost control as she was flying the plane in an upside-down loop. Bromwell was one of the best female stunt aviators in the United States when she died at the age of 23. Shortly before her death she set two flying records—one for flying the loop 199 times, and another for flying at 135 miles per hour.

Equipment firsts

❖ Besides sending astronauts into space, Ohioans have also provided some necessary space equipment. BFGoodrich engineer Russell Colley designed NASA's first space suits in the early 1960s at Akron. Peter Van Schaik—who got the idea for the Astronaut Maneuvering Unit from the Buck Rogers comic strip—invented the life support and propulsion backpack used during the space walks of the *Gemini* program. And the Helix antenna—now attached to all communications satellites NASA sends into space—was developed by Columbus engineer John Kraus in 1946.

Studying ice

❖ The NASA Lewis Research Center in Cleveland is the only NASA facility outside the South. It houses the biggest refrigerated wind tunnel in the nation where scientists can study the effects of ice in aviation.

Ohio's other astronauts

- James A. Lovell, Jr., flew on *Gemini 7* in December 1965, *Gemini 12* in November 1966, *Apollo 8* in December 1968, and *Apollo 13* in April 1970. Lovell is now president of Lovell Communications in Chicago.
- Charles A. Bassett II became an astronaut in 1963. He never flew any missions and was killed in a T-38 jet crash in 1966.
- Donn F. Eisele was chosen for the space program in 1963. His first and only mission was on the first manned *Apollo* mission—*Apollo 7*. He died in Tokyo, Japan, in 1987 of a heart attack.
- Robert F. Overmeyer became an astronaut in 1969. He flew on two shuttle missions, one in November 1982, and one in April 1985.
- Cleveland-native Kenneth D. Cameron joined the astronaut team in 1984 and flew on one mission as pilot in April 1991.
- G. David Low was a mission specialist twice—in January 1990, and in August 1991.
- Terence "Tom" Henricks became an astronaut in 1985. He piloted two space missions in 1991 and 1993. He was commander of the space shuttle *Discovery* that left Earth on July 13, 1995. Four of *Discovery*'s five-person crew hailed from Ohio. Cleveland's Donald Thomas, Ph.D., who flew as a mission specialist in July 1994, Troy's mission specialist Nancy Currie, whose first space flight was in June 1993, and Cleveland's mission specialist Mary Ellen Weber rounded out *Discovery*'s predominantly Buckeye crew.
- Astronaut Gregory J. Harbaugh lives in Willoughby. Selected for the space program in 1987, Harbaugh served as a mission specialist in April 1991.
- In 1990, Ronald M. Sega and Carl E. Walz joined the ranks of the astronaut corps. As of April 1995, they were serving as mission specialists and hope to take part in future flights. Sega and Walz were born in Cleveland.

Whirlybirds ❖ The national headquarters for the Vietnam Helicopter Pilots Association, with 6,000 members worldwide, is headquartered in Cincinnati's Federated Building.

A DESIRE TO LEARN

School bells ❖ In 1773, Ohio's first school opened in Schoenbrunn, but it was strictly for Native Americans. Five years later the first permanent white settlers established a school for whites at Belpre. Other education firsts include:

- First free public school system established in Cincinnati in 1825
- First kindergarten in the country began at Columbus in 1838 and the first junior high school—Indianola Junior High School—opened its doors on September 7, 1909.

Coonskin library

Young Thomas Ewing—Ohio University's first graduate and later a U.S. senator—contributed "all [his] hoarded wealth" of ten raccoonskins toward the Athens County "Coonskin Library." In 1804 Samuel Brown and Ephraim Cutler sold a wagonload of furs in Boston for $73.50 and returned with 51 books. Among the volumes—housed in Cutler's home two miles north of Amesville—were *Paradise Lost*, Gibbon's *Decline and Fall*, histories of Persia, Greece, and England, Irving's *Columbus*, Scotts' *Napoleon*, and Locke's *Essays*. Subscribers were fined if they got fingerprints on pages of the books. Incorporated as the Western Library Association in 1810, the library served patrons for 57 years. Some of the original books from the Coonskin Library— the first general library west of the Allegheny Mountains—can be found today at the Ohio Historical Society in Columbus.

The librarian's librarian

The non-profit Online Computer Library Center (OCLC), founded in 1967 by Federick Kilgour at OSU, is making the world's information available to libraries—and employing about 1,000 people in its Dublin headquarters. OCLC began the library computer revolution in 1971, when it devised a system that enabled libraries to catalog books and then order customized catalog cards. As of 1995, the OnLine Union Catalog holds 32 million bibliographic records, that can be accessed by 20,000 libraries in 61 countries. Touted as the largest service of its kind in the nation, OCLC also distributes several medical and technical journals online. *Applied Physics Letters*, a weekly publication, is the first magazine available through the World Wide Web. Online magazines will help OCLC meet its goal of providing information at a low cost—there are no paper, printing, or mailing costs involved.

A noble beginning

In 1824 Philander Chase, the first Episcopal bishop of Ohio, collected funds from English noblemen to found a school known as the Theological Seminary of the Protestant Episcopal Church. Lord Gambier, a participant in the peace negotiations with America after the War of 1812, reluctantly gave up his tract of land in Ohio, but consented to help establish the school. The town was named for him and the college for his friend, Lord Kenyon. Rutherford B. Hayes, 19th president of the United States, was among the first graduates of Ohio's oldest private college, Kenyon College.

Form follows function

❖ Higher education had its start soon after Ohio became a state. Ohio University in Athens received its charter in 1804. Planning for the school started several years earlier when the Ohio Company of Associates purchased the Muskingum Valley lands and set aside two townships for the establishment of a university. In 1800 General Rufus Putnam and several other persons from Marietta came to the valley to select a site for the university and to survey a town. That same year the territorial legislature approved the Putnam survey and named the village, comprising six cabins, Athens. Reverend Manasseh Cutler, agent for the Ohio Company, modeled the university's charter after Yale University's. Ohio University first opened as an academy in 1809 with three students and a small two-room building. It received the status of college in 1822 and became coed in 1869. Many of the elms on the campus were planted as a memorial to William Holmes McGuffey, president of the university from 1839 to 1843.

Head, heart, hands, health
School superintendent Albert Graham founded the 4-H Clubs of America in 1902 in Springfield. He wanted his students to have more hands-on experience.

Teaching America to read

❖ William Holmes McGuffey educated several generations of Americans with his popular series of six elementary-school readers known as "McGuffeys." The most successful first readers ever produced in the United States, *McGuffey's Eclectic Readers*, also imparted moral lessons and introduced children to good literature. Over 120 million copies were sold. "Only the Bible and *Webster's Dictionary* are believed to have been so widely influential as his little readers" were to American children.

Recent research suggests McGuffey was born in Ohio near Youngstown. Even as a young student, McGuffey memorized whole books of the Bible. In 1836, he became president of Cincinnati College. During his tenure, he helped organize Ohio's College for Teachers and published his first and second *Eclectic Readers* and successfully lobbied for legislation that organized the state's present-day public school system. In 1839, McGuffey was appointed president of Ohio University, where he stayed until 1843. He accepted a position at the University of Virginia where he taught until a few weeks before his death in 1873.

The Ohio State University

❖ The legislature established Ohio Agricultural and Mechanical College at Columbus in 1870. Seventeen students began classes in 1873. The institution changed its name to Ohio State University in 1878. Today, the Columbus campus—with over 50,000 students enrolled—is the largest in the nation. The value of the university's 1,600 acres, equipment, and 342 buildings approaches $3.25 billion. It is the only university in the nation where you can get a degree in geodetic science (science that deals with the size and shape of Earth) and welding engineering. Three campus buildings are listed on the National Register of Historic Places—Orton Hall, Ohio Stadium, and Enarson Hall. Orton Hall, completed in 1893, was built with 30 kinds of Ohio stone. The list of famous people who have attended OSU includes such luminaries as Leonard Downie, Jr., executive editor of the *Washington Post*; golfer Jack Nicklaus; basketball coach Bob Knight; track star Jesse Owens; actor/comedian Richard Lewis; president of LA Gear Mark Goldston; and Frank Stanton, president emeritus of CBS.

A research center

❖ Ohio State is known throughout the country for medical education—its program is ranked number two in the country by *U.S. News World & Report*. The Ohio State University medical complex, the first privately financed academic building on a state university campus, opened in December 1994. Funds were raised entirely by the faculty and by private contributors. Also unique is the fact that the $11.6-million building will be used exclusively for new and expanded programs rather than for existing programs. The building represents a shift in the college's focus—from treating patients to research. OSU's medical research budget in 1994 was approximately $52 million.

First coeds

Oberlin College became one of the first coeducational colleges in the United States in 1837 when four young women entered the four-year course leading to a bachelor of arts degree. In 1841, three female students became the first women in the United States to earn degrees on the same basis as men. Such an accomplishment, however, was not without its price. The young women were required to clean the rooms of the men students and wash and mend the young men's clothes. They were paid 2-3/4 cents an hour for their services. In addition, coeds were required to rise at 5:00 A.M., spend 30 minutes in prayer, and put their rooms in order before 8:00 A.M. The women students studied scientific courses as well as classical subjects, but in 1840 when the school acquired a telescope the girls' principal "was a bit hesitant about allowing lady students to stay up after hours to look at the heavenly bodies." In July 1994, Nancy Schrom Dye became Oberlin College's first female president.

❖ In 1863, Daniel A Payne, a free black from Charleston, South Carolina, became the first African-American university president in the United States when he was named head of Wilberforce University. Under the direction of the Methodist Episcopal Church, the university was opened in 1856 in Wilberforce, admitting both white and African-American students. In 1863 the institution was purchased by the African Methodist Episcopal Church and Payne was named president. The town of Wilberforce, the university's namesake, was named after William Wilberforce, an English reformer who fought the slave trade.

The ink is black, the page is white

❖ Antioch College, founded in 1853 at Yellow Springs, has earned national recognition for its practical but nontraditional education plan.

A plan for practical education

Antioch first came into the spotlight when Horace Mann, its president from 1853 to 1859, attempted to establish a nonsectarian school. In 1920, Arthur E. Morgan was named president of the college and the school revised its curricula to use the cooperative plan. Under this method, students spend part of their time in regular classwork and the remainder of the time working in a business or industry related to their studies. There are several advantages to this program. Two students fill one position; one works while the other studies. Students earn money for their tuition and expenses and gain valuable work experience. Finally, the employer benefits because two students are assigned to the same job for one year.

Did you know?
- Buchtel College, founded in 1870, became the University of Akron. It is the only university in the country that has a course in rubber chemistry.
- The first institution of higher learning in Cleveland—Case School of Applied Science—opened in 1880 through a gift from Leonard Case, Jr. In 1947 it became Case Institute of Technology. Western Reserve College was founded by Congregationalists in 1826 in Hudson. Renamed Western Reserve University in 1882, it moved to University Circle—a 500-acre site in Cleveland that houses more than 40 educational, medical, cultural, and social service organizations today. In 1967, the two schools joined to become Case Western Reserve University.

Soldier scholars

In 1943, 18 months after the start of World War II, 10 Ohio colleges—Ohio State University, University of Akron, Wilberforce University, Muskingum College, Kenyon College, Antioch College, Heidelberg College, University of Cincinnati, University of Dayton, and Western Reserve University—overflowed with soldiers enrolled in the Army Specialized Training Program (ASTP). Announced on December 17, 1942, the training program was supposed to provide a pool of college-trained officer candidates for the war. Just as the program reached its peak in late 1943, the Army decided to cut back. In February 1944, the number of trainees was cut 50 percent and instead of receiving officers' commissions, many ended up as privates. Despite its unfortunate conclusion, the ASTP was beneficial to higher education. Many young men who couldn't have gone to college without the program were given an opportunity to do so. The fact that so many Americans from varying backgrounds succeeded at the college level helped democratize American college education and laid the groundwork for the passage of the G.I. bill.

Get her a chair, not a stool

A 1993 *Cosmopolitan* article featured the University of Cincinnati as one of the "worst" places for women to work simply because one employee wrote: "I was assigned to a new office space—an unused restroom. I spent seven months typing while seated on the commode … [Then] I received an 'unsatisfactory' evaluation for keeping an untidy work area."

FREEDOM OF RELIGION FOR ALL

Spiritual moves

❖ In the early 1800s a group of new religious sects appeared in Ohio—the New Lights, Holy Rollers, Jerkers, Laughers, and Dancers. Perhaps the most turbulent was the New Lights, which first appeared in the winter of 1801 in Springdale at a great revival meeting. The sect had more than 3,000 followers in Kentucky and Ohio. The most fervid members experienced five distinct "hysterical" manifestations:

• falling, in which the subject collapsed in a state of suspended animation sometimes lasting for a day;
• rolling, in which the person, after being cast down rolled over and over rapidly;
• jerking, in which the member would experience powerful twitching of the muscles, usually of the neck and arms, sometimes the entire body;
• barking, in which the affected one barked like a dog and often moved about on all fours; and,
• whirling, in which the person spun like a top.

The disturbances usually passed away after a time, with the exception of jerking, which often lasted for years.

"God" moved to Philadelphia

Joseph C. Dylks—the "Leatherwood God"—appeared in Salesville in 1828 near the banks of Leatherwood Creek. Shortly thereafter in church one morning he announced he was God. Some of his listeners regarded him with equanimity, others believed him. In no time at all a new religious sect was started and, for a time, the group grew. However, when Dylks failed to perform a well-advertised miracle— constructing a seamless garment—he and his disciples conveniently disappeared. A few years later some of the converts returned to Salesville and reported that "God" had disappeared "somewhere in Philadelphia." William Dean Howells later told the story, with some embellishments, in his novel *The Leatherwood God*.

Wandering pilgrims

❖ Early in the winter of 1816-1817, a begging religious group called the Wandering Pilgrims came from somewhere in the east and stopped near Plain City. The group consisted of about 40 men, women, and children, each wearing a piece of canvas resembling sackcloth. They didn't wash their clothing or their bodies and didn't use eating utensils. What became of these curious people is not known. Local accounts state that they later established themselves along the Little Miami River, where their prophet amazed onlookers by walking on water. A skeptic discovered a plank walk just below the surface of the water and surreptitiously removed one of the planks. One night the prophet started to walk on the waters, sank out of sight, and was never seen again.

Dampened spirits

The Women's Temperance Crusade was formed in Hillsboro in December 1873 when Dr. Dio Lewis, a nationally known temperance lecturer, talked to the community's women about the evils of liquor. Many of them had husbands who drank too much, and the good doctor's comments affected them deeply. Before leaving the meeting the 70 women organized the Women's Temperance Crusade and put Mrs. Eliza Jane Thompson—daughter of former Ohio governor Allen Trimble—in charge. Early on December 24, the women met at the local Presbyterian church, ready to put their beliefs to work. Hillsboro's pastors addressed the group about the righteousness of their purpose and left the women in prayer. Guidance from above came, as a double column of women filed out of the church and down the street where they entered a saloon. The women sang a hymn, offered a prayer, and then asked the barkeeper to close his establishment. They continued their "march" until all of Hillsboro's 13 saloons, its drugstore dispensaries, and its hotel bars were visited. All of them closed or left town except one druggist. He continued to sell liquor by prescription so the female crusaders erected a canvas and frame tabernacle in front of his store where they sang and prayed fervently. The druggist sued them for trespassing and the court awarded the plaintiff $5 in damages. For a number of years the drugstore was the only oasis in Hillsboro's desert of prohibition. When repeal of the Prohibition Act came in 1933, an Ohio state liquor store was placed in the former quarters of Mr. Dunn's drugstore.

Communal corporation

❖ The Zoar Village State Memorial (10 restored and reconstructed buildings) preserves the village founded in 1817 by a religious group from southern Germany. They named their town after the Biblical city to which Lot fled after leaving Sodom. In 1819 the group formed a communal corporation and formally incorporated in 1832 as the Separatist Society of Zoar. By 1874 the Society had 300 members, owned 7,000 acres of land, and possessed property valued at more than $1 million. In addition, the Society operated numerous businesses, employed about 50 nonmembers, and rented some of its land. Despite its prosperity, the Society was disbanded in 1898 when younger members grew restive, demanding personal freedom and ownership of property. Today, all that remains of the Society is the Memorial at Zoar. Number One House, the residence of Zoarist leader Joseph Bimeler, is restored, as is Zoar Garden—a 2-1/2-acre garden patterned after the Bible's description of New Jerusalem—located in the center of the village. Zoar is also home to 177 permanent residents who own homes and shops.

Village agnostic

The grave of Chester Bedell in North Benton is marked by a life-size bronze male figure crushing a scroll entitled "Superstition." The statue holds high another scroll inscribed "Universal Mental Liberty." Since his death in 1908, fantastic accounts about Bedell's grave site have circulated. Bedell first gained local notoriety as the village agnostic, harboring a fierce hatred of ignorance and superstition. On his deathbed, so the story goes, he challenged God to prove His existence by placing snakes in his grave. According to the story, when Bedell was being buried the snakes were so thick they enmeshed the tools of the grave diggers. Accounts of snakes crawling in and out of the grave persisted for years. On the strength of those stories, visitors came from all over to see the grave. It was not uncommon for several hundred people to visit the site on Sundays.

Following simple ways

They travel in black buggies, take no "thought for the morrow," and don't like to "make talk" with outsiders. North-Central Ohio's Amish communities—the largest Amish population in the Ohio—are a step back to a simpler time. Concentrated in Wayne, Holmes, Coshocton, and Tuscarawas counties, the Amish don't use any modern equipment or motorized vehicles, don't go to court to settle disputes, and don't attend movies or athletic contests. And they don't buy insurance because they care for each other's needs. The sect broke away from the Mennonites in

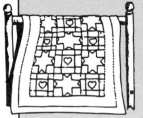

1609, followed Jacob Ammann (or Amen), and moved to Pennsylvania. In 1807, a group came down the Ohio River, looking for a less crowded place to settle. Arriving in Tuscarawas County, the first group welcomed an even larger Amish migration after the War of 1812. Although the Amish deny themselves worldly pleasures and affectations, visitors find it extremely pleasurable to eat their homemade bakery goods, ice cream, granola, butter, and cheese. The estimated Amish population in Ohio is 35,000.

The pope's pulpit

The Reverend Edward Fenwick was sent to Cincinnati in 1817 as the first Catholic priest assigned to an Ohio parish. City ordinances did not permit the erection of a Catholic church within the city limits (so much for religious freedom for all), so Fenwick built the church just outside the city boundaries. When the Cincinnati diocese was established on June 19, 1821, Father Fenwick was made a bishop. In the years before the Civil War the church fought openly against slavery and provided active support of the Underground Railroad. The church in Ohio also helped form the Prohibition Party in 1869, the Women's Crusade in 1873, and the Anti-Saloon League in 1893.

❖ Many of the state's colleges started as church-supported institutions.

• Otterbein College was founded in 1847 by the United Brethren Church.
• Hebrew Union College—the first Jewish college to train men for the rabbinate—was established in 1875.
• The only pontifical seminary outside Italy, Pontifical College Josephinum in Columbus, trains students for the Roman Catholic priesthood.

Religious leaders
• Catholic religious leader Cardinal John Krol was born in Cleveland on October 26, 1910. Cardinal Krol served as Archbishop of Philadelphia from 1961 to 1988 and was influential in the election of Pope John Paul II.
• In 1972 religious leader Sally Jane Priesand became the first ordained female rabbi. The author of *Judaism and the New Woman*, published in 1975, Priesand was born in Cleveland on June 27, 1946.
• Clergyman Victor Paul Wierwille was founder and director of the religious group The Way from 1942 to 1982. Wierwille was born in New Knoxville and died on May 2, 1985.

❖ Born May 31, 1898, in Bowersville, Norman Vincent Peale was a religious leader who developed a blend of psychotherapy and religion. In 1951, he helped found the American Foundation of Religion and Psychiatry and spread his message through his radio and television programs. Peale also wrote numerous self-help inspirational books, the most famous of which is *The Power of Positive Thinking*. The book was on the *New York Times* best-seller list for three years and was translated into 33 languages. Peale retired from the pulpit in 1985 and died on December 24, 1993.

HEALERS, LIFESAVERS, AND SCIENTISTS

❖ In 1826 Dr. John Harris established a school for teaching dentistry in Bainbridge. Harris's school was regarded as the "cradle of American dentistry." Chapin A. Harris, a graduate of the school, founded one of the first dental colleges in the world in 1840 at Baltimore and was editor of the first issue of the *American Journal of Dental Science*. James Taylor, also a graduate of Harris's school, founded the Ohio College of Dental Surgery at Cincinnati in 1845. Other notable graduates of the school included Edward P. Church, inventor of the forceps used for extracting upper third molars, and Wesley Sampler, the first dentist to pull a tooth from Abraham Lincoln's mouth.

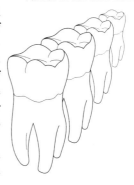

Today the small, white-brick house in which John Harris taught is a museum that showcases early dentistry tools. Although small, some look like pearl-handled hedge trimmers and ivory pliers.

Saves thousands each year

❖ The lifesaving technique known as the Heimlich Maneuver saves choking and drowning victims. Cincinnati surgeon Henry J. Heimlich introduced the technique in 1974. A specialist in thoracic surgery, Dr. Heimlich realized if he could develop a technique to prevent choking and aid drowning victims that he "could help more people in a few weeks than in [his] entire lifetime as a surgeon in the operating room." The Heimlich Maneuver confirmed this realization. He is also responsible for the development of an operation to replace the esophagus, and the Heimlich chest-drain valve. Founder of Computers for Peace—an organization that promotes world peace—Heimlich is currently seeking cures for cancer, AIDS, and Lyme disease.

Off with their heads

In 1974, Cleveland neurosurgeon Dr. Robert J. White surprised an international conference of organ transplant specialists in Fiuggi, Italy, when he boldly announced that, "We must, we want to think of transplanting the head." Since that time, Dr. White has performed 10 head transplants on monkeys, some of which have continued to function for as long as 36 hours after the transplant. In Dr. White's latest experiments, the transplanted head continued to see, smell, hear, and respond to stimuli.

Hospital food for 99 years

❖ Martha Nelson's hospital stay of 99 years was the longest in the country. In 1875, she was admitted to the Columbus State Institute for the Feeble-Minded. At age 103 years 6 months, she died at the Orient State Institution, ending her 99-year stay in Ohio hospitals.

The magic wand

❖ Kettering Medical Center is one of two medical centers in the United States that uses state-of-the-art Viewing Wand surgery—approved by the FDA in April 1994—for various types of brain operations. The surgery, which combines the use of the Viewing Wand with magnetic resonance imaging (MRI) and digital scanning procedures known as PET scanning, reduces risks, recovery time, and cost. The advanced procedure also makes it possible to treat patients whose conditions were considered inoperable. By combining the three technologies, the procedure gives surgeons a three-dimensional computerized road map of the brain as they operate. It also provides pinpoint accuracy. The surgery can  be performed on certain types of brain tumors, epilepsy, aneurysms, arterial venous malformations, and head and neck conditions.

Where the copy machine was born

The world's largest independent nonprofit research organization, Battelle Memorial Institute, was the birthplace of the copy machine. Originally, Mrs. Annie Norton Battelle and her son, Gordon, left money in their wills to establish an institute to foster and encourage research in metallurgy, fuels, and allied fields. The first building was completed in 1929. Over the years many foreign and national companies, organizations, and individuals have been Battelle clients. Engineer Chester Carlson came looking for help in 1949 when his electrostatic copying process had been rejected by numerous companies. Battelle allied itself with Carlson and the Haloid Company, which later became Xerox Corporation. In 1960, the first copy machine went on sale. Today, Battelle is the world's largest non-profit research organization—yearly revenues approach $1 billion.

❖ Sanford Hallock was a science whiz with a dream he couldn't forget. While he was working as an advertising executive in Columbus, he took a leave of absence to found COSI—the Center of Science and Industry. Opened in March 1964 with the motto "Science is fun," COSI was the nation's first science museum to use hands-on learning exhibits (right). If you wanted to learn about the brain, COSI put you inside one so you could hear and see how it worked. Today, COSI is one of 22 such science and technology centers in the world. The building boasts four floors of interactive exhibits and 140,000 square feet of space. The museum sponsors COSI on Wheels, a specially-equipped truck that brings science right to the classroom. COSI's "Mission to Mars" exhibit won a Computer World/Smithsonian Award in 1992.

Where science is fun

A shaky scale

Hamilton-native and physicist/seismologist Charles Richter developed the Richter scale with Beno Gutenberg in 1935. This is the scale used today to measure the intensity of earthquakes. At age 16, Richter moved to southern California with his family, where he got earthquake training firsthand. He mapped the country's earthquake regions, but always discouraged attempts to predict the occurrence of quakes.

❖ Born in Cleveland on September 21, 1926, physicist Donald Arthur Glaser was awarded the Nobel Prize in physics in 1960 for his invention of the "bubble chamber." He was one of the youngest recipients at age 34. Glaser's chamber was a sensitive device for detecting and making visible paths of nuclear particles.

Microbiologist Frederick Chapman Robbins of Cleveland shared the 1954 Nobel Prize in medicine and physiology with John Enders and Thomas Weller. Interestingly enough, in 1948, Robbins married the daughter of 1946 Nobel laureate for chemistry—John Howard Northrop.

Nobel briefs

Other Nobel Laureates

Charles Gates Dawes for peace, 1925
Arthur Compton for physics, 1927
Paul J. Flory for chemistry, 1974
William A. Fowler for physics, 1983

OHIO ONE DAY AT A TIME

An asterisk (*) after an item indicates that more information can be found in the index of this AWESOME ALMANAC.

JANUARY

1   Don Novello—Father Guido Sarducci of "Saturday Night Live"—born in Ashtabula 1943
2   One of the originators of the modern comic strip, Frederick Opper born in Madison 1857
3   Marty Balin (née Martyn Jerel Buchwald), founder of band Jefferson Airplane (1965 to 1971) and Starship (1975 to 1985), born in Cincinnati 1943*
    Senator Howard Metzenbaum retired from U.S. Senate 1995*
    "The Arsenio Hall Show" debuted on the Fox television network 1989
4   Football coach Don Shula born in Grand River 1930
5   Football coach Chuck (Charles H.) Noll born in Cleveland 1932
    Jazz great and cornetist William "Wild Bill" Davison born in Defiance 1906
6   Twelve white settlers massacred by Native Americans at Big Bottom on Muskingum River north of Marietta 1791
    Ohio State Capitol Building dedicated in Columbus 1859*
    Baseball Hall of Famer Byron Johnson born in Norwalk 1864
7   "Donahue" show began broadcasting from New York City 1985*
    Comedian George Burns and Gracie Allen married in Cleveland 1926
8   TV journalist Sander Vanocur born in Cleveland 1928
    Willard Kiplinger, journalist/publisher and founder of Kiplinger Washington Editors, Inc., in 1923, and publisher of *Kiplinger Washington Letter* and *Changing Times* magazine, born in Bellefontaine 1891
    President of IBM Thomas J. Watson, Jr., born in Dayton 1914
9   Wendy's award-winning "Where's the Beef?" advertising campaign featuring Clara Peller introduced 1984
10 John D. Rockefeller organized Standard Oil Company of Ohio in Cleveland 1870
    TV journalist Marlene Sanders born in Cleveland 1931
    Race-car driver and winner of the Indianapolis 500 Bobby Rahal born in Medina 1953
    Baseball Hall of Famer Elmer Flick born in Bedford 1876
12 Publisher/founder of *Who's Who in America* Albert Nelson Marquis born Brown County 1854
    Mormon leaders Joseph Smith and Sidney Rigdon left Kirtland to escape arrest because of banking irregularities 1838
14 One of the originators of the modern comic strip, artist Richard Outcault born in Lancaster 1863*

14 Trumpeter and jazz musician Billy Butterfield born in Middletown 1917
    State legislature passed the Job Creation Act—a comprehensive program of financial incentives to help businesses grow 1993
17 Rutherford B. Hayes died in Fremont 1893*
19 Cozy Cole, only drummer ever to sell over 1 million copies of a record—"Topsy" recorded in 1958—died in Columbus 1981
21 Golfer Jack Nicklaus born in Columbus 1940*
    Zanesville authorized building Y-bridge 1812*
23 The last streetcar run to Cleveland's Flats occurred 1954
24 Businessman Bernard H. Kroger born in Cincinnati 1860*
25 Governor Brown arrived at Dayton from Cincinnati, inaugurating boat service on Miami and Erie Canal 1829
    Actress Diana Hyland born in Cleveland Heights 1936
26 Actor Paul Newman born in Cleveland 1925*
    Author Leroy Lad Panek born in Cleveland 1943
    R & B singer Anita Baker born in Toledo 1958*
    Cleveland's Union Station, built by the Van Sweringen brothers, cost $119 million. A monument to the brother's financial success, it opened 1930
27 Football player Chris Collingsworth born in Dayton 1959
28 Astronaut Judith Resnik killed when the space shuttle *Challenger* exploded 1986*
29 Businessman John D. Rockefeller, Jr., born in Cleveland 1874
    Astronaut Robert F. Overmeyer born in Lorain 1936
    Explorer and mapper of western Canada, Mary Lee Jobe born in Tappan 1878
    Boxing promoter Don King first to promote boxing at Las Vegas MGM Grand Hotel and Casino 1994
    Barney Oldfield, early race-car driver and chief mechanic of Henry's Ford's racing team, born in Wauseon 1878*
30 Columbus-native and saxophonist George R. James, Sr., last living musician to perform with Louis Armstrong's original band and member of Fats Waller Orchestra, died in Columbus 1995
    Orville Wright died in Dayton 1948*
31 Songwriter ("It Had to be You") and bandleader Isham Jones born in Coalton 1894
    Author Zane Grey born in Zanesville 1875*

FEBRUARY

1   Actor Clark Gable born in Cadiz 1901*
2   Delia Bacon, author of theory that Shakespeare didn't write his plays, born in Tallmadge 1811*

3 Cincinnati Reds owner Marge Schott suspended from baseball for one year because of racially derogatory remarks 1993*

4 OSU football coach Woody (Wayne Woodrow) Hayes born in Clifton 1913*

5 Orval Hall, the Methodist Church's last circuit riding preacher, died in Columbus 1977
Quarterback Roger Staubach born Cincinnati 1942*
General William Tecumseh Sherman born in Lancaster 1820*

9 African-American poet Paul Laurence Dunbar died Dayton 1906*

10 Lowest temperature recorded in Ohio –39°F at Milligan 1899*

11 Inventor Thomas Alva Edison born in Milan 1847*

13 Dr. C.S. Beck performed the first heart operation for the relief of angina pectoris in Cleveland 1935

14 Clinton Cabinet member Donna Shalala born in Cleveland 1941
Baseball player Dave Dravecky born Youngstown in 1956
Series of sit-down strikes began in the rubber plants of Akron 1936
State capital established "on the high bank east of the Scioto River, directly opposite the town of Franklinton" at Columbus 1812*

16 Singer James Ingram born in Akron 1956*

17 Actor known for Mark Twain Tonight and TV sitcom "Evening Shade," Hal (Harold Rowe, Jr.) Holbrook, born in Cleveland 1925
Science-fiction/fantasy author Andre Norton, known for Iron Butterflies (1980), born Cleveland 1912

18 Pulitzer Prize-winning author Toni Morrison (Chloe Anthony Wofford) born in Lorain 1931

20 John Glenn, Jr., became the first man to orbit the Earth—three times in a five-hour flight in 1962*
Boxing promoter Don King staged the biggest show in boxing—"The Grand Slam of Boxing," featuring four world championships on one card, in Mexico City with 136,274 attending—1993*
Singer Nancy Wilson born in Chillicothe 1937*

21 Author Helen Hooven Santmyer, author of ... And Ladies of the Club died Xenia 1986*
Writer/humorist Erma Bombeck born in Dayton 1927*
PC Magazine awarded Upper Arlington-based CompuServe Editor's Choice Award as best on-line service for business subscribers 1995*

23 Charles M. Hall discovered the electrolytic process for making aluminum 1886

24 Hugh Downs, host of ABC's "20/20," born in Akron 1921
Pulitzer Prize-winning syndicated cartoonist Jim Borgman born Cincinnati 1954

25 Entertainer Jim Backus, voice of Mr. Magoo and star of "Gilligans Island," born in Cleveland 1913

27 Actor Howard Hesseman born in Lebanon 1940*

MARCH

1 Author William Dean Howells born in Martins Ferry 1837*

1 Tom Scholz, founder of hard rock band Boston in 1975, born in Toledo 1947. He also invented and made electronic equipment for musicians
Ohio became 17th state 1803*
Actress Catherine Bach born in Warren 1954

2 Phil Donahue interviewed Nelson Mandela on "Donahue"—the first and only talk-show appearance for the South African leader 1990

3 Rutherford B. Hayes became the first president to take the oath of office in the White House in a private ceremony 1877*
Rutherford Hayes finished term as president 1881
U.S. Grant finished term as president 1877

4 Boxer Ray "Boom Boom" Mancini born Youngstown 1961
The National Association of Professional Base-Ball Players organized 1871. The Cleveland Forest Citys finished sixth in the standings that year.
Ulysses.S. Grant began serving term as president 1869*
President Rutherford B. Hayes began term as president 1877
President James Garfield began term as president 1881*
Singer/songwriter Bobby Womack born in Cleveland 1944

7 The mayor of Cincinnati said women were unfit to drive cars 1908
The AFL and CIO joined forces in Ohio with total membership in the state of 722,000 1958
Alexander Graham Bell patented telephone. Elisha Gray didn't lost his patent battle—1876*

8 96 Christian Native Americans massacred by militiamen at Gnadenhutten, a Moravian mission in Tuscarawas Valley 1782*
Tragic school fire at Cleveland's Collingwood Elementary School killed 175 people 1908*

9 Congresswoman Frances Payne Bolton died in Lyndhurst 1977*

10 Journalist/columnist Bob Greene born in Columbus 1947

11 Actress Dorothy Gish, sister of Lillian born in Dayton 1898. One of the great silent film stars, she appeared in more than 100 films from 1912 to 1922

12 Adolph Simon Ochs, publisher of the New York Times from 1896 to 1935 and director of Associated Press from 1900 to 1935, born in Cincinnati 1858

13 Bandleader Sammy Kaye born in Lakewood 1913
Jurist Clarence Darrow died in Chicago 1938
Author Virginia Hamilton born in Yellow Springs 1936
Modern artist/painter Isabel Bishop, recipient of the Outstanding Achievement in Arts Award presented by President Jimmy Carter in 1979, born in Cincinnati 1902
Lynn St. James, race-car driver and, in 1992, second woman to qualify for the Indianapolis 500, born in Willoughby 1947

14 Legislature voted to make Columbus state capital 1812

15 TV producer/chairman of MCA Lew (Lewis Robert) Wasserman born in Cleveland 1913. A former movie usher described as "the last of the larger-than-life movie barons," Wasserman pioneered the miniseries, one-hour police show, and made-for-TV movies. Lyndon Johnson and Jimmy Carter tried to appoint Wasserman as secretary of commerce.

16 Race-car driver Barney Oldfield set a world speed record at of 131.724 mph at Daytona Beach, Florida, 1910*

18 Author Louis Brucker Bromfield died in Columbus 1956*

20 Art lover Maria Longworth Nichols Storer born in Cincinnati 1849. She established Rookwood, Ohio's first art pottery named after the family estate, in 1880

22 Cleveland Indians baseball players Steve Olin and Tim Crews killed in a boating accident 1993. Bob Ojeda survived.

24 Baseball Hall of Famer George Sisler born in Manchester 1893
Astronaut James A. Lovell, Jr., born in Cleveland 1928

25 First Medals of Honor awarded to Ohio participants in the Civil War's Great Locomotive Chase 1863*
Feminist Gloria Steinem born in Toledo 1935*
Dave Thomas, founder of Wendy's, received his high school diploma from Coconut Creek High School in Ft. Lauderdale, Florida, in 1993—45 years after he dropped out of high school*

26 Isaac M. Wise, founder of Reform Judaism in the United States, died in Cincinnati 1900

27 Mormon Temple at Kirtland dedicated 1836*
Helen H. Taft, wife of President William Taft, planted the first 300 cherry trees at the Tidal Basin in Washington, D.C., 1912*
Owens-Corning broke ground for new world headquarters building in Toledo 1995
Baseball Hall of Famer Miller Huggins born Cincinnati 1879

29 Baseball Hall of Famer Denton "Cy" Young born Gilmore 1867*
Last surviving soldier of the Revolutionary War, John Gray died in Hiramsburg 1868. He was 104*
Actress Eileen Heckart, Best Supporting Actress Oscar winner in 1972 for *Butterflies Are Free*, born in Columbus 1919

30 Businessman Bob (Robert L.) Evans born in Sugar Ridge 1918*

31 Politican James M. Cox, Sr., born Jacksonburg 1870

APRIL

1 Actor Gordon Jump (the Maytag man) born in Dayton 1927*
Baseball player Phil Niekro born in Blaine 1939
Cincinnati's firefighters became first to receive a salary 1853

2 Singer Herbert Mills of the Mills Brothers born in Piqua 1912*

3 Actress Doris Day born in Cincinnati 1924*

3 First church bell rang in Ohio country at Schoenbrunn 1772

4 Hank Aaron tieds Babe Ruth's all-time home run record (#714) at Riverfront Stadium in Cincinnati 1974
President William Henry Harrison became first president to die in office 1841*
U.S. Supreme Court Justice John McLean (1829-1861) died Cincinnati 1861

5 Astronaut Judith Resnik born in Akron 1949*

6 Doctor and murder suspect Samuel Sheppard died in Columbus 1970
Broadcaster Lowell Jackson Thomas born in Woodington 1892*

7 48 pioneers, led by Rufus Putnam, founded Marietta, first permanent white settlement in Ohio. Built Campus Martius as fortress 1788*

8 Basketball player John Havlicek born in Martins Ferry 1940

11 Actor Joel Grey (born Mickey Katz), Tony winner for *Cabaret*, born in Cleveland 1932

12 James Gamble and William Procter began a soap and candlemaking business in Cincinnati 1837*
Actor Ed O'Neill—Al Bundy on TV's "Married … with Children"—born in Youngstown 1946

14 Gas explosion in unfinished State Office Building at Columbus killed 11 and injured 50—1932
Adna R. Chaffee, who led U.S. troops during the Boxer Rebellion in capturing Peking, China, born in Orwell 1842
President William Howard Taft began the tradition of the President throwing out the first ball to open the baseball season in an American League game between Washington and Philadelphia 1910
Baseball player Pete Rose born Cincinnati 1942*

15 Canadian Prime Minister Pierre Trudeau and President Richard Nixon sign Great Lakes Water Quality Agreement 1972

16 Musician Henry Mancini born in Cleveland 1924*

17 Dennis and Cheryl Avery and their daughters killed in Kirtland by Jeffrey Lundgren 1988*
U.S. Supreme Court Justice William R. Day born in Ravenna 1849
Columbus-native Jerrie Mock became first female to fly around the world solo 1964

18 Lawyer Clarence Seward Darrow born in Kinsman 1857*

19 The Moravian mission of Lichtenau established near present site of Coshocton 1777

20 Twenty-third president of the United States Benjamin Harrison born in North Bend 1833*
After taking off from Cincinnati in his balloon, Thaddeus S.C. Lowe landed behind enemy lines and became the South's first prisoner in the Civil War 1861

21 Magician Dr. Eldoonie (Eldon D. Wigton) performed 225 tricks in two minutes at Kilbourne 1991
Donald Reibolt became last convicted murderer executed by electrocution in Ohio 1963*
Fire killed 320 prisoners at Ohio State Penitentiary in Columbus 1930*

24 Politician John M. Ashbrook died in Newark 1982

25   The *Scioto Gazette,* the oldest newspaper in Ohio retaining its original name, began publication at Chillicothe 1800*
Former OSU/Indianapolis Colts quarterback Art Schlicter born in Washington Court House 1953*
Actress Sara Jessica Parker born in Nelsonville 1965*

27   Television journalist John Scali born in Canton 1918
President Ulysses S. Grant born in Point Pleasant 1822*
Ground broken for Cleveland's Gund Area 1992*

29   Singer Donald Mills of the Mills Brothers born in Piqua 1915*
Cleveland's Public Square was lit in 1879 using Euclid Township-native Charles Brush's electric arc lights. Brush also invented the storage battery and first practical dynamo, allowing Cleveland to use the nation's first electric streetcar in 1884. Brush's company, along with Edison's, was part of the original General Electric Company
"The Phil Donahue show" moved from Dayton to WGN-TV Chicago and changed its name to "Donahue" 1974*

30   Actor Perry King born in Akron 1948

MAY

1   Famous American conductor Howard Barlow born in Plain City 1892
Terry Southern, author of script for the film *Easy Rider* (1969), born in Alvarado 1924*
TV talk-show host Jack Paar born in Canton 1918*

2   Author Susan Richards Shreve—known for children's mystery books—born in Toledo 1939
Herbert Faber and Daniel O'Connor opened their formica plant in Cincinnati 1913*

3   Earl Wilson, journalist known for gossip column "It Happened Last Night" (1943-1983), born in Rockford 1907

4   500 Kent State University students mount antiwar rally; 4 killed by National Guardsmen 1970*
Former Secretary of Education William. J. Bennett born in Salem 1944

5   Actor Tyrone Power, Jr., star of more than 50 films, born in Cincinnati 1914

6   Businessman/lawyer Joel Hyatt born in Cleveland 1950

7   Singer Theresa Brewer born in Toledo 1931*
FBI agent Elliot Ness died Cleveland 1957

8   Boxer Ray "Boom Boom" Mancini won the WBA lightweight title 1982*

9   Rock-country singer Richie Furay—with Buffalo Springfield, Poco, and The Southern-Hillman-Furay Band—born in Yellow Springs 1944
Cyrus Eaton, founder of Republic Steel Corporation in 1930, died Cleveland 1979, leaving an estate valued at $200 million*

10   John Sherman, U.S. senator, secretary of treasury and state, and brother of General William Tecumseh Sherman, born in Lancaster 1823*

10   The Harrison Land Law passed, making land more affordable in Ohio Country 1800*
Football coach/sportscaster Ara Raoul Parseghian born in Akron 1923*

11   Charles W. Fairbanks, vice president under Teddy Roosevelt, born Unionville Center 1852
Pitcher Roger Clemens called up from Pawtucket AAA team to joined the Boston Red Sox 1984*

13   Poet Jean Starr Untermeyer born in Zanesville 1886
Fantasy author Stephen R. Donaldson, known for *Chronicles of Thomas Covenant,* born in Cleveland 1947
Pitcher Roger Clemens started first game in the majors with the Boston Red Sox against Cleveland Indians in Cleveland 1984*

14   Cleveland Judge F.E. Allen became the first woman judge to sentence a man to death 1921*

15   Fire broke out at Cleveland Clinic. 125 peopled dead from poisonous fumes 1929*

16   George Andrew Horn and William Henry Gribben hanged near Ashland County Courthouse 1884*

17   Actress Debra Winger born in Cleveland 1955
Businessman Edward J. DeBartolo, Sr., (given name Anthony Paonessa), born Youngstown 1909*

18   The Libbey-Owens Glass Company organized in Toledo 1916*

21   Football coach Gerry Faust born in Dayton 1935*

23   Big band singer Helen O'Connell born in Lima 1921
The first airship to land on a roof and take-off again did so in Akron 1919

24   First major-league night-baseball game played at Cincinnati's Crosley Field 1935

26   CIO launched strike against "little steel" at Warren, Niles, and Youngstown 1937

27   Author Harlan J. Ellison born in Cleveland 1934
"The Arsenio Hall Show" went off the air 1994*

29   Entertainer Bob Hope born in London 1903*

30   The first successful U.S. Navy airship built in Akron 1917

31   Cleveland's Arcade—prototype for today's shopping malls—opened 1890
The trial of Mickey Monus, former Phar Mor president accused of 126 counts of fraud and embezzlement, began in Cleveland 1994*
Singer Johnny Paycheck born in Greenfield 1942*
Humanitarian Norman Vincent Peale born in Bowersville 1898*

JUNE

1   Businessman Harvey Samuel Firestone, Jr., died in Akron 1973
Cincinnati Reds played first official professional baseball game 1869*

2   James Murray Spangler patented his electric suction sweeper in Canton 1908*
Air Canada jet made emergency landing at Greater Cincinnati Airport; 23 people died from on-board fire 1983*

3   Businessman Ranson Eli Olds born in Geneva 1864*

3 The first airship with an enclosed cabin took flight in Akron 1925

Champion Paper Company received patent for machine paper-coating process 1933*

4 Hurdler Edwin Moses' winning streak ended at 122 victories. He was beaten by Danny Harris in the 400-meter hurdles 1987*

Former Senator Howard Metzenbaum born in Cleveland 1917*

6 Song-and-dance man Ted Lewis (born Theodore Friedman) born in Circleville 1891

Bob Evans Farms became a publicly held company 1963*

7 Baseball player Thurman Munson born in Akron 1947

11 Colonel William Crawford, leader of an expedition against Native Americans, burned at stake near Upper Sandusky 1782

Baseball Hall of Famer Roger Bresnahan born Toledo 1879

13 Congressman Wayne Hays—forced to resign from the House in 1976 after it was discovered his mistress Elizabeth Ray was on his payroll—born in Bannock 1911. He ran for the Ohio House in 1978 and won.

Actor Paul Lynde born in Mount Vernon 1926

Physicist Wallace C. Sabine, founder of the science of architectural acoustics, born in Richwood 1868. Boston Symphony Hall, the first building designed using his principles, opened October 15, 1900

14 A "one-in-500-years" storm hit Shadyside causing a flood that killed 26 1990

In 1870, the Cincinnati Reds lost to the Brooklyn Atlantics 8-7 ending the longest winning streak in baseball history—93-1-1.

The first air-rail passenger transcontinental service began in Cleveland 1929

15 Barney Oldfield became the first man to drive a mile a minute at Indianapolis 1903*

16 Pitcher Tom Seaver became first Reds pitcher to throw no-hitter at Riverfront Stadium. Beat Cardinals 4-0, 1978

17 Actor/singer Dean Martin born in Steubenville 1917

Paddle-wheeler *G.P. Griffith* burned in Lake Erie off Mendota 1850*

18 Actress Carol Kane born in Cleveland 1952

19 The Catholic Church established the Cincinnati diocese 1821*

Two strikers killed, 27 wounded, hundreds teargassed at Youngstown's Republic Steel plant during strike 1937

20 Football player Len Dawson born in Alliance 1935

Author Charles Chesnutt born in Cleveland 1858. He introduced the "new idea" in literature that African Americans were human beings—no white writer had done this before.

21 Editor of *Time* magazine (1943-1969), Robert T. Elson born in Cleveland 1906

First African-American mayor of any major U.S. City (Cleveland), Carl Burton Stokes born in Cleveland 1927*

23 Musical director of Metropolitan Opera in New York City, James Levine born Cincinnati 1943

A hung jury failed to convict former president of Phar Mor Mickey Monus on any of 126 fraud and embezzlement counts 1994*

25 William B. Saxbe, attorney general under President Nixon, born in Mechanicsburg 1916*

Cincinnati Daily Gazette, first daily newspaper west of Philadelphia, began publication 1827

Anti-feminist author Marabel Morgan, who developed the idea of the "total woman" through submission to husband, born in Crestline 1937

Traitor known as "Axis Sally" (Mildred Elizabeth Gillars), who broadcast Nazi propaganda and served 12 years in prison after WWII, died in Columbus 1988

26 Actress Eleanor Parker—the baroness in *The Sound of Music*—born in Cedarville 1922

Democratic presidential candidate William Jennings Bryan died in Dayton 1925

Businessman Henry Alden Sherwin born in Willoughby 1916*

27 Author Paul Laurence Dunbar born in Dayton 1872*

Sally Jane Priesand, the first ordained female rabbi, born in Cleveland 1946*

28 Tornado hit Lorain, killing 75 people and inflicting property damage of $25 million 1924*

Daniel D. Emmett, composer of "Dixie," died in Mount Vernon 1904*

Jeffrey Dahmer killed his first victim, Stephen Hicks, in Bath Township 1978*

29 Football player and TV-sports announcer Dan Dierdorf born in Canton 1949

30 The Cincinnati Reds moved into Riverfront Stadium 1970

JULY

1 Mezzo-soprano Jan De Gaetani born in Massillon 1933

The *Cleveland Gazette and Commercial Register* dropped the "a" in Cleaveland, giving the city name its present spelling 1832*

Actor Jamie Farr (Jameel Joseph Farah) born in Toledo 1934*

2 Author of *Little Big Man*, Thomas Louis Berger was born in Cincinnati 1924*

President James Garfield shot by Charles Guiteau, a disappointed office seeker, at the Washington, D.C., train station 1881*

Senator John Sherman introduced the Sherman Anti-Trust Act 1890*

3 The Schmeling-Stribling heavyweight championship fight opened Cleveland Stadium 1931

4 New York Yankee owner George Michael Steinbrenner III born in Rocky River 1930*

DeWitt Clinton, governor of New York, turned the first spadeful of dirt for the Ohio and Erie Canal at Licking Summit 1825*

Boxer Jack Dempsey defeated Jess Willard for the heavyweight title in the "battle of the century" at Bay View Park, Toledo 1919

4 Construction began on the Ohio State Capitol Building in Columbus 1839*

First sheet of formica came off press in Cincinnati 1914*

The Ohio Institute for the Blind—the nation's first school for the blind—opened in Columbus 1837

Poet and critic John C. Ramsom died in Gambier 1974

8 Football player Jack (John Harold) Lambert born in Mantua 1952

Philip Cortelyou Johnson, architect of the Glass House in New Caanan, Connecticut, born in Cleveland 1906

Elyria-native, playwright Robert E. Lee died 1994. In collaboration with Jerome Lawrence, he wrote *Inherit the Wind, Auntie Mame,* and *The Night Thoreau Spent in Jail**

Founder of Standard Oil Company—the first big U.S. business trust—John D. Rockefeller born Richford, New York 1839*

9 Football legend Paul Brown born in Norwalk 1908*

12 Heavest rainfall in eight hours (9.54 inches) at Sandusky 1966*

The first Etch A Sketch manufactured by Ohio Art Company 1960*

13 The Northwest Ordinance, which established rights later adopted in the Bill of Rights, became law two months before the Constitution ratified 1787*

14 Political activist Jerry Rubin—one of the Chicago Seven—born in Cincinnati 1938

15 Governor George Voinovich born in Cleveland 1936

Politician James M. Cox, Sr., died in Dayton 1957

16 *Apollo 11,* first moon-landing mission, launched from Kennedy Space Center with Wapakoneta's Neil Armstrong, and Edwin Aldrin, and Michael Collins 1969*

Marine Major John Glenn set transcontinental speed record—3 hours 23 minutes 8 seconds—in jet from California to New York 1957

Newburg-native D.R. Averill patented ready-mixed paint 1867

17 Bolivar Dam in Muskingum Watershed Conservancy District dedicated, completing the flood-control program in Muskingum Valley 1938*

Comedian Phyllis Diller born in Lima 1917*

Photographer Berenice Abbott born Springfield 1898

18 Pianist-singer Jay (Jalacy) Hawkins born Cleveland 1929

Astronaut/Senator John Herschel Glenn, Jr., born in Cambridge 1921*

First Ohioans to receive a patent were Sam C. Clark and Nathaniel Kirk from St. Clairsville for a "machine for breaking, hairing, and fleshing every species of hides" 1812

19 Major League all-time hit leader Pete Rose sentenced to five months in jail for tax evasion 1990*

20 Actress Theda Bara born in Cincinnati 1890

21 Highest temperature recorded in Ohio, 113°F at Centerville 1934*

Poet Hart Crane, known for "The Bridge," born in Garrettsville 1899

22 Ernest Ball, composer of "When Irish Eyes Are Smiling," born in Cleveland 1878*

22 Producer, singer, and composer George Clinton born Blainfield 1940. Produced such bands as Funkadelic and Parliament

Moses Cleaveland and his party of 50 reached mouth of the Cuyahoga River and surveyed the site for his capital city, Cleaveland 1796*

Baseball Hall of Famer Jesse Haines born in Clayton 1893

23 Internationally known for her research in spectroscopy, Emma P. Carr born in Holmesville 1880

Inventure Place, home of the National Inventors Hall of Fame, opened in Akron 1995*

25 Baseball player Nate Thurmond born in Akron 1941

World's biggest inland steamboat, the *Mississippi Queen*, commissioned Cincinnati 1976*

26 Ella Alexander Boole, president of the World WCTU from 1931 to 1947, born in Van Wert 1858

Confederate cavalry under General John Morgan captured 1863*

27 Singer Maureen McGovern born in Youngstown 1949

28 Entertainer Joe E. Brown born in Holgate 1892

30 Feminist leader Eleanor Smeal born in Akron 1939*

31 Born in Canal Dover in 1837, Confederate sympathizer Billy Quantrill—the "bloodiest man in American history"—led a mob of 450 men into Lawrence, Kansas, in 1863, killing 200 people and plundering and burning stores and homes.

Cleveland Indians played first game in their new home—Cleveland Municipal Stadium—1932

AUGUST

2 Baseball player Thurman Munson died in Canton 1979

Educator Horace Mann died in Yellow Springs 1859

Inventor Elisha Gray, involved in a legal battle with Alexander Graham Bell for telephone patent, born in Barnesville 1835*

3 Treaty of Greenville brought formal close to hostilities with Native Americans 1795*

Actor Martin Sheen born in Dayton 1940

Supreme Court Justice William B. Woods born Newark 1824

Justice Department ordered new investigation into murder of Kent State students by Ohio National Guardsmen 1973*

Harvey S. Firestone founded Firestone Tire and Rubber Company in Akron 1900*

4 Baseball pitcher Roger Clemens born in Dayton 1962*

5 Astronaut Neil Armstrong born in Wapakoneta 1930*

Football great Paul Brown died in Cincinnati 1991*

First electric traffic signals installed in Cleveland at Euclid Ave. and E. 105 Street 1914

6 Labor leader Jackie Presser born in Cleveland 1926

Republican party leader Ray C. Bliss died in Akron 1981

Actor Dorian Harewood born in Dayton 1951

7 Football Hall of Famer Alan C. Page born in Canton 1945

8   Charles Manson began a killing spree with cult members 1969*

The first fraternity west of the Alleghenies founded at Miami University in Oxford 1839*

Basketball coach Jerry Tarkanian born in Euclid 1930

10   Financier Jay Cooke born Sandusky 1821*

Leslie H. Wexner opened first Limited store at Kingsdale Shopping Center in Columbus 1963*

11   Businessman Frank Augustus Seiberling died in Akron 1955

Labor leader I.W. Abel born in Magnolia 1908*

12   Artist George W. Bellows born in Columbus 1882*

Radio station WJMP-AM in Akron began playing the song "Take Me Out to the Ballgame"—and nothing else—to register disgust over baseball strike 1994

13   Johnny Clem, famous "Drummer Boy of Shiloh" during the Civil War, born in Newark 1851

Sharpshooter Annie Oakley (Phoebe Moses) born in Darke County 1860*

14   Lee Adams, who wrote lyrics for successful Broadway musicals *Bye Bye Birdie* and *Applause*, born in Mansfield 1924

Actress Halle Berry born in Cleveland 1968*

16   Dancer Suzanne Farrell born in Cincinnati 1945*

Tennis great Tony Trabert born in Cincinnati 1930

Cleveland Indians player Ray Chapman died as a result of being hit in the head with a wild pitch—the only player ever killed in a major league game 1920*

The Libbey Glass Company opened in Toledo 1888*

18   Record executive Enoch Light born in Canton 1907

First cross-country air competition for women—the Women's Air Derby from Santa Monica to Cleveland—began 1929*

The game show "Concentration" debuted with Hugh Downs as its first host 1958

19   Singer Harry Mills of the Mills Brothers born in Piqua 1913*

Eric Carmen of The Raspberries born in Cleveland 1949. Band had hit singles "All by Myself" in 1975 and "Make Me Lose Control" in 1988

Orville Wright born in Dayton 1871*

20   Mad Anthony Wayne broke the power of British-Native-American confederation at the Battle of Fallen Timbers, ending 20 years of bitter frontier fighting 1794*

Boxing promoter Don King born in Cleveland ghetto 1931*

21   Heisman Trophy winner Archie Griffin born in Columbus 1954*

Mystery writer Robert L. Fish (penname Robert L. Pike) born in Cleveland 1912

22   Businessman Vernon Stouffer born in Cleveland 1901*

23   Baseball player Pete Rose banned from baseball for gambling 1989*

24   David Zeisberger and band of Native-American Christians established Moravian community at Schoenbrunn 1772*

25   Baseball pitcher Rollie (Roland Glen) Fingers born Steubenville 1946

25   Businessman William Cooper Procter born in Glendale 1862*

27   Nobel laureate (for the Dawes Plan after WWI) and first director of the Bureau of the Budget (1921) Charles G. Dawes born in Marietta 1865. He also wrote the music for the hit song, "It's All in the Game"*

First autogiro looped the loop publicly in Cleveland 1932

29   The first dirigible passenger transfer to an airplane took place in Cleveland 1929

Charles Kettering, engineer who invented automobile self-starter, born in Loudonville 1876*

31   Glenn H. Curtiss made the first over-water flight in a plane at Cleveland 1910

Olympic intermediate hurdling gold medalist Edwin Moses born in Dayton 1955*

Actor Richard Basehart born in Zanesville 1914

SEPTEMBER

1   Last passenger pigeon in the nation—Martha—died at Cincinnati Zoo 1914*

Pontifical College Josephinum established in Worthington 1888*

2   Moses Cleaveland's Connecticut Land Company bought the Western Reserve Land except for Fire Lands 1795*

3   Al Jardine, guitarist and singer with The Beach Boys, born in Lima 1942

Dirigible *Shenandoah* crashed near Ava killing 14 people 1925*

First Labor Day celebrated in Ohio 1890—four years before the national holiday*

5   By noon on this day radio station WJMP-AM of Akron had played "Take Me Out to the Ballgame"—and nothing else—15,366 times to protest baseball strike 1994

7   The Professional Football Hall of Fame opened in Canton 1963*

Christine E. Hynde, founder of the British rock group The Pretenders, born in Akron 1951*

Thomas Hendricks, vice president under President Grover Cleveland, born near Zanesville 1819

George Ligowsky of Cincinnati received patent on "clay pigeon" target 1880*

Pianist and recording artist Michael Jay Feinstein born in Columbus 1956

8   President Rutherford B. Hayes became first president to visit the West Coast 1880

9   Jimmy the Greek, TV sports announcer fired for racial remarks, born in Steubenville 1919

10   Isaac K. Funk, founder of Funk and Wagnalls Company and publisher of *Standard Dictionary of the English Language* (1893), born in Clifton 1839

Oliver Hazard Perry defeated British flotilla near Put-in-Bay and wrote, "We have met the enemy and they are ours" 1813*

11   Baseball player Pete Rose made hit number 4,192 in Cincinnati, boosting him to all-time hit leader. Passed Ty Cobb 1985*

12 Bank robber John Dillinger broke out of Lima jail 1933*

Best known for her role as Wicked Witch of the West in *The Wizard of Oz*, Margaret Hamilton born in Cleveland 1902

13 Former governor James A. Rhodes born in Jackson 1909

Michael Owens, glassblower extraordinaire, patented his first invention—a mechanical dummy that opened and closed glass molds—1892*

Canton-native and TV anchor Christine Craft fired at station KFBK in Sacramento in 1993 on tenth anniversary of her famous sexual harassment law suit against a Kansas City TV station

15 Boxing promoter Don King staged a record six title fights on one card—"Unfinished Business"—1994*

Children's author/illustrator Robert McCloskey born in Hamilton 1914

Twenty-seventh president of the United States William Howard Taft born in Cincinnati 1857*

The first jet-propelled four-engine plane tested in Columbus 1947

16 Actor George Chakiris born in Norwood 1934

Cincinnati Reds pitcher Tom Browning pitched first perfect game in Reds' history 1988

Mob boss Thomas Licavoli, head of crime in Detroit during Prohibition, died in Columbus 1973

17 The American Professional Football Association founded in Canton 1920*

Cincinnati Reds player Johnny Bench hit last home run of his career (#389) at Riverfront Stadium 1983

Author Vance Bourjaily born in Cleveland 1922. Best known for *Brill among the Ruins* (1970) and *A Game Men Play* (1980). His most recent work was *Old Soldier* (1990)

Ohio Farm Bureau incorporated Farm Bureau Mutual Automobile Insurance Company 1925. Name changed to Nationwide Insurance in 1955.

18 Supreme Court Justice John Clarke born in New Lisbon 1857

19 President James Garfield died 1881

"Black Monday," the day the Lykes Corporation—parent company of Youngstown Sheet & Tube—announced the closing of their steel mills 1977*

21 First Monday-night football game TV telecast pitted the Cleveland Browns against the New York Jets 1970. Cleveland won 31-21

Politician John M. Ashbrook born in Johnston 1928

Nobel prize physicist Donald Arthur Glaser born Cleveland 1926*

22 Israeli Supreme Court released retired Cleveland auto-worker John Demjanjuk 1993*

Pretty Boy Floyd gunned down by police near East Liverpool 1934*

Procter and Gamble announced recall of Rely tampons when government studies showed use increased chances of toxic shock syndrome 1980

23 Female presidential candidate Victoria Claflin Woodhull born in Homer 1838*

Wendy's first international restaurant opened in Canada 1975*

24 Political boss/businessman Mark (Marcus Alonzo) Hanna born in New Lisbon 1837*

Publisher Adam Willis Wagnalls founded publishing company Funk & Wagnalls with Isaac Funk in 1890. Born in Lithopolis 1843

27 Baseball Hall of Famer Mike Schmidt born in Dayton 1949

Actor Greg Morris of TV's "Mission Impossible" born in Cleveland 1934

30 The Ohio Turnpike opened 1955

OCTOBER

1 Ralph Sockman, popular pastor in New York City from 1916 to 1961, born Mount Vernon 1889

2 Actress Beverly D'Angelo (originally a rock singer) born in Columbus 1952

3 Eighty-four-year-old Mel Harder, former Cleveland pitcher who opened Cleveland Stadium in 1932, threw ceremonial last pitch at the stadium 1993

4 Nineteenth President of the United States Rutherford Hayes born in Delaware 1822*

The 55,555,555th Goodyear tire produced in Akron 1923*

5 Antioch College—first nonsectarian college to give women equal rights with men—opened in Yellow Springs 1853

6 Businessman Frank Augustus Seiberling born in Western Star 1859

8 Pilot Eddie (Edward Vernon) Rickenbacker born Columbus 1890*

Dennis J. Kucinich, youngest mayor of Cleveland, born in Cleveland 1946*

Author R.L. Stine born in Columbus 1943*

9 American Humane Association organized in Cleveland 1877

Baseball Hall of Famer Richard W. "Rube" Marquard born in Cleveland 1889

"Dr. Spock," an NBC-TV show broadcast from KYW-TV in Cleveland, went on the air in 1955. Spock taught at Western Reserve University College of Medicine and gave parents over-the-air tips on childcare. The show ended August 9, 1956.

10 Cleveland Indian Elmer Smith hit the first World Series grand slam and Cleveland won title, 5-2, against the Brooklyn Dodgers 1920*

11 Actor Luke Perry born in Mansfield 1966*

Cleveland Indians won the World Series, 4-2, beating the Boston Braves 1948*

Inventor Thomas Alva Edison, holder of 1,093 patents, died in West Orange, New Jersey, at age 84 1931*

12 Charles A. Wick (known as Charles Zwick), director of U.S. Information Agency and Reagan confidante, born in Cleveland 1917

13 Jazz great/pianist Art Tatum born in Toledo 1910

14 Children's author/illustrator Lois Lenski born in Springfield 1893

John W. Dean, White House counsel for President Richard Nixon and author of *Blind Ambition* (1976), born in Akron 1938

15 Pulitzer Prize-winning historian and assistant to Presidents Kennedy and Johnson, Arthur Schlesinger, Jr., born in Columbus 1917. He wrote *A Thousand Days* (1965) and *Robert Kennedy & His Times* (1978)

17 Gallipolis founded by band of 500 French artisans and craftsmen 1790*

Entertainer Tom Posten born in Columbus 1927

Baseball Hall of Famer Buck Ewing born in Massillon 1859

18 Author and dramatist Fannie Hurst born in Hamilton 1889. She never lived in Ohio, however.

20 Fire raged through a 50-block area of Cleveland 1944*

22 Pretty Boy (Charles Arthur) Floyd—Public Enemy No. 1 in 1933—died near East Liverpool 1934*

23 Football great John William Heisman born in Cleveland 1869*

24 Baseball player and author Jim Brosnan born in Cincinnati 1929

Last of the great silent film stars Lillian Diana Gish born in Springfield 1896. She starred in movies, television, and plays for 85 years until her death in 1993

25 Baskbetball coach Bobby (Robert Montgomery) Knight born in Orrville 1940*

Erie Canal, the country's first manmade waterway, opened 1825

26 Cardinal John Krol, archbishop of Philadelphia from 1961 to 1988, born in Cleveland 1910

Sister of female presidential candidate and social reformer Victoria Woodhull, Tennessee Claflin born in Homer 1846

27 Actress Ruby Dee (Mrs. Ossie Davis) born in Cleveland 1924

29 Daniel Emmett, writer of song "Dixie," born in Clinton 1815*

Arctic Pacific Airlines plane crashed in Toledo, killing 16 players on the California Polytechnical College football team 1960*

30 Baseball Hall of Famer Ed Delahanty born in Cleveland 1867

31 Natalie Barney, hostess of famous literary salon in Paris in 1920s and 1930s, born in Dayton 1876

William Procter and James Gamble signed a formal partnership as Procter & Gamble in Cincinnati 1837*

NOVEMBER

2 Twenty-ninth president of United States Warren G. Harding born in Corsica 1865*

Annie Oakley died in Greenville 1926*

Nation's first titanium mill opened in Toronto 1957

Peter G. Thomson incorporated Champion Coated Paper Company in Hamilton 1893*

Edward W. Scripps began publishing *Penny Press* (later the *Cleveland Press*) in Cleveland 1878, beginning the Scripps-Howard communication and newspaper business

3 Founder of *Cincinnati Post* in 1879 Walter Wellman born in Mentor 1858

4 Baseball great Cy Young died in Peoli 1955*

General Arthur St. Clair defeated in attempt to destroy the confederation of Native-American tribes in the Northwest Territory at site of Fort Recovery 1791

5 Worst mine disaster in state's history killed 82 at Millfield 1930*

6 Robert H. Smith, founder of Alcoholics Anonymous in 1935, died in Akron 1959*

Althea Leasure Flynt, wife of *Hustler* publisher Larry Flynt, born in Marietta 1953

Edward J. DeBartolo, Jr., businessman and owner of the San Francisco 49ers, born in Youngstown 1946*

"The Phil Donahue Show" premiered as the first audience-participation TV talk-show on WLWD-TV in Dayton 1967*

7 Actor Dean Jagger, winner of Best Supporting Actor Oscar for *Twelve O'Clock High* (1949), born Lima 1903

Carl B. Stokes elected mayor of Cleveland, first African-American mayor of a major U.S. city 1967*

8 Ray "Boom Boom" Mancini won WBA lightweight boxing title in first-round knockout 1982*

9 Actress Dorothy Dandridge born in Cleveland 1922

The *Centinel of the North-Western Territory*, first newspaper north and west of the Ohio River, published by William Maxwell at Cincinnati 1793*

Golfer Tom Weiskopf born in Massillon 1942

10 The Stern-Auer Company and the United States Shoe Company of Cincinnati merged to become U.S. Shoe Corporation, headquartered in Cincinnati 1931

11 Murderer Charles Manson born in Cincinnati 1934*

Politician Richard F. Celeste born in Cleveland 1937

14 Ernest Kent Coulter, founder of the first Big Brother agency in New York City in 1904, born in Columbus 1871

Politician Frank Lausche born in Cleveland 1895*

15 Former Air Force Chief of Staff Curtis Emerson LeMay, who once said he wouldn't hesitate to use the atom bomb," born in Columbus 1906. He commanded the Strategic Air Command (1948-1957) and was a vice-presidential candidate on the Independent Party ticket with George Wallace in 1968.

The first Wendy's restaurant opened at 257 E. Broad Street in Columbus 1969*

Columnist Elizabeth Drew born in Cincinnati 1935

Phil Donahue celebrated 25th anniversary on the air with a two-hour NBC-TV prime-time special 1992*

16 Actor Burgess Meredith born in Cleveland 1909

17 The first shipment of plate glass left Edward Ford Plate Glass Company of Toledo 1899*

18 Businessman James S. Kemper born in Van Wert 1886

First national women's temperance society organized Cleveland 1874

19 Twentieth president James A. Garfield born in Orange 183 *

19   Author of *Shane* (1949) Jack Schaefer born in Cleveland 1907

Founder of CNN in 1980 and pioneer of the superstation concept in 1975 with WTBS, Robert Edward Turner II (Ted Turner) born in Cincinnati 1938

20   Entertainer Kaye Ballard born in Cleveland 1926

First commissioner of baseball Kenesaw M. Landis born Millville 1866*

23   Main strategist for the Navy during WWII Ernest Joseph King born in Lorain 1878

25   William Riley Burnett, author of *Little Caesar*, born in Springfield 1899*

Helen Hooven Santmyer, author of *...And Ladies of the Club*, born in Xenia 1895*

Former Cleveland Browns quarterback Bernie Kosar born in Boardman 1963

DeHart Hubbard, first African American to win an Olympic gold medal, born in Cincinnati 1903*

Inventor and businessman Charles Kettering died in Dayton 1958*

28   Football Hall of Famer Paul D. Warfield born in Warren 1942

Early Zionist Abba Hillel Silver died in Cleveland 1963

29   Billy Strayhorn, arranger, pianist, and member of Duke Ellington's band, born in Dayton 1915

DECEMBER

1   Baseball Hall of Famer Walter Alston born in Darrtown 1912

3   Oberlin College became the first coeducational college in the nation 1833*

4   Coroner's report revealed that 1932 Olympic track star Stella Walsh was a man Cleveland 1950*

11 people trampled to death in rush to get seats at The Who concert in Cincinnati 1979

5   General George Armstrong Custer born in New Rumley 1839*

6   The *Canton Repository* first mentioned the idea of a Professional Football Hall of Fame in Canton 1959*

Charles Hall, who brought aluminum into general use, born in Thompson 1863

7   Party of emigrants left Ipswich, Massachusetts, for Ohio country 1787

8   Author James Thurber born in Columbus 1894*

Oberlin College graduated the first African-American woman 1850

9   Louis Kronenberger, drama critic for *Time* magazine (1938-1961) and author of numerous novels, born in Cincinnati 1904

Bandleader Freddy Martin born in Cleveland 1906

10   The American Federation of Trades and Labor founded in Columbus with Samuel Gompers as president 1886

11   "The Mike Douglas Show" began on Cleveland's KYW-TV 1961

13   Early social reformer Fanny Wright shocked America by speaking openly about birth control. She died in Cincinnati 1852

Actor Tim (Thomas Daniel) Conway born in Willoughby 1933

14   First Siamese twins to survive a separation and live for one year operated on in Cleveland 1952

15   President U.S. Grant received King David Kalakaua of Hawaii 1874. First president to have a reigning king visit the United States

16   Republican party leader Ray C. Bliss born in Akron 1907. He rebuilt the Republican party after Barry Goldwater was badly defeated in presidential election of 1964

17   Wilbur and Orville Wright flew the first motorized airplane at Kitty Hawk, North Carolina 1903*

18   Moviemaker Steven Spielberg born in Cincinnati 1947*

19   President Lincoln's Secretary of War Edwin McMaster Stanton born in Steubenville 1814*

Pioneer of shopping malls Edward J. DeBartolo, Sr., died in Youngstown 1994*

Actor Robert Urich born in Toronto 1947

20   Tire magnate Harvey Samuel Firestone born in Columbus 1868*

Baseball Hall of Famer W. Branch Rickey born in Stockdale 1881

21   Sterling Tucker, civil rights leader and executive director of Urban League of Washington, D.C., born in Akron 1923

Talk show host Philip John Donahue born in Cleveland 1935*

22   First gorilla born in captivity—Colo—born at Columbus Zoo 1956*

23   Actress Elizabeth Hartman, nominated for Academy Award for her first film *A Patch of Blue* (1965), born in Boardman 1941. She committed suicide June 1987

25   Football player Larry Csonka born in Stow 1946

The first soccer game held in Cleveland 1905

Actor Gary Sandy of TV show "WKRP in Cincinnati" born in Dayton 1945*

26   President Richard Nixon's loyal secretary Rose Mary Woods, best known during Watergate for the mysterious 18-1/2-minute gap in a White House tape, born in Sebring 1917

27   Author/ecologist Louis Brucker Bromfield born in Mansfield 1896*

28   Mt. Vernon-native William Semple patented chewing gum 1869*

29   Bridge collapsed under the Pacific Express train in Ashtabula, killing 84 and injuring 160 people—1876*

30   Golfer Jack Nicklaus made his professional golf debut in Miami 1961. Lost to Gary Player*

Western Ohio Map

LAKE ERIE

North Bass I.

Middle Bass I.

South Bass I. • Put-in-Bay

• Columbia

Sylvania •

Toledo

Kelleys I.

• Holland

Wauseon •

• Perrysburg

• Woodville

• Marblehead

Maumee R.

• Sandusky

Fremont •

• Defiance

• Bairdstown

• Norwalk

• Fostoria

Findlay •

Tiffin •

Sycamore •

• Van Wert

• New Washington

Lima •

Bucyrus •

• Mansfield
• Lexington

Wapakoneta •

• Johnsville

Coldwater •

• New Knoxville

Marion •

Richwood •

• Mt. Vernon

• West Mansfield

Great Miami R.

Bellefontaine •

Woodington •

Marysville •

West Liberty •

Greenville •

• Piqua

• Middletown

• Pitsburg

Clayton •

Springfield •

London •

⊙ **Columbus**

• New Paris

• Vandalia

Trotwood •

Dayton •

• Yellow Springs

Camden •

Xenia •

• Cedarville

• Circleville

Miamisburg •

• Wilberforce

Darrtown •

• Centerville

• Bowersville

• Franklin

Middletown •

• Oregonia

New Miami •

• Washington Court House

Mason •

• Lebanon

Hamilton •

• Chillicothe

Fairfield •

• New
Vienna

Little Miami R.

• Bainbridge

Cincinnati

• Miamiville

• Rainsboro

• Plainville

Hillsboro •

Wayne National Forest

• New Richmond

Point Pleasant •

• Felicity

Portsmouth •

• New Boston

Ripley •

Wayne National Forest

Aberdeen •

• Manchester

• Hanging Rock

Scioto R.

Darby Cr.

Legend

- ⊙ State Capitol
- • City or town
- ▲ Mountains

Bold type
indicates National
Park or Land

Italic type
indicates body of
water or island

Great Miami R.

Little Miami R.

Springdale •

Wyoming •

• Blue Ash

Mt. Healthy •

• Silverton

North Bend •

Cincinnati

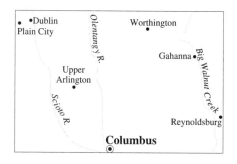

• Dublin

Plain City •

Olentangy R.

• Worthington

Gahanna •

Big Walnut Creek

Upper
Arlington •

Scioto R.

• Reynoldsburg

Columbus
⊙

Eastern Ohio Map

These maps shows the main cities of the state and most places mentioned in the book. If you cannot find a specific place on one of these maps, it may be found on one of the special supplementary maps found throughout the book. Every effort has been made to include everything; however, in some cases we were not able to list every entry because of space limitations. If the place you seek is not listed, we apologize.

SELECTED REFERENCES

Allen, Hayward. *The Traveler's Guide to Native America: The Great Lakes Region*. Minocqua, Wi.: North Word Press, 1992.

Asimov, Isaac. *Asimov's Biographical Encyclopedia of Science and Technology*. Garden City, N.Y.: Doubleday, 1972.

Barth, Jack. *Roadside Hollywood*. Chicago: Contemporary Books, 1991.

Collins, Louise Mooney, ed. *Newsmakers: The People Behind Today's Headlines*. Detroit: Gale Research, 1991 through 1995.

Coyle, William, ed. *Ohio Authors and their Books: 1796-1950*. Cleveland: The World Publishing Company, 1962.

Current Biography (Numerous volumes). New York: The H.W. Wilson Co.

Federal Writers' Project. *The Ohio Guide*, 1940.

Freidel, Frank. *The Presidents of the United States of America*. Washington, D.C.: White House Historical Association, 1981.

Garrison, Webb. *A Treasury of Ohio Tales: Unusual, Interesting, and Little Known Stories of Ohio*. Nashville: Rutledge Hill Press, 1993.

Gunther, John. *Inside U.S.A.* New York: Harper, 1947.

Hoover, Earl. *Cradle of Greatness: National and World Achievements of Ohio's Western Reserve*. Cleveland: Shaker Savings Association, 1977.

James, Edward T., ed. *Notable American Women*, 3 vols. Cambridge, Ma.: The Belknap Press of Harvard University Press, 1974.

Jordan, Philip D. *Ohio Comes of Age, 1873-1900*. Vol. 5 of *The History of the State of Ohio*. Columbus, Oh.: Ohio State Archaeological and Historical Society, 1943.

Klapthor, Margaret Brown. *The First Ladies*. Washington, D.C.: White House Historical Association, 1981.

Lorant, Stefan. *The Glorious Burden: The History of the Presidency and Presidential Elections from George Washington to James Earl Carter, Jr.* Lenox, Ma.: Authors Edition, 1976.

Lucaire, Ed. *The Celebrity Almanac*. New York: Prentice Hall, 1991.

McNeil, Alex. *Total Television: A Comprehensive Guide to Programming from 1948 to the Present*. New York: Penguin Books, 1991.

Menke, Frank G. *The Encyclopedia of Sports*, 4th ed. New York: A.S. Barnes, 1969.

Moorehead, Warren King. *The Indian Tribes of Ohio*. Columbus, Oh.: Ohio Archaeological and Historical Publications, 1899. Clarified and copyrighted 1992 by Arthur W. McGraw.

The Ohio Sports Almanac. Wilmington, Oh.: Orange Frazer Press, 1992.

Pierce, Neal R. and John Keefe. *The Great Lakes States of America*. New York: W.W. Norton, 1980.

Roseboom, Eugene H. *The Civil War Era: 1850-1873*. Vol. 4 of *The History of the State of Ohio*. Columbus, Oh.: Ohio State Archaeological and Historical Society, 1944.

Siebert, Wibur H. *The Underground Railroad in Ohio*. Columbus, Oh.: Ohio Archaeological and Historical Publications, 1895. Map credited to *The Mysteries of Ohio's Underground Railroad*. Columbus, Oh.: Long's College Book, 1951.

Stewart, George Rippy. *American Place Names*. New York: Oxford University Press, 1970.

Vonada, Damaine, ed. *The Ohio Almanac*. Wilmington, Oh.: Orange Frazer Press, 1992.

Vonada, Damaine, ed. *Ohio: Matters of Fact*. Wilmington, Oh.: Orange Frazer Press, 1990.

Weisenburger, Francis P. *The Passing of the Frontier: 1825-1850*. Vol. 3 of *The History of the State of Ohio*. Columbus, Oh.: Ohio State Archaeological and Historical Society, 1941.

The author used various issues of the *Cincinnati Enquirer, Columbus Dispatch, Cleveland Plain Dealer, Youngstown Vindicator, Timeline, Cincinnati Magazine, Cleveland Magazine, Ohioana Quarterly, Ohio Magazine, Saturday Evening Post, Sports Illustrated, Wild Ohio, Twine Line*, and *People*. Numerous individuals were also interviewed.

INDEX

natural resources 79, 84–85
Nature Conservancy, The 25, 26, 31
Nelson Kennedy Ledges State Park 27, 33
Nelson, Martha 180
Nelsonville 184
Ness, Elliot 185
New Albany 99
New Athens 70
New Berlin 81
New Bomb Turks 121
New Boston 70, 192
New Concord 193
New Connecticut 12, 65
New England 8, 39
New France (Canada) 42, 43
New Holland 70
New Knoxville 179, 192
New Lebanon 70
New Lexington 17, 70, 104, 193
New Lights 176
New Lisbon 50, 189
New London 70, 193
New Madrid earthquake 45
New Miami 70, 192
New Orleans 69, 130, 189
New Paris 70, 192
New Philadelphia 17, 75, 193
New Richmond 49, 70, 192
New Rumley 51, 191, 193
New Vienna 70, 192
New Washington 70, 192
New York City 110, 113, 118, 182, 189
Newark 14, 17, 185, 187, 188, 193
Newberry Medal 113
Newburg 187
Newcomerstown 193
Newman, Paul 75, 121, 132, 182
Newman, Steven 151
newspapers 104–105
Nicklaus, Jack 150, 174, 182, 191
Niehaus, Charles 20
Niekro, Phil 138, 184
Niles 123, 185
Nixon, Richard 25, 55, 59, 63, 132, 159, 184, 186, 189, 191
Nobel Prizes 181, 188, 189
Noble County 17, 152
Noble, Edward 86
Noble, Warren P. 17
Noll, Charles H. (Chuck) 140, 182
North Bass Island 7, 84, 192
North Bend 52, 62, 184, 192
North Benton 178, 193
North Coast Harbor 66, 126
North Country National Scenic Trail 32
North, Paul 151
Northrop, John Howard 181
Northwest Ordinance of 1787 5, 8, 11, 13, 45, 187
Northwest Territory 5, 9, 11, 12, 13, 19, 44, 46, 62, 190
Northwest Territory maps 11, 12
Norton, Andre 183
Norwalk 17, 115, 138, 140, 182, 187, 192
Norwalk, Connecticut 12
Novello, Don 182
Nusbaum, Jay 85

O

O. Henry 116
Oak Openings 22
Oakar, Mary Rose 57
Oakley, Annie 121, 130-31, 188, 190
oatmeal 85
Oberlin 57, 78, 143, 161, 193
Oberlin College 57, 167, 174, 191
obscenity 107
Ochs, Adolph S. 183
O'Connell, Helen 185
O'Connor, Daniel 100, 185
Ohio Agricultural And Mechanical College 174
Ohio and Erie Canal 48, 70, 187
Ohio and Erie Canal National Heritage Corridor 28
Ohio Art Company 98, 187
Ohio Book Fair 103, 109
Ohio Caverns 22
Ohio College of Dental Surgery 179
Ohio Company of Associates 12, 46, 69, 173
Ohio Constitution 9
Ohio Division of Forestry 31, 33
Ohio Division of Natural Areas and Preserves 26, 37
Ohio Division of Wildlife 33, 34
Ohio Film Bureau 123
Ohio Fish Commission 33
Ohio Herb Education Center 74
Ohio Historical Center 23
Ohio Historical Society 172
Ohio Insitute for the Blind 187
Ohio Land Company 41, 42, 43
Ohio maps 192, 193
Ohio Natural Areas Act 26
Ohio Oil Company 90
Ohio Penitentiary 116, 153, 154, 155, 156, 160, 162, 166, 184, 185
Ohio River 4, 6, 8, 11, 12, 21, 25, 41, 42, 46, 48, 50, 69, 77, 79, 121, 193
Ohio River Sternwheel Festival 69
Ohio Stadium 145, 174
Ohio State Buckeyes 139, 140, 142, 144, 145, 146
Ohio State University medical complex 174
Ohio State University, The 23, 57, 58, 67, 108, 111, 118, 119, 148, 172, 174, 175, 183, 185
Ohio Turnpike 189
Ohio University 31, 172, 173
Ohioana Library 103
oil industry 89, 90
O'Jays (band) 125
Old Man's Cave 27
Old Woman Creek State Nature Preserve 26
Oldfield, Barney 149, 182, 184, 186
Olds, Ranson Eli 95, 185
Olentangy Scenic River 24, 192
Olin, Steve 184
Olsen, Harold 146
Olympics 135, 138, 140, 148–149, 188, 191
O'Mic, John 154
Oneida tribe 40

O'Neill, Ed 184
Online Computer Library Center (OCLC) 172
Onondaga tribe 40
Ontonagon (ship) 92
Oorang Indians 140
opera 107
Oppenheim, Joseph 83
Opper, Frederick 108, 182
Orange 53, 190
Oregonia 22, 192
organized crime 155, 158, 189
Orient State Institution 180
Orr, Carey Cassius 109
Orrville 87, 141, 144, 193
Orwell 184
Orzechowski, Benjamin 125
Osborn, Charles 49
Ottawa 17, 28
Ottawa County 17
Ottawa National Wildlife Refuge 28
Otterbein College 178
Ottowa tribe 41
Outcault, Richard 108, 182
Overmeyer, Robert F. 171, 182
Owens, Jesse 32, 148, 174
Owens, Michael 90, 189
Owens-Corning 184
Oxford 114, 188

P

Paar, Jack 133, 185
Page, Alan C. 140, 187
Page, Clarence 105
Paige, Satchel 138
Painesville 17, 85
paint 80, 187
painters 110–111
Palace Theater 127
Palmer, Arnold 150
Panek, Leroy Lad 182
Paonessa, Anthony 101, 185
papermaking 85, 115
Parent, Steven 163
Paris (Ohio) 193
Parker, Eleanor 186
Parker Hannifin Corporation 92
Parker, Sarah Jessica 121, 130, 185
parks and preserves 26-29
Parma 62, 145, 193
Parrot, Jacob 60
Parseghian, Ara 145, 185
passenger pigeons 34, 151, 188
patents 81, 82, 86, 90, 96, 151, 168, 187
Patterson, John 80
Paulding 17
Paulding County 17
Paulding, John 17
Paulin, Asariah 160
Paycheck, Johnny 127, 185
Payne, Daniel A. 174
Peale, Norman Vincent 179, 185
Pei, I.M. 126
Pelisipia 8
penalty flags (football) 146
Pennsylvania 11, 12, 42, 43, 178
Penny Press (newspaper) 190
Peoli 190
peregrine falcons 33, 34
Perez, Tony 136

PHOTO CREDITS

Courtesy of the University of Akron: 112

©Archive Photo: 19, 55

Bettmann: 129

BFGoodrich Company: 97 top

BP America Inc.: 89

The Charles Rand Penny Collection of the Works by Charles E. Burchfield–Penny Art Center, Buffalo State College, Buffalo, New York: 110

Cincinnati Convention and Visitors Bureau: 63

Courtesy of the Cleveland Indians: 137 top

©Columbus Zoo/Michael Pagany: 34

Courtesy Jerry Devol: 166

©1983 Eastern National: 46

Courtesy of Elektra Entertainment/Jeffrey Scales: 125

Dan Feicht: 134

©V. Scott Gilmore: 145

Courtesy of Golden Bear/©Kufner: 150

©1991 Gund Arena: 142

Indiana State Library: 162

Don King Productions: 147

Kevin Kitzsimons: 108

Library of Congress: 50, 72, 154

Courtesy of The Loral Defense Systems-Akron: 170 top

Marietta Area Tourist and Convention Bureau: 4

Arthur E. Morgan: 30

©The Museum Center: 107

NASA: 170 bottom

©Nesnadny & Schwartz: 66

Courtesy of the Office of the Governor: 10

Ohio Department of Natural Resources: 27

Courtesy of the Ohio Division of Travel and Tourism: 40

The Ohio Historical Society: 177

Photo courtesy of The Ohio State University Photo Archives: 81, 104, 118, 144, 148

Ohio University: 173

Pro Football Hall of Fame: 141

©1994 The Rock and Roll Hall of Fame and Museum: 126

Greg Sailor: 181

William Howard Taft National Historic Site: 54

Courtesy of the Toledo Mud Hens Baseball Club: 138

Courtesy Tower City Center: 67

U.S. Department of the Interior, National Park Service, Negative #68-WRBR-1-CP.N.: 168

U.S. Department of the Interior,, National Park Service, Edison National Historic Site: 82

UPI/Bettmann: 164

Special Collections of the Military Library at West Point: 59

Courtesy of The Wilds: 36

Wisconsin Center for Film and Theater Research: 131,132

Youngstown State University: 146